PIONEER PROGRAMMER

Betty Jean Jennings [Bartik], 1924–2011

Pioneer Programmer

JEAN JENNINGS BARTIK AND THE
COMPUTER THAT CHANGED THE WORLD

Jean Jennings Bartik
AUTOBIOGRAPHY

Edited by **Jon T. Rickman** and **Kim D. Todd**

Truman State University Press
Kirksville, Missouri

Copyright © 2013 Truman State University Press, Kirksville, Missouri 63501
All rights reserved
tsup.truman.edu

Cover art: Details from February 1946 photo by *Science Illustrated* magazine for a May 1946 article. Copy in Jean Jennings Bartik Computing Museum.

Cover design: Teresa Wheeler

Library of Congress Cataloging-in-Publication Data

Bartik, Jean.
Pioneer programmer : Jean Jennings Bartik and the computer that changed the world / Jean Jennings Bartik ; autobiography edited by Jon T. Rickman and Kim D. Todd.
    pages cm
Includes bibliographical references and index.
ISBN 978-1-61248-086-2 (paperback : alkaline paper) — ISBN 978-1-61248-087-9 (ebook)
1. Bartik, Jean. 2. Women computer scientists—United States—Biography. 3. Computer scientists—United States—Biography. 4. Women computer programmers—United States—Biography. 5. Women inventors—United States—Biography. 6. ENIAC (Computer)—History. 7. Computer industry—United States—History—20th century. 8. Women in science—United States—History—20th century. 9. Glass ceiling (Employment discrimination)—United States—History—20th century. 10. Sex discrimination against women—United States—History—20th century. I. Rickman, Jon T. II. Todd, Kim D. III. Title.
QA76.2.B27A3 2013
004.092—dc23

2013031857

No part of this work may be reproduced or transmitted in any format by any means without written permission from the publisher.

The paper in this publication meets or exceeds the minimum requirements of the American National Standard for Information Sciences—Permanence of Paper for Printed Library Materials, ANSI Z39.48–1992.

Dedication

I dedicate this book to J. P. Eckert and John W. Mauchly, who were not only brilliant and inventive, but were also good and honest men. They were born to inspire and teach and lead. And so they did. They gave far more than they received and deserve a far better tribute than I can give them. I am thankful to have known them.

In Tribute to the Other ENIAC Women

Kathleen "Kay"
McNulty
[Mauchly Antonelli]
1921–2006

Frances Elizabeth
"Betty" Snyder
[Holberton]
1917–2001

Ruth Lichterman
[Teitelbaum]
1924–1986

Frances "Fran" Bilas
[Spence]
1922–2012

Marlyn Wescoff
[Melzer]
1922–2009

Contents

Illustrations xi
Foreword by Dr. Jon T. Rickman xv
Preface xix
Acknowledgments xxiii
Prologue: The Start of Something Big 1
1: The Originators, the Women, and the ENIAC 5
2: My Story: How It All Began 27
3: Human "Computer" to ENIAC Programmer 57
4: Apricot Brandy and Nighttime Logic 91
5: Surrounded by Brilliance 121
6: Moving On, and the Glass Ceiling 143
7: The Trial to Overturn the ENIAC Patent 166
8: The ENIAC Women in the Spotlight 179
Epilogue: Looking Back 195
Afterword by Kim D. Todd 203
Notes 209
Index 221

Illustrations

Unless otherwise noted, all images are courtesy of Jean Jennings Bartik Computing Museum, Northwest Missouri State University.

Prologue
Betty Snyder and Betty Jean Jennings, December 14, 1946 1
Betty Snyder and Betty Jean Jennings working with the ENIAC, 1946. John Mauchly Papers, Department of Special Collections, University of Pennsylvania Library. Used with permission 3

Chapter 1
John Mauchly, co-inventor of the ENIAC, ca. 1944. Courtesy of Bill Mauchly 6
J. Presper "Pres" Eckert, co-inventor of the ENIAC, ca. 1945 6
The Ballistic Research Laboratory's Scientific Advisory Committee, September 1940. Courtesy of the U.S. Army (ARL Technical Library) 9
The EDVAC installed at Aberdeen Proving Ground, 1948. U.S. Army photo 15
Moore School of Electrical Engineering, University of Pennsylvania, ca. 1944 23

Chapter 2
Lula Spainhower [Jennings], ca. 1906 27
Betty Jean Jennings with family, ca. 1932 32
Betty Jean Jennings with classmates and teacher Bill Gage at the Jennings School, ca. 1936 35
Betty Jean Jennings with her high school sophomore class, 1938–39 38
Gretchen Jennings Kirby, ca. 1932–37 40
Lou and Harold Jennings, 1942 45
Betty Jean Jennings and a friend, ca. 1942–43 47
Lieutenant Commander Robert Jennings, 1944 48
The girls' basketball team at Northwest Missouri State Teachers College, ca. 1943 56

Chapter 3
Betty Jean Jennings's appointment as a "computer" for Aberdeen Proving
 Ground in 1945 59
Beatrice Ficaro and Betty Jean Jennings, ca. 1945. 63
Harold Jennings, ca. 1945–53. 73
Betty Snyder and Kathleen McNulty, fall 1946. Photo by Betty Jean Jennings. 75
Diagram taken from the ENIAC Patent application, showing the units of
 the ENIAC. 77
Senior engineer Arthur Burks and Betty Jean Jennings in front of the
 ENIAC, February 1946 78
Betty Jean Jennings and Frances Bilas working with the ENIAC.
 Courtesy of the U.S. Army (ARL Technical Library) 81
The ENIAC women, 1946. 89

Chapter 4
ENIAC Programming Sheet (Pedaling Sheet) 93
The ENIAC, 1946. Courtesy of the U.S. Army (ARL Technical Library Archives) . . . 100
Kay McNulty and John Mauchly, ca. 1946–47. Courtesy of Bill Mauchly. 110
John Mauchly and Betty Jean Jennings, December 14, 1946. 111
Betty Jean and Bill's wedding reception, December 14, 1946 112

Chapter 5
The Binary Automatic Computer (BINAC) on the test floor, ca. 1946. Courtesy
 of Joe Chapline and the Jean Jennings Bartik Computing Museum 123
The Eckert-Mauchly BINAC, 1949, that went to Northrop. Photo donated
 by the UNISYS Blue Bell Retirees Group to the Jean Jennings Bartik
 Computing Museum. 124
BINAC Engineering Team, 1949 129
The Eckert-Mauchly UNIVAC Crew, 1949. Photograph by B. Victor 133
Jean and colleagues from Eckert-Mauchly, ca. 1950. 136

Chapter 6
Walter Cronkite with J. Presper Eckert, Harold Sweeney, and the UNIVAC I,
 fall 1956. AP photo, courtesy U.S. Census Bureau 145
UNIVAC I with console, printer, and four UNISERVOS (tape devices), ca. 1950s. . . 147
"UNIVAC I installations." #2011001, Jean Jennings Bartik Papers 149
Mary, Tim, and Jane Bartik, ca. 1967–68. Photo by Jean Jennings Bartik 152
John Mauchly and Kay McNulty on the day they wed in 1948. Courtesy of
 Bill Mauchly 153

Chapter 8

Final picture of all six ENIAC female programmers together, November 1985....... 180
Jean's Women in Technology International (WITI) Hall of Fame award............. 183
The last official resume of Jean Jennings Bartik, 1996............................... 186
Dinner at Bunratty Castle in Ireland during a three-university speaking
 tour, 1998... 189
Jean cuts the ribbon at the grand opening of the Jean Jennings Bartik
 Computing Museum, April 2002 190
Jean Jennings Bartik receives the 2008 Fellow Award in Mountain View,
 California, October 21, 2008 192
The inductees into the Computer Museum of History's Hall of Fellows, Mountain
 View, California, October 21, 2008. Photo by Dr. Jon T. Rickman 192
Group at the Hall of Fellows awards ceremony at the Computer History Museum
 in Mountain View, California, October 21, 2008 193
Marker designating the Eckert-Mauchly building as a historic site. Photo by
 Jon Rickman 193
Bill Mauchly, Jean Jennings Bartik, and Chris Eckert, 2006........................ 194

Foreword

If you are a woman who ever felt you were working in a man's world, this author meets that environment head on. If you are a person who works with technology, especially computers, this author was there at the birth of the first successful electronic computer.

The author describes her creative efforts to program the first successful computer and later transform it into the first stored-program computer. The author programmed the first hardware-based stored-program computer, the BINAC, and helped design the first successful commercial computing system, the UNIVAC. Jean Jennings Bartik often said proudly, "I was there when we programmed the Electronic Numerical Integrator and Computer (ENIAC)."

Jean's autobiography describes growing up in rural northwest Missouri and living on a farm with a father who was a schoolteacher and a farmer. The sixth of seven siblings, she learned how to work and complete difficult tasks. She earned her ticket to participate in the birth of electronic computing by completing a degree during World War II that included mathematics and science courses at Northwest Missouri State Teachers College.

In the spring of 1945, she boarded a Wabash train at midnight that steamed its way toward Philadelphia and a new and exciting life in the city. She was anxious to start her new job as a "computer" using electromechanical calculators to produce artillery firing tables for the U.S. Army.

Soon after she understood the process of computing artillery firing tables, she was hired to become one of six programmers for the world's first electronic computer. According to Merriam-Webster's Dictionary, a computer must be "programmable" to be considered a computer, and the ENIAC was programmable.

Jean found herself working in a man's world dominated by male engineers and military managers. She describes writing the first program to demonstrate the power of the ENIAC to the world. She tells of the frustrations the programmers experienced when the media thought of them as just models needed to stand by and sell the newest household appliance.

This autobiography describes the atmosphere of a new company started in a new computing industry by Eckert-Mauchly. It was a continuation of the excitement of working with intelligent people performing new and very complex tasks. She loved the work and the coworkers, but lawyers, patents, and buyouts changed everything. She worked for several computer companies in a competitive time and several publishing firms where she experienced executives with large egos and companies with glass ceilings for female managers. Jean seemed to always take away valuable lessons for living from most of her home and work experiences.

There has been a long debate about who invented the electronic computer, or who invented parts of early computers. It's been analogous to analyzing the invention of the automobile. Does the first automobile need to be driven by steam, batteries, gasoline, or diesel? Does it need to have three wheels or four? I would say it is most important that is has systems for a driver to control both direction and speed. Similarly, I believe the marvel of a computer is that it can be controlled and its function can be changed, or programmed, not whether it uses decimal or binary arithmetic. I also believe that the next most important attribute of computers is their continued miniaturization, permitting them to be programmed for more and more mobile, even exploratory, applications.

I certainly don't need to weigh in on the first electronic computer debate. Jean does that in her unique style. I do know that the ENIAC was the first electronic computer that needed the first computer programmers, including Jean Jennings and others who were there to program it for the first large public demonstration of an electronic computer solving a very complex problem! It is also evident that the ENIAC was the first electronic computer that was programmed to solve a wide variety of problems and was the first electronic computer to be programmed to run stored programs. Jean was there again to design the program for the ENIAC to convert it into an electronic stored-program computer, the configuration in which it was used for most of its problem-solving life.

This autobiography is about a tough personality, a person who displayed a lot of common sense and never minced words, never avoided a challenge, worked to understand the truth, and was always quick to identify unfair situations. Sometimes her life was changed quickly by her actions. She could match any man's logic and any man's street language. As a computing pioneer she expresses her love for her colleagues, and as a grandmother she shows enormous pride in her active family.

I am proud to have known Jean and have always enjoyed our conversations. She always kept me thinking, and I had to be careful in making sure my statements about computer architecture were precise. It was a joy to watch her talk to a large crowd and answer questions from students studying computer science. It was a class act when Jean and Kay McNulty Mauchly Antonelli made a presentation together. They complemented each other perfectly. Jean received a rare standing ovation at Northwest Missouri State University for her commencement speech in 2002. It was an honor to watch Jean accept the prestigious Computing History Museum Fellow Award in 2008. Finally, I invite you to come see the Jean Jennings Bartik Computing Museum at Northwest Missouri State University or visit our virtual museum at www.nwmissouri.edu/onlinemuseum. Read and enjoy this book about the fascinating life of Jean Jennings Bartik.

      Dr. Jon T. Rickman, Vice President of Information Systems
      Northwest Missouri State University
      February 15, 2011

Postscript

I completed the foreword on the anniversary of the historical demonstration of the ENIAC to the world. Just one month later, on March 23, 2011, Jean passed away.

As Jean wanted, all profits derived from her autobiography will go to the Jean Jennings Bartik Scholarship for Women in STEM (Science, Technology, Engineering, and Mathematics), and the Jean Jennings Bartik Computing Museum at Northwest Missouri State University.

After thirty-five years of service to Northwest, I retired on January 1, 2012. I truly enjoyed the good times I had with Jean and will greatly miss her.

      Jon Rickman
      September 11, 2012

Preface

In a perfect world, Presper Eckert and John Mauchly's company would have become the greatest and most successful computer company of all time, and Eckert-Mauchly would be as familiar today as Hewlett-Packard. Also, in a perfect world, the "Sensational Six"—Kay McNulty, Betty Snyder, Ruth Lichterman, Marlyn Wescoff, Fran Bilas, and me—who were originally hired with a sub-professional rating and the title of "computer," would have ushered in an era of computer programming in which women led the way, or were at least on equal footing with men, and worked in equal numbers with them.

But we do not live in a perfect world. Presper Eckert and John Mauchly, the brilliant co-inventors of the ENIAC, were betrayed as others took credit for their ideas or tried to force them to sign over patent rights, and a trial judge in Minneapolis ruled that the ENIAC was not their invention, but was based on a machine that had been thrown away by Iowa State University. As for the ENIAC women, we were lost in the shuffle when World War II, which had ushered women into many non-traditional roles, ended and the country reverted to its comfortable, male-dominated mode. When histories of the ENIAC were written, the ENIAC women were seldom even mentioned. For example, Herman Goldstine, the liaison between the U.S. Army and the ENIAC project team, helped to obscure and devalue the importance of our role as programmers by always referring to us as nameless project members with such references as "John Holberton and his girls," "Holberton and his group," and "Holberton and his people" in his flawed but influential book *The Computer from Pascal to von Neumann*. Goldstine also took credit that should have rightly gone to others in that same book.[1]

The impulse that led me to write this book probably had its germination back in 1975. I was working in northern New Jersey, and at nearby Fort Monmouth, the regional chapter of the Association of Computing Machinery (ACM) was preparing to host a seminar on the history of computing. The seminar was to be chaired by Dr. J. G. (John Grist) Brainerd of the University of Pennsylvania's Moore School of Electrical Engineering, who had been Penn's liaison with Aberdeen on the ENIAC project. I was invited to attend and when I received the program, I noticed that no women were scheduled to speak. ENIAC technicians were speaking, but no ENIAC programmers, who had all been women. I wrote to Dr. Brainerd saying that I thought it was a disgrace that no women were on the program, and as a result, I was asked to speak at that event. I was honored to stand in for the other women programmers of the ENIAC, but it was clear that evening that we women had fallen through the cracks of history.

Eleven years later at the University of Pennsylvania's celebration of the fortieth anniversary of the introduction of the ENIAC, Kay McNulty Mauchly Antonelli was finally invited to be a guest speaker. But she was asked to speak as John Mauchly's widow and not as an ENIAC programmer. Most of the six ENIAC women attended that fortieth anniversary luncheon, with the exception of Ruth, and there we met Kathryn Kleiman, a Harvard University student who was writing a thesis on women in computing. Because of Kathryn's interest and inquiries about the ENIAC women, *Wall Street Journal* columnist Tom Petzinger came on the scene to write articles about Betty Holberton and me. Thus the women of the ENIAC were rediscovered.

As a result of Kathy Kleiman's efforts and Tom Petzinger's articles, people became intrigued by the notion that, at a time when men dominated business and science, a group of women had been responsible for programming the "Great Brain." Intrigue turned to interest and interest turned to acknowledgment of our historical significance. The "ENIAC Six" were suddenly plucked from obscurity and began receiving the kind of respect and recognition that we had perhaps always deserved, but had never dreamed was even possible. With this new validation of our contributions to computing history, I began re-examining my responsibility to that history. I decided to write a firsthand account of my time working on the ENIAC, even though there had been quite a few books and documentaries published already about the electronic computer. But my initial motivation was spurred by the fact that many of those previous histories, while well-intentioned, had inaccurate information. For instance, many claimed that the ENIAC was not a stored-program computer, but that is not true. The ENIAC was the world's first stored-program computer and I should know, because I led the team that turned the ENIAC into a stored-program computer. The majority of mistakes in previous histories about the ENIAC were honest mistakes. The authors were telling secondhand stories without actual firsthand experience and in some cases, perpetuating faulty information because they had used a source that had inaccurate data. Errors perpetuated themselves and myths propagated over the years until history really became (as Napoleon said) "a set of lies agreed upon."

More recently, some books have discussed the role of the ENIAC women. I'm sure that Ethlie Ann Vare and Greg Ptacek, in their 2001 *Patently Female: From AZT to TV Dinners, Stories of Women Inventors and Their Breakthrough Ideas*, had the best of intentions, but the book contains inaccuracies because the authors did not actually interview any of the four remaining ENIAC women when they were writing the book. Unfortunately, the book is so well written that other authors will no doubt use the book for source material and thus perpetuate the errors as truth.

Nancy Stern published *From ENIAC to UNIVAC: An Appraisal of the Eckert-Mauchly Computers* in 1981. Like *Patently Female*, Stern's work also has incorrect information, and in my opinion, seems to confuse the BINAC with the EDSAC (designed at Cambridge University by Maurice Wilkes, and first run in May 1949).

When my dear friend Kay McNulty Mauchly Antonelli died on April 7, 2006, after a short battle with cancer, I felt even more strongly about telling the story of the ENIAC and the ENIAC women programmers for three primary reasons. First, I wanted to correct previous literary inaccuracies. Second, I wanted to recognize the largely undocumented and overlooked contributions of the six ENIAC women programmers, who were there practically from the beginning. We programmed the ENIAC and in my case, the BINAC and UNIVAC as well, but firsthand accounts of our experiences were practically nonexistent. And third, I wanted to inspire young women who might be interested in the math and computing fields.

Most of the improvements to our standard of living have come from engineers and scientists. Such individuals are the world's true dreamers and adventurers; they forge into frontiers to find realms that sensible people know are impossible to reach. I would like to see more women blaze new trails into these unknown frontiers to discover that "all things are possible to those who believe."

Over the years, while I contemplated and talked about writing a book or books, I continued to collect memories and conversations the way some people might collect coins or stamps. While John Mauchly, Kay McNulty Mauchly Antonelli, Pres Eckert, and Betty Snyder Holberton always supported my literary endeavors, I didn't feel equipped to tell my own story because it was a story about all of them and how they had impacted my life. It wasn't just my story, it was our story, and I didn't know if I was the appropriate person to tell our story. So I didn't begin to write my own story until well after 1996.

The process of writing wasn't an easy one. The story of my life, which was interwoven with the lives of so many others, seemed too large and messy to organize into a single manuscript. Also I was determined that any story I wrote would help clear up inaccuracies and right old wrongs whenever possible, especially with regard to Pres Eckert and John Mauchly. Kay did not feel that I needed to defend either men or their work. She believed that things would work out without my input. But I believe that Dick Clippinger and our team didn't get the credit that we deserved for all our hard work in turning the ENIAC into a stored-program computer. And I honestly believe that Pres Eckert and John Mauchly were unfairly denied credit and patent rights for their inventions. Perhaps I may be forgiven for taking pot-shots at sacred cows, since Pres and John inspired and lifted me beyond myself, but then Presper Eckert and John Mauchly were great teachers who inspired many others to succeed and pursue their dreams.

In truth, there are many tales to be told of the invention of the computer and there are many unsung heroes—women and men—who were part of this invention that has revolutionized the world. Many have proclaimed their contributions, which were often far more modest than they later advertised, but there is credit enough to go around, and I am proud to have been there and been a part of it.

Like most people's stories, mine is mixed up with others—the stories of those I worked with in those heady days. Unfortunately some stories will never be told by the people who could have told them best. My story, no doubt the last to be told by one who was actually there, could not be told without telling about the other people behind the extraordinary electronic machine that changed the world. I hope this story offers a firsthand glimpse into a time when the impossible became possible and life as we knew it changed forever with the turn of a switch.

Acknowledgments

I would like to thank the following people for their help in making this autobiography possible. Without each one of them, my story (our story) could not have been told: Kay McNulty Mauchly Antonelli, Betty Snyder Holberton, John Mauchly, Presper "Pres" Eckert, Ruth Lichterman, Marlyn Wescoff, Fran Bilas, Hester Eckert (Pres's first wife), J. William "Bill" Mauchly (John's son with Kay), Chris Eckert (Pres's son with Hester), Judith Eckert (Pres's second wife), Bob Shaw, Jeffrey Chuan Chu, Kite Sharpless, Harry Husky, Jack Davis, Adele Goldstine, Joe Chapline, Edward Schlain, Paul Chinitz, and Dick Clippinger.

I want to take this time to also thank Benjamin Jones, Dr. Jon T. Rickman, and Kim D. Todd for helping me with my autobiography. Kim and Jon's enthusiasm and editing skills were invaluable to the completion of this manuscript and I am grateful for their support. I also want to acknowledge the first-rate assistance provided by Benjamin Jones. Jon hired Jones to be my personal assistant during my early development of the manuscript. Jones helped me organize my thoughts and notes, and motivated me to expand some of my incomplete narratives.

A special thank you also to Dr. Jon T. Rickman and Kim D. Todd for all their hard work in establishing the Jean Jennings Bartik Computing Museum located on the campus of Northwest Missouri State University.

A very special thank you to Tom Petzinger and Kathy Kleiman. You both changed my life!

Lastly and most importantly, I want to thank my family, especially my children Tim, Jane, and Mary, for their love and support over my lifetime.

Prologue
The Start of Something Big

We were known as "the two Bettys." One of us had dark brown hair; one of us had auburn hair that, in childhood, had been carrot-red. One of us had grown up on the Main Line railroad of Philadelphia, the daughter of a highly respected astronomy teacher at a prestigious boys' school. And one of us had grown up on a Missouri farm, the daughter of a hardscrabble farmer who had also once taught in a one-room schoolhouse. What brought us together initially was an advertisement for recently graduated female math majors. But what brought us to this moment was a remarkable fate. It seemed to open doors at every turn and usher us through them until there was just the two of us, Betty Snyder and Betty Jennings, alone in a room with the largest and most impressive electronic machine ever created.

Betty Snyder and Betty Jean Jennings, December 14, 1946.

We were the best of friends, and we were on the verge of making history. It was late—quite late, in fact— on a frigid February night in 1946. Betty and I (I went by my first name then, although now I use my middle name, Jean) were holed up on the first floor of the Moore School of Electrical Engineering on the campus of the University of Pennsylvania, in Philadelphia. Betty was twenty-eight, and I had just turned twenty-one a few weeks earlier.

It happened to be the night of Valentine's Day, but we were unconcerned about that. Besides, we had no boyfriends at the moment. We were serious young ladies with important things on our minds. For that reason, we did not resent having to spend the evening cooped up in the Moore School working. Most people consider Valentine's Day a romantic day. But we never gave a thought that evening to valentines or romantic dinners. What we were thinking of was an all-important demonstration we were to run the next day for the world.

We were all by ourselves, except that we weren't. There was something else inhabiting that space. Like the proverbial elephant in the room, it was hard to miss. In fact, it took up most of the room, surrounding us on all sides. Standing nearly nine feet tall, it towered over us, its forty panels—each measuring two feet wide and a foot deep—looked like some strange sci-fi floor-to-ceiling cabinetry. And stretching, all told, eighty feet in length, it not only took up three entire walls, but there were also rolling islands of function tables on wheels in the center of the room that could be turned this way and that. The fourth wall was covered with its power supplies, which were also housed in big, black panels.

Counting all of its panels and parts, it weighed thirty tons, or the equivalent of about forty-five of the horses I had ridden and driven as a teenager on the farm in Missouri. As Betty and I worked on it that night, its vacuum tubes flickered like distant lightning. A storm was rolling in, one might say—if one were given to poetical fancy—and in its wake, twentieth-century technology would never look the same again.

The machine was the reason we were there that night—now past eleven p.m., long after the city's couples had gone home from their Valentine's Day dinners out—and the reason we had been in that room for countless hours over the previous two weeks. But this was the final night; tomorrow all of our hard work would be put to the test—and before some of the greatest minds in the United States.

What was this behemoth that surrounded us as we plugged cables into its circuitry, with more than two thousand neon bulbs flashing as we ran the test problem again and again, searching for the final piece of a puzzle? It was the world's first electronic computer—or, to use its official name, the Electronic Numeric Integrator and Computer. But that's a mouthful, even to designate something as complex and revolutionary as this was, and no one actually called it by that name, not even the mathematicians. Instead, the world would soon come to know it as the ENIAC.

There had been other computers of a sort, but they weren't nearly as impressive or as capable as the ENIAC. Today, of course, a silicon chip smaller than the tip of a pencil can hold the same capacity as the ENIAC, which occupied a large

Betty Snyder (left) and Betty Jean Jennings (center) working with the ENIAC, with two unknown women at right, 1946. Courtesy of John Mauchly Papers, Department of Special Collections, University of Pennsylvania Library. Used with permission.

room. But at that time, the ENIAC left all the other prototype "computers" in its dust with its power of computation and speed. As mathematicians, we were awestruck to work with such power in harness. It felt how I imagine it might have felt to Thomas Watson when he heard Alexander Graham Bell say over the first telephone, "Come here, Watson—I want you." It was a thrilling experience to work with the ENIAC.

But just now, it was more like a curse, because the great machine was giving us trouble. Our task, which we had been given a little over two weeks before, was to program the ENIAC to calculate the trajectory of a shell fired from an artillery gun. We had one major problem with our program, which we were trying to fix the evening of February 14, 1946.

While we had made the ENIAC trace the actual flight path just fine at the point in the simulation where the shell should have hit the ground and stopped, it kept going, as if it were tunneling under the earth at the same velocity that it had traveled through the air. We couldn't stop the shell on impact. Unless we solved that problem, we knew the demonstration would be a dud, and the ENIAC's inventors and engineers would be embarrassed. Now it was the last night before the ENIAC would be unveiled to the scientific community, and while we knew we were close to solving the problem, we couldn't find the magic fix for which we were searching.

We worked and worked that night, checking and adjusting the myriad settings for the computer, but we couldn't find the answer. Finally, with the clock nearing midnight, we shut off the lights, locked up, and left the building, terribly discouraged. Betty lived in the suburbs, and the last train for her home departed at midnight. I left her on Walnut Street, a block from the train station, and walked home, she going one way and I the other. I don't know what her thoughts were as she rode the Main Line out to Narberth, but mine were gloomy.

In the morning, which was bitterly cold, Betty and I returned to the Moore School with the problem still before us. But not for long: Betty walked up to the computer, flipped one switch, and the program ran perfectly. We were suddenly in business; the shell now stopped on impact. And a good thing, too—the demonstration was only a few hours away.

How had Betty done it? How had she known which switch was set wrong, out of the thousands that were on the ENIAC? What I called her "nighttime logic" had been at work. Betty often solved logical problems by sleeping on them. While she slept, her subconscious untangled the knot that her conscious mind had been unable to. She was the best I ever saw at this.

We were now ready for the eminent mathematicians and other distinguished guests who would soon descend on the room. It was nearly time for the ENIAC to make history.

CHAPTER 1

The Originators, the Women, and the ENIAC

Many men built early "computers" of one sort or another during the World War II years. It's probably a stretch to call them tinkerers, yet some of their machines were of pretty humble construction. In the 1930s, British mathematician Douglas Hartree built a differential analyzer, which England used during the war, out of parts from a Meccano set (a British version of the Erector set). Another fellow, John Vincent Atanasoff, aided by graduate student Clifford Berry, built an electronic computing device in 1937 to 1942 in the basement of the physics building at Iowa State College (now University) in Ames.[1]

In England, there was the Bletchley Park code-breaking computer, the Colossus, inspired by the work of Alan Turing. And Hitler had Konrad Zuse's Z3 in Germany, used for designing the planes of the Luftwaffe. Neither came to light until well after the war. In 1944 Howard Aiken devised the IBM-built electromechanical Mark I for Harvard. And George Stibitz, a scientist at Bell Laboratories, in 1937 built an electromechanical relay machine, which he called Model K. He constructed most of it at his kitchen table, using relays, flashlight bulbs, and strips cut from tin cans.

However, for all of the ingenuity of these various comers, there were two men who were at the center of the design and construction of the world's first real electronic computer capable of solving myriad problems, the ENIAC, and the successors to that computer, the EDVAC, BINAC, and UNIVAC. They were John Mauchly and J. [John] Presper Eckert, known as Pres. If the invention of the electronic computer and the subsequent sea change it ignited can be credited to any two individuals, it is these two men. For reasons this book will chronicle, John and Pres were denied the full credit and renown (and, yes, riches) they deserved for their invention. Nevertheless, they were the men who were responsible for the most astounding invention of the twentieth century: they were the originators.

John William Mauchly, born in 1907 in Cincinnati and raised in Chevy Chase, Maryland, developed an interest in computing when he was still very young. His father was physicist Sebastian J. Mauchly, who was chief of the Terrestrial Electricity and Magnetism Section at the Carnegie Institute in Washington, D.C. While in high school, John did calculations for his father. In 1925, by virtue of having won the Engineering Scholarship of the State of Maryland, he earned a full scholarship to Johns Hopkins University to study electrical engineering, but after two years he decided the work was too cut-and-dried for him. The university allowed him to switch to another major, so he enrolled directly in a PhD program in physics and got his doctorate. He only received one degree—that being the PhD—because he never bothered to complete the paperwork necessary to qualify for his bachelor's and master's degrees. John completed his PhD in 1932 and the following year became a professor of physics at Ursinus College near Philadelphia, where he taught until 1941.

John Mauchly, co-inventor of the ENIAC, ca. 1944. Courtesy of Bill Mauchly.

Pres Eckert, who was nearly twelve years younger, grew up in a large house in Philadelphia's Germantown section, the son of wealthy real estate developer John Eckert. A chauffeur drove him to elementary school at William Penn Charter School. In high school, he joined the Engineer's Club of Philadelphia and, after school, hung around

J. Presper "Pres" Eckert, co-inventor of the ENIAC, ca. 1945.

the electronics laboratory of Philo Farnsworth, the inventor of the television, in Chestnut Hill.

Pres scored second in the country on the math portion of the College Board examination. At the urging of his parents, he started out studying business at the University of Pennsylvania's Wharton School. However, in 1937—still just eighteen—he transferred to Penn's Moore School of Electrical Engineering. At the age of twenty-one he applied for his first patent, "Light Modulating Methods and Apparatus."

In the summer of 1941, having graduated, Pres was working on radar projects and getting his master's degree. That summer, the United States was using the lend-lease program to help Great Britain and France survive in their desperate struggle against Nazi Germany. This effort created a shortage of engineers in the United States. To help overcome this shortage, the U.S. Department of War launched a program that summer known as the Engineering Defense Training Program. Under this umbrella, the University of Pennsylvania offered a program called Electrical Engineering for Defense Industries, an intensive, ten-week course for college graduates who had majored in mathematics or physics. The course was tuition-free and its laboratory instructors were C. Bradford Sheppard and J. Presper Eckert.

John Mauchly, chairman of physics at Ursinus College in Philadelphia, took the course at the Moore School in 1941 along with Arthur Burks, Lou Wilson, and Al Auerbach, all of whom figure into this story. John had given the lab experiments used in this course to his own classes in physics at Ursinus; thus he had time to discuss with Pres Eckert what he was really interested in: computers. He was fascinated by weather problems, such as calculating the effect of sunspots on the weather on earth, for which he had done calculations with his students using hand calculators. John wondered if vacuum tubes could be used to do the calculations on a computer.

Pres was already recognized as an engineering genius around the Moore School. Even his professors consulted with him on electrical circuit designs. Pres told John that he thought vacuum tubes could be used if one was careful. It was Pres's carefulness in designing the ENIAC that made it work. It used vacuum tubes that everybody, including the professors at the Moore School, knew were too unreliable to use as computing devices; however, Pres designed the circuits so that the vacuum tubes didn't have to work very well. In fact, they had to work at only 10 percent of their capacity. These conversations between Pres and John began their long association designing computers that changed forever the course of computer history and our everyday world.

John and Pres became friends as well as close associates through their work designing computers. When Pres gave his eulogy of John in 1980, he called John Mauchly the most brilliant man he had ever met.[2] And John, in memoirs he recorded in 1978, said that, when it came to designing computer components, Pres was the greatest engineer of the twentieth century. Chris Eckert, Pres's son, said that his father told him that he had never had a serious conflict with John in all the years they worked together.

The Moore School had a computer called the differential analyzer in its basement running trajectories for the Aberdeen Proving Ground. The differential analyzer was a mechanical, analog computer—that is, it solved problems by using gears and shafts to provide an analogy to the problem. It was based on the design of a differential analyzer at Aberdeen Proving Ground that was, in turn, based on the differential analyzer Vannevar Bush had invented and built at the Massachusetts Institute of Technology (MIT) in Cambridge in the 1920s.

The differential analyzer could be set up to run the trajectories needed for the firing tables of big guns for the war. It took about two days to set it up for a particular gun, and then it took about half an hour to run each trajectory. However, trajectories done on the differential analyzer were not very accurate. Thus, Aberdeen Proving Ground had set up a group of about one hundred human computers who used mechanical calculators to compute trajectories. It took a human computer about forty hours to compute a trajectory. These trajectories were quite accurate and were interspersed with those from the differential analyzer, and the results were "smoothed" to produce the final firing table.

The human computers were mostly women. Initially, Aberdeen recruited women math majors, but not many women at that time majored in math. Eventually, they resorted to recruiting women who had any math background at all, and Aberdeen trained them in the mathematics needed for the job. Of the original ENIAC programmers, Kay McNulty, Fran Bilas, and I were math majors; the other three had some math in their background and were trained by Aberdeen.

After John Mauchly took the engineering course at the Moore School from Pres and Brad Sheppard in that summer of 1941, Harold Pender, dean of the school, hired him away from Ursinus to teach at Penn. John learned all about the differential analyzer and the human computers who were calculating trajectories. He wondered whether these trajectories could be calculated electronically using vacuum tubes.

Colonel Herman Goldstine, the military liaison between Aberdeen Proving Ground and the Moore School, was being pressured by Aberdeen to get the trajectories calculated faster because so many new guns were being produced and they all needed firing tables for the soldiers or sailors who would man them. Joe Chapline was the maintenance engineer for the differential analyzer and a close friend of John Mauchly. Chapline said he clearly remembered the day John Mauchly conceived of the idea for ENIAC. According to Chapline, John Mauchly had an idea to speed up the way they calculated firing trajectories, so John dictated his idea for building an electronic computer to do the trajectories to his secretary, Dorothy Shisler. Dorothy then typed up a memo for John to give to Professor John G. Brainerd, who was the University of Pennsylvania civilian liaison with Aberdeen.[3]

One day, during a conversation between Joe Chapline and Herman Goldstine, Goldstine said to Chapline that he wished there was some way to speed up the way they calculated firing trajectories. Chapline, remembering John Mauchly's idea, said he then told Goldstine about John Mauchly's idea for an electronic computer. Chapline told Goldstine that John had written up a memo on his idea for Dr. Brainerd. Herman Goldstine immediately met with John Mauchly to discuss John's idea. Strangely, John's memo to Dr. Brainerd could not be located. Fortunately, however, Dorothy Shisler came to the rescue and the memo was recreated from her shorthand notes.[4]

Herman Goldstine was very excited about John's idea, so he asked John and Presper Eckert to write a proposal to build such a computer and said he would arrange for them to present it to Aberdeen's Scientific Advisory Board,

The Ballistic Research Laboratory's Scientific Advisory Committee, September 1940. Courtesy of the U.S. Army (Aberdeen Research Laboratory Technical Library).

which controlled its operation. After Pres and John had given their presentation, Oswald Veblen, a veteran ordnance expert from World War I, said, in effect, "Give them the money"—and so the board did. The contract was signed in 1943, and engineers were hired to form teams to design and build the ENIAC. Pres Eckert was the chief engineer and John Mauchly the principal consultant. The other engineers who designed the logic and electronics of the ENIAC were Arthur Burks, Jeffrey Chuan Chu, Jack Davis, Harry Husky, Thomas Kite Sharpless, and Robert "Bob" Shaw.

After the design of the ENIAC was frozen and it was being built, Pres and John had time to think of what they would want in their next computer. When they were building the ENIAC they were under severe time constraints, so they didn't have the chance to put many of their ideas into the ENIAC. But during this breathing space, in between designing the ENIAC and testing the machine after it had been built, they began to have meetings on what the design of the next machine, the EDVAC (Electronic Discrete Variable Computer), would look like. For example, Pres Eckert and John Mauchly saw the need for an automatic regulation or control of electronic calculations, which is an implicit statement of need for a stored-program computer as early as December 1943.[5] More importantly, Presper Eckert wrote about the concept of a stored-program computer on January 29, 1944.[6]

A "stored-program" computer is one that stores the program in the computer in the same memory as data, so that the stored program can be operated on and changed in the same way as data. In contrast, the program of the original ENIAC was contained in the nature of how the different functions of the computer were wired to each other, so the original ENIAC had to be rewired to execute a new program. One can well understand that this put enormous pressure on the programmers to get a program right, or at least nearly right, the first time.

The importance of the stored-program concept in the early development of the computer is impossible to estimate. Brian Randell once wrote that the "final major step in the development of the general-purpose electronic computer was the idea of a stored program." The innovation allowed a program to change itself during its execution. The ability was critical back in the early days, when programmers had to rely on cumbersome hardware because they lacked any kind of software support. However, self-altering programs are seldom used, since today's universal machines can be made to do specialized functions simply by downloading a program. Nevertheless, Pres Eckert and John Mauchly's concept of the stored program was the key to unlocking future innovations in computer science. Unfortunately, others would attempt to take credit for their concept. As a result, the history of computing became disputed and distorted by individuals such as Herman Goldstine.

When I first met Herman Goldstine, the U.S. Army liaison to the ENIAC project, I had no idea he would become a fox in the ENIAC henhouse. Over the years, Herman Goldstine made multiple claims about the ENIAC that were inaccurate. Some claims are about small issues, others are about large issues. Goldstine's claims have been passed on by scholars and the media until they have helped form one version of the conventional wisdom about who did what in computer history.

According to Goldstine, he and his wife, Adele, taught the ENIAC women to program the ENIAC, when in fact, they had nothing to do with teaching us to program the ENIAC. Actually, *I* taught *Adele* to program the ENIAC. She knew the ENIAC technology because she had written the operator's manual, but she had not done a real program before I took her under my wing. Goldstine also claimed that he and Adele programmed the ENIAC for the February 15, 1946, demonstration to the scientific community. In truth, Betty Snyder and I were authorized to program it, which we did successfully. Goldstine furthermore asserted that Adele Goldstine and Abraham Taub of Princeton programmed and ran what was known as the Taub Problem.[7] Actually, Adele and I ran the program for Professor Taub.[8]

In his influential 1972 *The Computer from Pascal to von Neumann*, Goldstine claims that famed Hungarian-born mathematician John von Neumann thought up the idea of the stored-program computer concept for the EDVAC in September 1944. According to Goldstine, von Neumann then thought of converting the ENIAC into a stored-program computer in 1947 and gave the idea to Adele to implement. But this was not the case at all. In reality, Dick Clippinger, a manager with Aberdeen's research and development division, was the first to conceive the idea for converting the ENIAC into a stored-program computer.[9] He then brought up the idea to Pres Eckert and John Mauchly, who were instantly receptive to the idea. Pres and John, you see, had already seen the need for a stored-program computer as early as December 1943,[10] and Pres had written about such a concept in January 1944.[11] What I remember being told when I joined the ENIAC project is that John von Neumann had come on the scene around September 1944. John and Pres were building the ENIAC at that time and were already working on the designs for the EDVAC. So it is impossible that the idea of the stored-program computer or the architecture of the EDVAC could have originated with von Neumann, since he was not involved in the project when that work began. John von Neumann only became involved in converting the ENIAC into a stored-program computer because Dick Clippinger and my team (I was project team leader in charge of the programming team that would program the ENIAC to be a stored-program computer) sought out his help in 1946 with questions about what instruction set to implement. Adele and Herman Goldstine sat in on our sessions with von Neumann in Princeton when my team, which included two other mathematicians from Aberdeen Proving Ground as well as Dick Clippinger, consulted with him about the instruction set. I go into more detail about this issue in a later chapter. Consequently, Goldstine should have been very aware that the stored-program computer idea, especially in connection with the ENIAC, did not originate with von Neumann; I can only assume that Goldstine admired von Neumann so much that he decided to attribute the invention to von Neumann regardless of the facts.

To understand, we need to go back to the summer of 1944. Col. Herman Goldstine, the liaison to the University of Pennsylvania for the project from Aberdeen Proving Ground, was standing on the railroad platform in Aberdeen waiting for the train to Philadelphia when he spotted the renowned Hungarian-American mathematician Dr. John von Neumann on the same platform. Goldstine saw von Neumann as larger than life, a mover and shaker in the scientific community, and Goldstine's personal golden ticket to professional success by association. John von Neumann was a diminutive man, but he cut a giant figure in the world of science. His colleague Paul Halmos regarded him as "one of the greatest minds of this century" and called the 1944 *Theory of Games and Economic Behavior*, which von Neumann wrote with Oskar Morgenstern, "one of the major scientific contributions of the first half of the twentieth century."[12]

Janos von Neumann was born in Budapest, Hungary, in 1903 to a wealthy Jewish family. Janos, nicknamed Jancsi (later called John, or Johnny), showed signs of genius from the time he was a child. According to Halmos, "At six, he could divide two eight-digit numbers in his head; by eight he had mastered calculus; by twelve he was at the graduate level in mathematics. He could memorize pages on sight."[13] When von Neumann was ten, the Austro-Hungarian government conferred nobility upon his father, Miksa, for the service that he, a lawyer, had rendered to the Austro-Hungarian Empire, and the Austrian nobility designation "von" was added to the name. Johann, as he now called himself, earned a PhD in mathematics from the University of Budapest in 1926 at the age of twenty-three. At the same time, he earned a degree in chemical engineering from the Swiss Federal Institute of Technology in Zurich to please his father, who thought mathematics was not a sound career.

By 1929, von Neumann was at work on quantum mechanics, and three years later he came out with his classic book *The Mathematical Foundations of Quantum Mechanics*. By that time, he had published nearly three dozen major papers. He was not yet thirty years old. By 1930, von Neumann and his mother and brothers had immigrated to the United States to escape the growing specter of Nazism, and John (he anglicized his first name) had been made a professor at the Institute for Advanced Study in Princeton. When the Institute for Advanced Study was established in 1933, von Neumann numbered among the six mathematicians who made up its staff. One of the other five was the Swiss mathematician and physicist Albert Einstein.

Skip forward a decade. In 1944, John von Neumann was a consultant to Aberdeen, Los Alamos, and various other government laboratories. Surprisingly, until that day on the railroad platform, no one at Aberdeen had ever told von Neumann about the ENIAC—probably because the Aberdeen scientists were afraid it would not work. Herman Goldstine had never met John von Neumann, but that didn't stop him from going up to the great man and introducing himself. After the two had chatted for a few moments, Goldstine brought up the ENIAC and began to tell von Neumann about it. Goldstine asked von Neumann if he would like to come see it. Of course von Neumann said he would, and Goldstine arranged for him to come in September 1944.

When von Neumann showed up, the ENIAC engineers demonstrated the two-accumulator test for him. Pres and John had designed it to prove their ideas about the accumulator design. Kay McNulty (who later married John Mauchly) was there for the two-accumulator test. At the time, she was working at the Moore School and had heard rumors about a "Project X" or PX, which would become known as the ENIAC.

According to Kay, the first time she really knew anything about the ENIAC was in early 1944.

> Pres Eckert and John Mauchly came into the analyzer room one night all excited and asked us—Alice Snyder and me—to come and see this. They took us to an enclosed area in front of the room where the PX was being built. The enclosed area was about 6 or 8 feet square with a big sign saying, "High Voltage, Keep Out." Inside, they had two accumulators connected together with a long cord attached that had a control button on it (a remote control). They said, "Look at this." One accumulator had a five in it. One of them pushed a button and the five appeared in the other accumulator three places over, thus reading as 5,000. We were perplexed and asked, "What's so great about that? You used all this equipment to multiply five by 1,000." They explained that the five had

been transferred from the one accumulator to the other a thousand times in an instant. We had no appreciation at all of what this really meant. That this was the famous two-accumulator test that proved their idea for the PX (the ENIAC) would work. No wonder they were excited.[14]

When Pres Eckert was told that the great von Neumann was coming to see the ENIAC run the test, he was unimpressed. He had known many noted scientists who didn't live up to their billing. So Pres made a pronouncement to those around him: If von Neumann asked the particular question Pres deemed crucial to understanding the ENIAC, Pres would know he was worth knowing. After seeing the test, von Neumann asked one question: "How do you control it?" As far as Pres was concerned, that was the right question.

After that, Pres and John were willing to open up to von Neumann and discuss their ideas with him, including their ideas for the EDVAC. Intrigued with the group's work, von Neumann asked to join Pres and John Mauchly's meetings on the EDVAC design. He was accepted into the group and was very active in the discussions. In fact, John Mauchly, in his video memoirs, said that von Neumann was one of the men he admired most in his life. John von Neumann, he said, understood things almost instantly and made contributions.

That fall of 1944, von Neumann attended several weeks' worth of meetings but then had to go to Los Alamos, New Mexico, because the scientists at Los Alamos Laboratory were conducting tests for dropping an atom bomb.[15] While there, John von Neumann wrote a document that would be entitled "First Draft of a Report on the EDVAC." Despite its boring title, this document would become famous and influential; it was the first public description of the logic—the "architecture"—by which stored-program computers would work.

John von Neumann sent Herman Goldstine a copy of the "First Draft" report. Pres Eckert and John Mauchly said that Goldstine did tell them about von Neumann's report; however, according to Pres and John, Goldstine initially told them that the von Neumann document was nothing more than the minutes of their meetings, organized so that members of the group could read about the EDVAC and have a better grasp of its design.

Dr. Reed Warren had replaced Dr. John Grist Brainerd as the University of Pennsylvania's liaison with Aberdeen Proving Ground after the engineers had almost revolted against Dr. Brainerd because of his bureaucratic style.[16] Goldstine told Warren, his civilian counterpart, that the report was for internal distribution, which was consistent with what he had told Pres and John. After all, the ENIAC and the EDVAC projects were both classified. However, instead of giving it only

The EDVAC as installed in Ballistic Research Laboratory at Aberdeen Proving Ground, 1948. Unknown man at the console (left); Richard Bianco at the paper tape machine (right). U.S. Army photo.

to the engineers working on the EDVAC project, Goldstine distributed the report widely to various U.S. government agencies and to a number of universities. Not only was this wide distribution a blatant violation of the project's military classified status, but it also effectively squelched any chance John and Pres had to patent the EDVAC, since the information had now become broadly disseminated.

Strangely, John von Neumann never mentions electronic circuits in the "First Draft" document. He uses the word "neurons" to describe electronic circuits. In a February 1973 oral history interview for the Smithsonian Institution, John Mauchly said, "There is some evidence…to indicate that von Neumann chose to use neurons as the elements of his computer rather than vacuum tubes just to make it possible to say that they saw no need for classifying this. We were not consulted. We were not advised even. We didn't know these things were happening. So it was only some years later that we began to realize the full impact of this."[17]

The "First Draft" report certainly didn't give appropriate credit for what was learned from the Aberdeen team meetings, and without those meetings, von Neumann would have had nothing to write about. Some statements I've read over the years seem to indicate that John von Neumann believed, and probably Goldstine with him, that the greater good for science and possibly for the United States would be achieved by having this report disseminated as widely as possible. Consequently, I believe that von Neumann deliberately used the word "neuron" in place of "electronic circuit" to try to distance his report from Eckert and Mauchly's work. In this rather underhanded way, the EDVAC architecture described in the report became known as the "von Neumann architecture" and unfortunately, computer historians most often say that early stored-program computers used a "von Neumann architecture." Thus, credit for the invention of the computer, at least in the general parlance, shifted from Eckert and Mauchly to the latecomer, von Neumann.

John von Neumann's report had no footnotes and no references to the EDVAC group from which he got the design. What von Neumann really did was rename components of the EDVAC and write a well-organized paper giving a clear description of the EDVAC architecture, which he was intimately acquainted with as a result of sitting in on the Moore School meetings. Adding to this betrayal, von Neumann ever afterward accepted credit—falsely—for the work of the Moore School group. It is interesting that, in later years, whenever John Mauchly attended any lecture by John von Neumann (and Mauchly attended many of them), von Neumann never even acknowledged Mauchly's presence from the lectern. It's hard to believe that von Neumann could have missed him, since Mauchly always made it a point to sit on the front row.

Why would a world-famous mathematician and universally admired figure do such a thing? Well, I believe that John von Neumann was a brilliant man who realized that electronic computers would have more effect on the world than any of his mathematical contributions and he wanted to be known as a key contributor to the computer. John Mauchly, in my opinion, was as much of a logician as von Neumann. Moreover, Mauchly had brilliant, original ideas. My belief is that von Neumann didn't have original ideas in computing, just a brilliant ability to take original work on computing and expand upon it. More importantly, von Neumann had the wisdom to be the first to write it down. In addition, John von Neumann had a willing disciple in Goldstine, who idolized him. Goldstine's ambition, along with his hero worship, skewed history, shaping events into what he preferred should have happened rather than what actually happened.

In Goldstine's book *The Computer from Pascal to von Neumann*, he includes an anecdote that is similar to an event that happened to Betty Snyder Holberton and me. We frequently and publically recounted this incident to our colleagues. The incident that happened to us is that one night, as Betty and I were working on getting the trajectory debugged on the ENIAC, Dean Pender came down and asked us how we were doing. We said that we were doing okay. He then gave us a paper bag with a bottle of liquor in it and said, with a wink, "Hop to it." In the book, which was published twenty-seven years later, Goldstine wrote that the incident happened to him and Adele, but this was the first instance that Betty and I had ever heard about him receiving liquor from Dean. I think Goldstine appropriated what happened to Betty and me to add a little human interest to his story.

The actions of von Neumann and Goldstine with regard to Mauchly and Eckert were unethical. Herman Goldstine, who viewed von Neumann as a mentor, enthusiastically supported von Neumann's wrongful claims and essentially helped the man hijack the work of Eckert, Mauchly, and the others in the Moore School group. The truth may be hard to swallow, but it is the truth. I apologize right now for whatever sacred cows I may be tipping over in order to set the record straight; nevertheless, the record needs to be set straight.

I personally liked John von Neumann, despite his less-than-stellar conduct with regard to taking credit from Mauchly, Eckert, and the other hard-working members of the Moore School team. And I initially liked Herman Goldstine, especially since Adele and I always got along famously. However, while I have a dim view of Herman Goldstine for various reasons, I have a generally good opinion of von Neumann, who was always gracious to me. John von Neumann was, without doubt, a shining star in the scientific universe. It is just unfortunate that some of his starlight had to be appropriated from others. Together, von Neumann and Goldstine let the cat out of the bag on the EDVAC with the unauthorized release of von Neumann's report. The leaked report helped to cement von Neumann's claim to fame, giving him the credit and glory that rightfully should have gone to Mauchly, Eckert, and the Moore School group.

Herman Goldstine was quick to assure everyone that von Neumann would have given John Mauchly, Pres Eckert, and the rest of the Moore School team credit had von Neumann known that it would be distributed widely. I find that difficult to believe since von Neumann, in a signed affidavit dated May 8, 1947, which was notarized by a New Jersey Notary Public who was also a secretary for the Institute for Advanced Study at Princeton, stated that Herman Goldstine asked him to write the document for the Moore School group for publication.[18]

> During the first half of 1945 it was felt desirable by Dr., then Captain, H. H. Goldstine, as that time the technical representative of the Office of the Chief of Ordnance on the ENIAC and EDVAC projects, as well as by myself, to write a report which summarized the general ideas dealing with the overall organization of a high speed computer, of the type which the projected EDVAC was conceived to represent.[19]

Whatever the case, von Neumann never made an effort to dispel the general acclaim in the years that followed. He accepted the accolades as his due and thrived on them for the rest of his life. And Goldstine helped to keep up his idol's charade. Forty years later, in recordings made for MIT's oral history project, Herman Goldstine was still doing so, much to Kay McNulty Mauchly's dismay. The two tangled over the issue, but Goldstine held firm. As novelist Stephen King once said, if you repeat a lie long enough, it can become your truth. Enough said.

I guess the quintessential historic declaration would have to be, "I was there." Tenzing Norgay could say it about accompanying Edmund Hillary up Everest. Thomas Watson could say it about assisting Alexander Graham Bell in the invention of the telephone. And the six Marines shown raising the flag on Iwo Jima in the famous photograph could certainly say it. Well, I was there in 1945 when the ENIAC was programmed. And there were women in the room.

Betty Snyder and I programmed the problem the ENIAC ran that first day of the computer era. We were two of a team of six computer programmers for the ENIAC—all women. We six women were the first computer programmers in the world. The role we played in history was due largely to good fortune. When I worked as a programmer for the ENIAC from 1945 to 1947, I was happy just to be there and doing the job I was hired to do. I always felt that I had merely happened to land in the right place at the right time.

But how did Betty and I get there? We had been among dozens of female "computers" working on the campus of the University of Pennsylvania for the Aberdeen Proving Ground. We calculated trajectories for shells fired from large guns, using Friden, Monroe, and Marchant hand calculators. Out of those dozens, Betty and I were picked to set up and run the ENIAC, along with Ruth Lichterman, Kay McNulty, Marlyn Wescoff, and Fran Bilas.

The human computers, numbering about one hundred, were almost exclusively women. Initially, Aberdeen had recruited only women math majors for these posts, but not many women at that time majored in math. So eventually they began recruiting women who had any math background at all, and Aberdeen trained them in the mathematics needed for the job. Of the original ENIAC programmers, Kay McNulty, Fran Bilas, and I had been math majors. The other three had some math in their background and were trained by Aberdeen. Women did many things during those years, because we were in a terrible war and almost all the able-bodied men were in the armed services fighting the war. The women were left to rivet together aircraft, build tanks, or do a hundred other formerly male tasks.

For similar reasons that the vast majority of computers were women, all of the first programmers were women. Despite our coming of age in an era when women's career opportunities were generally quite confined, we helped initiate the era of the computer. Through a series of fortuitous circumstances, we were allowed to play an important technical role during a time when American society, as well as American science and engineering, was even more sexist than it is today.

Yet even before we were allowed to program the ENIAC, women had had a long and storied association with the computer, dating back over one hundred years. Probably the earliest was Ada Lovelace, Lord Byron's daughter by a female mathematician, Anne Isabella Milbanke, whom he had married in a hurry to hush up a scandal about his having a relationship with his half-sister. Byron wooed Anne Milbanke by talking of parallel lines and parallelograms, but he left her when Ada was born in 1815, moving to the Mediterranean, and neither Ada nor her mother ever saw him again.

Nonetheless, Anne Milbanke taught her daughter mathematics. At the age of seventeen, Ada became acquainted with Charles Babbage, who was twenty-five years her senior. Babbage (1791–1871) was the English engineer who originated the concept of a programmable computer and designed several mechanical computers, such as his difference engine. Babbage talked to Ada Lovelace about another machine he had conceived and was working on called the analytical engine, which was designed to use punch cards of the Jacquard rug mills for control. It was programmable, and Ada programmed a problem for it.

An Italian mathematician, Luigi Menabrea, wrote a paper on Babbage's analytical engine, and Baggage asked Ada to translate it. As Ada did so, she made so many additions and corrections to Menabrea's paper that Babbage suggested she write her own paper about it. She did. Her paper on the analytical engine came out in 1843 and was published under only her initials, because a woman would not have been taken seriously. Indeed, for many years male historians, in their desire to discount the accomplishments of women, have said that she only translated Menabrea's paper. Regardless, Ada Lovelace is considered to have been the first programmer.[20] One of the highest awards that the Association for Women in Computing can bestow on women in the technology industry is called the Ada Lovelace Award. My co-programmer Betty Snyder Holberton received the Ada Lovelace Award in 1997, a few years before her death.

I find it remarkable how many programming pioneers were women. For instance, Grace Hopper worked on the Mark I calculator at Harvard and developed the first compiler for a computer programming language. During World War II, women ran the code-breaking programs on the Colossus machines at Bletchley Park in England for Prime Minister Churchill's secret intelligence group, which has been credited with shortening the war by eighteen months. These women were generally never named and were not allowed to tell anyone—not even family members—what they were doing during the war.[21] Immediately following the war, American women programmed the Whirlwind at MIT, which was completed in 1951, the first computer to display real-time video.[22]

When the other five ENIAC women and I answered an advertisement for female math majors, we stepped into the midst of this lineage. Our official job title was "computer"; no one thought of the title of "programmer" until well after the ENIAC was in operation. Initially all our job description called for us to do was to set switches and plug in cables to represent the problem being calculated. You see, originally, the designers and planners of the ENIAC thought that mathematicians would design the setup for their own problems, and we women would just set up the hardware of the ENIAC and run the problem. But it quickly became clear that planning the program setup was too complex for mathematicians to learn easily, and they had neither the time nor the inclination to do so. The Ballistics Research Lab at the Moore School proceeded to select six women to receive training to become ENIAC programmers starting in June 1945, and the ENIAC women became the programmers who designed the flowcharts and formats for planning the programs that ran on the ENIAC. Actually, only two scientists, Nick Metropolis and Stan Frankel from Los Alamos, designed and ran their own problem—with help from ENIAC programmers Kay, Fran, Ruth, and Marlyn.

In a way, women became the first programmers by accident. If the ENIAC's administrators had known how crucial programming would be to the functioning of the electronic computer and how complex it would prove to be, they might have been more hesitant to give such an important role to women. I believe that Herman Goldstine was having difficulty with programming, and that is why he invited Betty and me to his apartment in West Philadelphia on February 2, 1946. Whatever the real reason, Betty and I were quite surprised to be invited to coffee with him and his wife, because neither one had interacted with us very much before. Consequently, the invitation was a pleasant surprise.

At the apartment, Herman asked Betty and me if our trajectory program was ready to run on the ENIAC. We told him that it was indeed ready to go. Goldstine then invited Betty and me to run the program on the ENIAC for the first public demonstration on February 15, 1946. As you can imagine, we were thrilled and delighted that our program would be the one to be demonstrated.

The reason Betty and I were the ones chosen to program the trajectory problem was that, shortly after our programming group of six women had been assembled, Ruth Lichterman and Marlyn Wescoff had been assigned the job of manually calculating a trajectory exactly the way the ENIAC would do it, add time by add time. The time it took to do an addition was the basic timing element of the ENIAC. Betty and I used this calculation by Ruth and Marlyn to test the ENIAC's accuracy as well as our own in programming the trajectory. It was a very valuable tool for us, and it would prove to be a gateway to our getting the respect of the engineers and the other men around us. It allowed us to debug the ENIAC down to a vacuum tube, and there were about 18,000 of them in the ENIAC.

In October 1945, Metropolis and Frankel had made a trip to Philadelphia to learn about the ENIAC from Pres and John and the engineers. In December 1945, they had come back to put a problem for Los Alamos on the ENIAC. ENIAC programmers Kay, Fran, Ruth, and Marlyn were assigned to help them. On March 18, 1946, Dr. Norris Bradbury, Director of the Los Alamos Laboratory, acknowledged that having the ENIAC perform the calculations was of tremendous value to the Los Alamos project.

While Kay, Fran, Ruth, and Marlyn were helping Nick and Sam, Betty and I were programming a trajectory for the ENIAC. That trajectory program would be the one used as the test program for the ENIAC. In order for Aberdeen to accept the computer—thus allowing Penn to fulfill its contract with Aberdeen—the test had to succeed. It succeeded.

Our test program for the trajectory was the one used for the formal scientific demonstration on February 15, 1946. After that exciting ENIAC demonstration, the men all went out to eat and celebrate together. However, the ENIAC women were left behind with barely a word of congratulations for our many contributions to the success of the project. The ENIAC female programmers had always felt respected and valued by our male coworkers. Yet that night we were forgotten, even by them. Why? I don't have an adequate answer other than to say that it was a different time and society at large expected us to stand behind our men and silently support them. Like every other American woman, the ENIAC women played the role society had assigned to us and we played it well and generally without rancor, although not without some hurt feelings.

While it would have been nice to be included in the festivities and receive our own accolades for a job well done, at least all of us knew the truth about our contributions. Each of us women could also feel a quiet satisfaction in being able to say, "I was there." We had tamed a mechanical beast and made it purr.

The ENIAC was the first electronic computer built and demonstrated to the world. Computers like the Z3 in Germany and the Colossus in England had been built and run secretly during World War II, but nobody outside of a small circle had heard of them. All other predecessors of the ENIAC, such as Harvard's Mark I and the Stibitz machine from Bell Laboratories, were electromechanical. The ENIAC opened the gateway to electronic computing, which eventually led to the computing industry we know today. It is hard to imagine, but the behemoth ENIAC had less computing power than a laptop or palm-held computer of today. It ran at 100 kilocycles (100,000 cycles per second), while today's personal computers run at several gigahertz (billions of cycles per second)—more than 10,000 times as fast as the ENIAC. Yet only sixty years ago such computing power was even more breathtaking than the computing speeds of the PCs used today.

The ENIAC's forty panels, which almost covered the walls of its forty-by-thirty-foot room, contained the electronics and controls of the various units needed to do calculations: twenty accumulators (each of which could add or subtract a ten-decimal-digit number carrying a positive or negative sign), a multiplier, a divider/square-rooter, three function tables (each of which could store 102

Moore School of Electrical Engineering, University of Pennsylvania, ca. 1944.

twelve-decimal-digit numbers), a card reader, a card punch, a master programmer (the control unit for programs), a cycling unit, and power supplies.

The press hailed the ENIAC as a "giant brain" and scientists from around the world came to see this marvel and learn whether it could help solve some of the millennium problems—ones that would take a thousand years to compute using a hand calculator—that plagued them.

The public demonstration on February 15, 1946, was designed to assure the U.S. Army, which was purchasing the computer, that the ENIAC could perform the operation it was designed for. During World War II, many new guns were developed, and servicemen needed to know at what angle of elevation to set a particular gun for the shell to reach a distant target. While the ENIAC was being built, Aberdeen had to produce firing tables by combining results from a mechanical "differential analyzer" computer with results from human computers. The highly accurate trajectories were interspersed with the less accurate trajectories from the mechanical, analog differential analyzer, and the results were smoothed to produce the final firing tables. This process worked, but it took a human about forty hours to compute a trajectory. That was too long to keep up with all the new guns being produced and the varied conditions under which they would be used.

In 1945, prior to the ENIAC being completed, we "human computers" had to calculate trajectories for each gun, which were collected into tables and bound in a handbook that soldiers could take out in the field and use for aiming and firing their guns. Later, when the ENIAC programmers went from the Moore School to Aberdeen for training, we met some of these soldiers. They teased us by saying that they had never used the tables, but finally they admitted that when they went out in the field they always grabbed the firing table for the gun they were going to use and found them very reliable. Unfortunately, the ENIAC was not completed until several months after WWII ended and was not used to actively produce firing tables during the war.

Both the human computers and the ENIAC for demonstration purposes calculated the trajectories using numerical integration, which is a mathematical method by which the arc of a circle is replaced by a series of straight lines. The shorter the lines—that is, the interval of integration—the more accurately the calculation represents the true arc. At that time Aberdeen Proving Ground consisted of 32,000 acres of mostly swamps. Aberdeen did several test firings of new guns out over the firing range using various measuring devices to obtain the altitude of the shell at timed intervals and the distance it traveled. The scientists there also measured atmospheric conditions such as temperature, barometric pressure, and sea level. Aberdeen did only a few test firings for each gun; these test firing data were used as the input for performing the calculations of the hundreds of trajectories that made up the firing table for that gun.

The distance the shell travels when fired from the gun depends on a number of factors: the angle of elevation of the gun, the velocity of the shell as it leaves the muzzle of the gun, the altitude of the gun, and the drag of the air on the shell. The drag of the air on the shell likewise depends on several factors, such as temperature, height above sea level, and barometric pressure. The most important factor, however, is the speed of the shell as it pushes on the envelope of air in front of it. As the shell speed increases, the amount of air that it pushes in front of it becomes greater and greater, offering more and more resistance, until the shell reaches the speed of sound. Then, remarkably, when the shell surpasses the speed of sound, the air is no longer pushed ahead of the shell but streams smoothly along its sides, producing much smaller amounts of drag on the shell.

When this change occurs, however, tremendous forces are put on the shell, causing it to yaw (wiggle and waggle). This is known as breaking the sound barrier. It is called the sound barrier because at one time scientists believed that an object could not travel faster than the speed of sound. The speed of sound is dependent on the temperature, but it is about 758 miles per hour when the temperature is at 68 degrees Fahrenheit. As most of us know, breaking the sound barrier produces a loud boom that can be heard for miles. The speed of sound is called Mach 1, named after the nineteenth-century physicist Ernst Mach. Subsonic speed is less than Mach 1, transonic speed is at Mach 1, and supersonic speed is greater than Mach 1. Hypersonic speed is greater than Mach 5, or five times the speed of sound.

For our calculation of the trajectory, the drag function was stored in the three function tables of the ENIAC, and we merely calculated the speed of the shell in order to find out the amount of drag. Each of the twenty accumulators contained ten columns in its upper half and ten columns in its lower half. Each of these ten columns had ten rows of electronic vacuum tubes with a neon bulb to display the status of each vacuum tube. These neon bulbs peeked through holes drilled in the front panel. Thus each accumulator stored a ten-digit number. Another column of two rows in each panel represented the sign of the ten-digit number, either positive or negative.

As the ENIAC made the calculations for the trajectory, its calculations were shown in the lights of the accumulators, which flickered and flashed as the numbers were built up in the accumulators and transferred from one accumulator to another and finally to the card punch to output the result. The tops of ENIAC's neon bulbs were small and nothing spectacular to look at, which was unfortunate, since a movie crew would be there to film the ENIAC in action. Consequently, for several accumulators, Pres and John (the ENIAC's inventors) placed halves of Ping-Pong balls over the tops of the neon bulbs and painted a large number on each one; the numbers denoted the row each vacuum tube represented (an integer from 0 to 9). The numbers showed up clearly, especially since the room's lights were turned off for the demonstration, and the brightly lit, flashing "bulbs" gave viewers something dramatic to view.

The demonstration proved to be spectacular. As Pres had promised those in attendance, the ENIAC raced through the calculations of the shell's arc faster than the time it took the shell to trace it. It was unheard of that a machine could reach such speeds of calculation, and everyone in the room, even the great mathematicians, were in complete wonder and awe at what they had just seen. The ENIAC used IBM punched cards to hold input and output data and for printing, so following the demonstration we—Betty and I and perhaps Kay—took the output punched cards to the IBM tabulator and printed them out as souvenirs for the attendees. The tabulator read the punched cards and printed the output on ordinary paper in ordinary language that described the trajectory calculation.

Some in that august assembly to whom we handed the printed output merely glanced at it and slipped it into their inside breast pocket; others studied it curiously, as if trying to fathom its mysteries. That seemingly ordinary piece of paper was a kind of Rosetta stone, providing the key not to the past, but to the future—a future so breathtakingly innovative that it has produced wondrous wireless, mobile communication devices and other technological achievements that in 1945 were either undreamed of or the stuff of science fictions. However, before we journey into the future, let us take a trip back in time to the year 1927 and a small farm in northwest Missouri. Surprisingly, my years growing up in a rural community prepared me to become a pioneer in the field of computing.

CHAPTER 2
My Story
How It All Began

I consider that I am a most unlikely person to have been there for the birth of the computer, which just goes to show that the Fates can weave an intricate path to one's destiny. Believe me, as a young girl growing up on a farm in Missouri, I never dreamed of having a destiny. But, oh, did I dream! As much as I loved my family, I dreamed of going to far-off places and being independent. When I first got to Philadelphia, I would walk the streets thinking, "Nobody here knows anyone from my family." I loved it, because I wanted to make my life my own. I had never had a separate identity in Missouri—I was always the relative of someone. It was only natural, since I was the sixth of seven children of Bill and Lula Jennings, born on December 27, 1924.

My father, William Smith Jennings, was a schoolteacher and a farmer. He had started first grade when he was four years old. By the

Lula Spainhower [Jennings], Betty Jean's mother, ca. 1906.

time he was seventeen, he was teaching in a one-room school. My mother was very intelligent, but she had only gone as far as eighth grade. She could, however, do algebra and geometry as well as my father.

My mother met my father when she was twenty-six and he was twenty. She had gone around with a neighbor boy since they were children, and this neighbor boy had given her a ring. I suppose they were considered engaged. So when my dad began going out with her, he immediately told her to get rid of the other man's ring. Mom, deciding that she liked my father far more than she liked the neighbor boy, threw the ring in a well. As children, we knew where the well had been (it no longer existed) and considered the story very romantic. My maiden aunt Elsie always said that Mom made a fool of herself over Dad. She said he would come riding up on his horse and whistle, and Mom would come running. I thought that was the way it ought to be: if you can't make a fool of yourself over him, don't marry him.

Since I was the sixth of seven children, my older brothers and sisters had already done what I was doing, so I always felt like nobody, including my parents, was interested in my stories and that nobody listened to me at the dinner table. Of course, we children had a life that our parents never knew about, as I'm sure children still do today. Our father was a strict disciplinarian, but we considered that what he didn't know wouldn't hurt him—or us, for that matter! When we were disobedient, my mother saved the discipline up for Dad to dispense when he got home, and he would spank us with a razor strop. Needless to say, we were often not happy to see him come home.

I never knew my oldest brother, William, very well. He was older than me and was married at nineteen when I was in the fifth grade. But I do remember that when Dad told him to do something, he would say, "I was just planning to do that." My oldest sister, Erma, eight years older than me, was the cook for the family. She was truly a good person, and everyone loved her.

My next oldest brother, Bob, was six years older than me, was the goody-two-shoes of the family and a charmer, although I considered him a brownnoser. Every old person in the neighborhood thought Bob was wonderful. When I followed Bob to high school and college, all of those spinster English and math teachers remembered Bob fondly, but I certainly didn't measure up to his charm. He had a couple of janitorial jobs—first for our little one-room school and later in high school. Then he worked his way through college being a butler, chauffeur, companion, and all-around gofer for a rich lady, Old Lady Townsend. He planned to be a doctor, so he caponized chickens and worked on any injured animals. When I was young, he was my favorite.

He did have one characteristic that didn't fit with the goody-two-shoes image: when he became angry, he would go on a tear until he managed to destroy at least three things. Not that he intended to—he would just get so frustrated that he would wind up breaking a gate or a glass or ripping a shirt. Other than that, he was pleasant and mild and helpful with most any task. He had auburn-red hair. I also had red hair, but it was carrot-red, not beautiful auburn like Bob's.

Next in line was my sister Lula May, four years older than me. We called her Lulu or Lou because she had a boyfriend who imitated Bing Crosby crooning "Lulu's Back in Town," a hit song from the 1935 movie *Broadway Gondolier*. Lulu was Mom's housekeeper and a holy terror. She threw fits when we messed up the house, which we did all the time because it was a four-room house for nine people. She was very attractive and always had lots of boyfriends. Lulu was also a good fighter. One time, when she came home from college, my brother Raymond said something she didn't like. She whirled around, threw him to the floor, and sat on him. He was sure surprised.

Next was Raymond, who was a macho male and two years older than me. He worked very hard, played rough games, and tried to live pretty close to the edge. Raymond, I felt, was determined to kill me—or at least maim me. At different times, Raymond challenged me to climb to the top of the windmill, jump off the roof of a barn, and see how close to my fingers I could chop an ear of corn with a corn knife. For some reason I accepted all of his dares. One time, I was drawing water from an open well; it was about three feet in diameter and its top was level with the ground. Raymond pushed me, and I very nearly fell in. It scared the life out of not only me but him too, and ever after that he drew the water for the cows himself.

Raymond was not an outstanding student, but I think his IQ was perhaps higher than any of the rest of us. He always used his head in ordinary life and became a very successful farmer. When he was about eighteen, he went into a venture with my brother-in-law, Forrest Alldredge, to go up to Minnesota to head bluegrass on the farmers' pastures there. Heading bluegrass means to strip off the bluegrass heads using a header (stripper). Raymond borrowed money to lease the pastures and rent bluegrass strippers and the tractors to pull them. The strippers were about eight feet wide with a cylinder of teeth that ripped off the heads as the cylinder rotated and funneled them into a catcher. When the catcher was full, Raymond and Forrest would empty it in rows on a tarpaulin placed on the ground, where the heads were dried in the sun. They raked the rows of bluegrass heads over and over again each day until the heads gave up the seeds. They could then rake off the chaff, because the seeds would fall to the bottom, and gather up the seeds in sacks ready for market. The price of the seed was higher if the seed was cleaner, containing very little chaff. About fourteen miles from my hometown of Stanberry is King City, Missouri, which was called the Bluegrass Capital for the many companies there that processed bluegrass seed. The town even has a museum displaying various types of strippers that were used over the years. At the end of the summer, Raymond had a profit of about two thousand dollars, which was a lot of money in 1941. He bought a little Ford coupe, which attracted a lot of my girlfriends that fall. He gunned it as we went over the top of hills and as it left the ground and fell back, just over the crest, it took my breath away. He was also pretty dashing because he was taking civilian pilot's training.

I was next in line. Mom already had a cook (Erma) and a housekeeper (Lou), so I always worked outdoors with the men. That didn't prevent me from being responsible for washing the dishes and the separator (a machine that used centrifugal force to separate the cream from the whey in milk), even if I had worked outside with the men all day. It was a male chauvinist environment. In the evenings my brothers would sit reading the paper, while I was expected to wash the dishes. The inequality really galled me. Later on, my Uncle Fred would pay the boys a dollar a day to hoe corn for him while he paid me fifty cents, even though I hoed as much corn as the boys. The unfairness of his treatment was not lost on me, and to this day, whenever I perceive a situation to be unfair—toward others or myself—I become genuinely enraged.

Fortunately, the male chauvinist attitudes did not spill over to the intellectual sphere. Women in my family were considered to be as bright as the males, if not brighter. My Grandma Jennings—Eliza Jane Coffey Jennings—had been a schoolteacher. She claimed that education had gone to hell when the old McGuffey Readers were abandoned in favor of newer books. Grandma had also been a heroine once when my grandfather was county sheriff. My grandfather was out and some prisoners tried to break out of jail. She held them at gunpoint until my grandfather returned. Grandma's example proved what we had always been told: that we Jennings girls could do anything if we worked hard enough.

The last and best of the family was my younger sister Kathleen, born four years after me. We called her Tommy for a while, but later, and for the rest of her life, she was Kackie. Her various nicknames came from Kathleen herself. She couldn't pronounce Kathleen when she was little and could only say Kackie. Then one day she was wearing overalls and said she was a boy called Tommy. Kathleen was adorable and we all loved her to pieces. Kathleen was not only delightful, but she was very pretty, intelligent, and fun to be with. We caused her no end of anxiety because we fought over who would get to be with her. I loved her more than anyone in my life until I had children. She was a truly good person who experienced a lot of adversity in her life. Kathleen married a football player who went into the U.S. Army and became a Green Beret. He cheated on her. They adopted two children, but parenthood didn't solve their marriage problems, which continued to get worse with time.

In the 1960s, Kathleen was an English teacher for the U.S. Army and taught the men whom Secretary of Defense Robert McNamara had recruited under the philosophy that anyone and everyone can serve in the Army. Many couldn't read or write when they came to her, yet she had fabulous successes with some of them. When Kathleen died of a heart attack in her mid-fifties, a piece of my heart died with her.

Although I had a very nice family growing up, I have never cared for large families. This may be surprising in light of my big, boisterous clan, but it's true. I think it is almost impossible for children to have a close relationship with parents who have their attention divided so many ways. There just isn't enough time in the day to spend very much of it—or any of it—with each of the children. I do realize there are many advantages to being part of a large family, especially if the siblings include both boys and girls. I learned about how each gender acts and how to react to them. I learned to get along with people with different ideas, even crazy and bizarre ones. I learned how to survive without getting my own way. I learned how to compete and be heard and to fight for myself. Plus, I learned that I could trust any member of my family with my life. What they said they would do, they did. What they said was true, was true. Those last two things have not always helped me. I find it almost impossible to believe that people do not keep their word and do lie. I am an easy mark, but I would rather be that than a suspicious, paranoid person.

Growing up in this family sounds wonderful as I write it, yet I was often lonely. I felt that whenever I expressed myself, somebody in the family always had some criticism. So I spent a great deal of my time in a fantasy world. I would go out in the pasture, lie down, look up in the sky, and dream. Sometimes I went up in the hayloft to dream. Things in my daydreams always turned out as I wanted them to. Sometimes when the family went out for some reason, such as to clean up the churchyard or cemetery (there was no lawnmower, so we used sickles and scythes and clippers), I would stay home. I loved the feel of the house when it had only me in it. I could do as I pleased and no one had anything to say about it. I often imagined that I was an only child, that my parents had left me at this farm temporarily and would come back for me someday. I wanted to be an only child, and not have to compete with all those brothers and sisters. On those days when

Betty Jean with family, ca. 1932. Front row (left to right): Kathleen "Kackie" Jennings (sister), Betty Jean Jennings, William Jennings (father), Glen Grantham (relative), Bobbie Grantham (relative), and Bob Jennings (brother). Back row (left to right): Lula May Jennings (sister) and Neal Best (relative).

I was alone in the house, I was allowed to live this fantasy. I always prepared a good dinner, such as an old hen with noodles and dressing and a cake for dessert (I could cook by the time I was ten or eleven) and Mom was always delighted to come home and find that she didn't have to prepare dinner. Because dinner was already ready when they returned from the churchyard or cemetery, nobody minded that I stayed home.

Our Grandma Jennings was very important in our lives. Grandma was widowed when my dad was twelve years old. Dad was the sixth of eight children, five boys and three girls. So Grandma had small children and a large family to support on her own. She had a farm of about three hundred acres. Uncle Fred farmed it on the shares with her when I was young, but earlier, she did it herself with the help of her five sons. All the children who were interested were educated. Back in those days, one could teach school after going one or two years to a normal school, which trained teachers. Dad's older brothers Pat and Egbert became schoolteachers, as did my Aunt Gretchen.

Grandma lived in a large farmhouse about one-and-a-half miles from our house. Later, we moved to a farm within a quarter mile of her house. I went to see her every day. I rode our pony, Beauty. We were too poor to afford the St. Joseph *News-Press*, but Grandma took the paper, and she assured us that she had it read by four in the afternoon, so one of us always went to pick up the paper. I'm sure she was too busy most days to have it read by four, but she also took the weekly *Kansas City Star*. She said that anything that was very important was in the weekly newspaper, which she read thoroughly.

Grandma would always ask me to gather eggs from her hayloft because she didn't want to climb up the ladder. It was a straight wood ladder with slats, nailed to the frame of a square hole in the loft floor that was used to throw down hay for the horses and cows housed below. There were no cages up there for roosting hens—they just sneaked up there to make nests in the hay to lay eggs in. I would gather the eggs for her every few days. For that and other chores, she would give me a dime. And she always had pound cake in her pantry, and she would tell me to go get a piece after the work was done. Everyone in the family looked up to Grandma and loved her. As a child, I'm sure I told her all the family secrets, for she always listened to what I had to say, usually without comment.

When I was five years old, I had appendicitis. Old Doc Williamson, the local doctor, assumed the pain in my stomach came from eating green apples or something equally as bad, and he gave me a laxative. Shortly thereafter, my appendix ruptured, resulting in peritonitis, which was almost always fatal back in that era before penicillin. The Wallace brothers, doctors who shared a practice in St. Joseph, Missouri, operated on me, placing small rubber drainage tubes in my side. Sometimes one of them would come to see me and sometimes the other—and although I liked one of them much better than the other, I'm not sure I ever knew their first names.

The two physicians told my mother that she must make me lie on that side twenty-four hours a day to drain out the infection. She stayed with me for twenty-four hours a day except for about an hour when she went out to a local drugstore for lunch. She slept on a cot in my room and ate one meal a day. Everybody in the hospital thought I was a brat because I would scream when my mother left me to go to lunch. But actually I was just scared. You see, what no one knew was that one of the janitors would come into my room whenever my mother left and no one was around and tell me he was going to cut off my ears and nose. He also warned me that I had better not tell anybody about his visits or I would be sorry, and so I didn't. In fact, I didn't tell anyone until I was much older and had children of my own. Seeing me so upset when she would leave for lunch, Mom began to have an aunt or uncle from St. Joseph come in and stay with me while she was gone. I really liked it when Uncle Roy came because of the fun way he teased and baited me.

I was in the hospital for a month. The doctors credited my mother with saving my life, because she kept me on that side until the tubes came out, even though I developed bedsores. I started first grade that fall several weeks after school had started, but I went on to second grade the next year. In the one-room schools around our area, the teacher taught first, second, third, and fourth grades every year but would alternate the higher grades, teaching fifth and seventh grades one year, sixth and eighth the next. When I was due to enter fifth grade, it happened to be the year for the sixth grade course of study. My teacher told me that if I would do both fifth and sixth grade math that year, he would promote me to seventh grade the next year. I did that, so I basically skipped a grade. This acceleration of a year changed so many things in my life, but maybe the biggest thing was that it led to my being in the right place at the right time to get hired for the ENIAC project.

The one-room school had its advantages. The classes went up to the front of the room to recite lessons. When I was through with my work, I could sit and listen to the recitations of the older students. Also, to have enough players for a softball team, every age group had to play, so I played softball from the time I was in first grade. The game was underhand fast-pitch, and I practiced pitching until I became better at it than the boys. Eventually I became the team pitcher when we would play against other schools.

The town of Stanberry, which was nine miles away, had a girls' softball team. Someone there heard about my pitching, and the manager came to ask my father if I could play on Stanberry's team. My father gave his consent, but said my sister Lou would have to drive me to the games. Before she could do that, he made us prove that we could change a tire in case we ever had a flat. We changed a tire all right, but as we drove down the highway outside of Stanberry later that day, the car suddenly began to bump along jarringly. We then watched our tire run down the highway ahead of us! You see, no one had told us that we needed to tighten the nuts alternately so the tire wouldn't wiggle itself loose!

When I was eleven or twelve, I began to pitch and play with the team, as did Lou. I think I was the youngest one playing. One time before a game we stopped by the house of my sister Erma and my brother-in-law Forrest, and Forrest dared us to smoke a cigar. We did and got sick and threw up shortly before a game. Lou hit two home runs that night, and I hit one. Even so, we never smoked another cigar. As I began to pitch winning games, people around town, especially the men, would stop

Betty Jean with classmates and teacher Bill Gage at the Jennings School, ca. 1936. Betty Jean (who was in eighth grade) is in the middle of the back row; Kackie is third from the left in the front row.

me and make comments on the last game. Some would critique the game and tell me what to do differently next time. One day when I was in town with Mom, the owner of the pool hall stopped me and began talking about my pitching. After we had walked on, Mom had a fit, saying, "That ornery man dared talk to you! I'm not going to town with you if you keep talking to people like that!" I didn't even know the man, but lots of people I didn't know talked to me about softball.

This was in a small, rural town, before television. There wasn't even much radio. Everybody came out to watch the girls play. The boys' team liked to play doubleheaders with us because we drew a large crowd. We played against teams from the other little towns around: King City, Albany, Bethany. One time, a team from Kansas City came to Stanberry to play us. That team had been runner-up to the national championship team. They whipped us good. Their pitcher could throw an underhand curve ball. I had never before seen a ball do that—it just wasn't where it seemed to be! Another time, we went to Tarkio, Missouri, for a game. We rode in the back of a truck, the kind that would haul cattle and hogs to market. It was late as we drove home after the game. The driver thought that he knew a shortcut, but he went over a bridge that collapsed under the back wheels. It took several hours for us to get out and get back to town—at first they tried to pry the truck out with boards, then finally someone went to get a farmer to pull us out with horses. When we arrived back at town, about four in the morning, there stood Dad by our car. He just said, "Get in the car. This is the end of your softball career." He had awakened in the middle of the night and realized we weren't home. He walked to my Uncle Fred's house, and Uncle Fred drove Dad to Albany, where we had left the car. Dad drove home and made Lou and me do the chores before we could go to bed. I really thought that was it for my softball career, but my Uncle Fred came to tell Dad that he would take us to the games. Dad finally relented and let Lou and me continue as before.

This softball experience was the first time that I really got any recognition in the family. I nailed a flattened-out tin can to the door of the smokehouse and practiced my control by pitching at it. All the practice paid off: I actually did pitch one no-hit, no-run game. Later another girl came along who could pitch with a windmill windup. She was harder to hit than I was, so she did most of the pitching from then on. I loved playing softball and seeing my name in the *Stanberry Headlight* newspaper. But I quit playing when I was fourteen and got interested in boys. The truth is, I quit because I had a boyfriend smaller than me, and I was embarrassed to be so big and strong. It affected my play, too. So I quit.

We grew up on horses in my family. We had a pony named Beauty, who was half Shetland and half pacer. He was a lot bigger than Shetlands, and four of us would ride him when we were little. He was like a member of the family. We fed him everything. My sister Lou, who liked sour things and never much liked dessert, would feed him her dessert almost every night. We fed him apples, carrots, and even leftover peanut butter and jelly sandwiches. He was a wonderful horse, and we lived on him. One time, we looked out, and there was my little sister Kackie lying down on his back sound asleep. She had been astride him holding onto the reins, and she just lay back on his rump and fell asleep.

Dad always kept a long-legged riding horse. Dad taught school, and we lived on a dirt road. In bad weather, he rode the horse to school. One of these riding horses was named Rex; another was King. Dad gave them names like that because they were big and fast, serving as his commuter horse. King was a light gray horse that had been a racehorse. He was a fine horse except, when another horse came running up behind him, he would think he was back in a race and would take off. There was no telling when he would stop.

One day, we decided to ride down to Grandma's house. Raymond, Lou, and Kackie were on Beauty; Erma and I were on King. She rode in the saddle, and I sat behind the saddle. We were walking down the road, but Beauty, with his short legs, fell behind King. Someone kicked Beauty in the ribs, and he came running up behind King. King thought he was in a race and he took off. Erma could not get him to make the turnoff to Grandma's house. He tore down the road over a little hill, past the cemetery, and down a long hill, at the bottom of which was a sharp left turn. Dad was in a field at the bottom of the hill and saw King running. He knew King was going too fast to make the turn and would get tangled up in the barbed wire fence bordering the road. Dad ran to the road, stood out in the middle of it, and caught King's reins. King reared up in the air. I fell off and was knocked unconscious; Erma was thrown around in the saddle and cut her leg on a buckle. I thought Dad was the bravest man in the world for that, and I still do.

Another time, Bob offered to gentle a bay riding horse owned by a girlfriend's family. It had been in her family for a long time, but it never was gentle enough for the kids to ride. Dad was annoyed with him bringing the horse to our farm without getting permission. Bob took a job on a farm away from home and wasn't there to ride the horse, so I rode her. Dad noticed that when she balked at going somewhere I wouldn't make her go there; he told me I was ruining the horse and to stop riding her. One day, he went off to spend the day working at the church, but before he left, he specifically told me not to ride the bay horse. Well, later that day a neighbor boy asked me to go with him to visit a cousin. I went to the barn and bridled the forbidden horse and rode her out to the field where my brother Raymond was working, which was on the way to the cousin's house. Raymond said, "I thought Dad told you not to ride that horse."

I replied, "What he doesn't know won't hurt him."

On the way out of the field and into the road, we had to go over a barbed wire fence that had fallen down and was partially covered with dirt. On the other side, we had to jump a ditch beside the road. When we came to the ditch, my horse didn't want to jump, so she began to back up, dragging her front feet on the ground. As she did this, she pulled the barbed wire up from the ground and caught it on the joints just above the hooves on her front legs. She apparently had been cut by wire before, because she went wild. She reared up in the air, sawing on the wire, and the barbs began to cut her feet.

I screamed and slid off her back and held onto her reins as she reared up in the air with me going with her. Finally the wire broke, and I knelt on the ground wrapping the skirt of my dress around her feet to stop the bleeding.

My Uncle Egbert from Arkansas was visiting my Grandma Jennings, whose house was maybe an eighth of a mile from this field. Hearing my screams and the horse's neighing, he jumped in his car and raced over. He bound up her feet and took me home. I was hysterical and Mom put me to bed. When Dad came home, he spanked me, but that was nothing compared to the months of seeing that poor horse limping around the farm. I also had nightmares for years, reliving flying up and down in the air with that horse.

I stayed in town with my sister Erma and her husband, Forrest, for my freshman and part of my sophomore year. I didn't like that arrangement very much. Forrest sometimes teased me about my dusting or cooking. Plus he hunted, so he kept hounds in the shed out back, and I had to cook big pots of oatmeal for them. But Forrest also once spent half an hour getting a comb untangled from my thick hair without saying a word of criticism. Forrest bought my softball uniform, which had

Betty Jean Jennings with her high school sophomore class, 1938–39. Betty Jean is in the second row, the second girl on the left.

the name of his store on the back, Alldredge Feed and Seed. Erma adored him. During my sophomore year in high school, I was able to move back home because the school bus started coming to Alanthus, which was about two miles from the farm. One day, I was working out in a field with Dad. He asked me if I knew how to drive a car. My brother Raymond had let me drive a few times, so I said, "Yes." The car was parked by the side of the road on a downhill slope. Dad said, "Show me. Back up the car." I got in, started the engine, put it in gear, and tried to back up. I killed the engine. Started it up and killed the engine again. I started it up a third time and sort of jumped backward. Dad said, "I see you can drive a car. You can drive it to Alanthus tomorrow to catch the bus."

My trip to Alanthus was the only driver's test I have ever taken. I was fourteen at the time but couldn't get a driver's license until I was sixteen. I only drove around the dirt roads and stayed off the main highway until then. In Missouri, all one had to do to get a license was show proof that you were sixteen. The state didn't have a speed limit until long after World War II. The only rule was to go a "reasonable speed," and those old farmers drove like maniacs once they got fast cars.

I was a good student, especially in math, and Miss Madeira was my favorite teacher. Amelia Madeira taught English and really set high standards in the school. At the time, I thought I would be a nurse and work with my brother Bob, who was going to be a doctor. Lots of medical terms are derived from Latin, so I decided to study Latin, which wasn't offered by the school. However, Miss Madeira came to my rescue, offering to refresh her Latin and study it with me. I went over to Miss Madeira's house one night a week and sometimes after our lessons, Miss Madeira would listen with kind understanding and encouragement to my fantasies and ambitions.

Miss Madeira had been a friend of my Aunt Gretchen when they were in high school. Aunt Gretchen had left Missouri to teach in Illinois and eventually in Cleveland. Unfortunately, Miss Madeira wasn't able to follow in Aunt Gretchen's footsteps, even though she'd wanted to travel. You see, Miss Madeira had a brother who was not quite "right"—he sort of slinked around town with a shifty look in his eyes, acting sort of paranoid—and she felt she could not abandon him, so she stayed behind in Missouri to look after him. Now, Aunt Gretchen was an amazing woman and my role model. She was an English teacher and had gotten her master's degree. She became superintendent of schools for Gentry County, Missouri. After that she left Missouri, but she came home every summer. It was one of the three highlights of the year. The other two were Christmas dinner at Grandma Jennings's house with all my aunts, uncles, and cousins and the Fourth of July in Stanberry, when the carnival came to town.

Aunt Gretchen would correct our grammar and anything else she felt like correcting. She wore Hammacher suits, jewelry, and lipstick. I thought she was the most glamorous woman in the world. Why she felt such responsibility for her nieces and nephews, I'll never know, but she offered to loan any of us twenty-five dollars a month to go to college for two years. That amounted to two hundred dollars per year. She had nineteen nieces and nephews. How she managed on a teacher's salary is beyond me. Her salary at that time could not have been more than two thousand dollars per year. Of course, we were strung out in our ages so only two or three were borrowing money from her at a time.

Gretchen Jennings Kirby, Betty Jean's aunt, ca. 1932–37.

She got married when she was forty to Forrest Kirby, an industrial arts teacher. He was a bachelor and an only child, and he took to us like a real uncle. He told how he and Aunt Gretchen went to a county fair shortly after they met. She told him she could milk a cow. He said, "Show me," and she did, right there at the fair! Eventually, they moved to California, where he opened an automobile agency. One summer, they went to Detroit and bought two white Mercurys for his agency. They decided they would drive them back so they wouldn't have to pay the freight. They drove them to Missouri first. What a sensation they were! I had never ridden in a new car before (I must have been eight or nine at the time). In the evening, we would drive to town for ice cream cones.

During World War II, Aunt Gretchen and Uncle Forrest worked in defense plants. Afterward, Uncle Forrest became a builder and made lots of money. He and Aunt Gretchen adored each other, but Aunt Gretchen never forgot us. When she died, after leaving special grants for scholarships and money to various people, she left the residue of her estate to us, her nieces and nephews. Aunt Gretchen also used to send us her old clothes. She cleaned out her clothes closet regularly. If she liked something, she kept it for up to three years; if she didn't like it, she gave it away in a year. Some of the nicest clothes I wore in high school came from Aunt Gretchen. I never minded wearing her old clothes. In fact, I liked it. Mom altered them—she was a superb seamstress and could make patterns and fix anything. Even when she was an old woman, Mom's granddaughters came to her to make them suits or evening gowns for special occasions. She didn't much like altering Aunt Gretchen's clothes, however. I imagine it was because it reminded her of how poor we were. I imagine she wanted to buy our clothes herself. And I imagine she hated being dependent on Aunt Gretchen, because Mom wasn't as educated as Aunt Gretchen. Mom was very bright, but her family didn't have the push to educate their children. But she liked school so much that she went for two more years even after she had graduated from eighth grade—the one-room schools allowed that.

In high school, my brother Raymond was a year ahead of me. When I was a sophomore and he was a junior, my class served for the Junior/Senior Banquet, which was held in the gymnasium. It had a Hawaiian theme, and we girls wore hula skirts made out of rolls of crepe paper. When I passed Raymond's table, he grabbed my skirt and the waist came loose and almost fell off! Aside from that incident, I enjoyed high school. I became editor-in-chief of our little school paper, which was published as a section of the *Stanberry Headlight*. I was also president of the student council. Throughout high school, I never talked to any teacher on a personal level except Miss Madeira—not even the math teacher or the physics teacher, although I was the best math student in the school. Because of her connection to Aunt Gretchen and my father, I think Miss Madeira was interested in me. She saw that I was good in English and encouraged me. She was also sponsor of the newspaper, so as a staff member I worked under her guidance.

The superintendent of schools was an old fool named Zeliff. He was an old bachelor who shut himself in his office and smoked. When not doing that, he stalked the halls with a cane. We always had a "walkout" day in the spring. Zeliff would always try to stop us, but nobody paid him any attention. We just left. Once, we also walked out to go see *Gone with the Wind* when it came to town. I never talked to the principal. He was such a nonentity, I can't even remember his name. The school actually was a good school with some good teachers: Mr. Campbell for math, Mr. Craig for physics, Mr. Johnson for social studies, and Miss Madeira for English.

I was a good student, and nearly everyone expected that I would be valedictorian of my class, but I wasn't. The principal changed the way he calculated it, and I was salutatorian. Miss Madeira lobbied on my behalf, and Dad went to the school and protested the choice, but to no avail. I was devastated, mainly because I thought there was a scholarship to Northwest Missouri State Teachers College attached to the honor. There wasn't, because the nonentities, namely Zeliff and his principal, never even had us take the test for it. Anyway, I decided I would never study for an honor again. Very early on in my college career, I decided to learn for myself only. I thought, "Nobody will really care what honors I get in school; they will care only about what knowledge I have in my head." So in a way I was lucky not to have been valedictorian. But I still felt angry and cheated about how my high school career had ended, and I was determined not to let others have that power over me in the future. With this mind-set, I was happy to leave Stanberry High School behind and move on to college in Maryville, Missouri.

I absolutely loved college. I went to Northwest Missouri State Teachers College in Maryville (now Northwest Missouri State University), where many, many Jennings family members and relatives had gone before me, including my father, uncles, cousins, brothers, and sisters. In the early 1900s, Missouri had set up five state teachers colleges, one in each corner of the state and one in the center. That system supplied plenty of teachers to Missouri, as well as to Kansas and Iowa, and the colleges gradually expanded to include many other fields of study. In 1941, I was a sixteen-year-old freshman, and I lived in the Holt house. Arlettie Holt rented out rooms to college students—twelve girls in all. We had kitchen privileges in the basement. I shared a two-room suite with my roommate Joyce Cox and two juniors, Connie Bolar and Dorothy Steeby. They, like me, were from small towns in northwest Missouri.

Connie and Dorothy were wonderful to Joyce and me. Dorothy was the most organized person I've ever met. She got up early to serve in the men's dining hall of the Quad Building. She attended classes and did her homework right on schedule. Connie, on the other hand, never had a class before noon and was always in bed when we left. I had a class in French with her; she was adorable and always had her homework done although she never seemed to study. I was convinced that she jumped out of bed as soon as we left and studied like mad. I think she just liked the image of being lazy.

Joyce was the most beautiful girl in our freshman class. She had a boyfriend still in high school, Melvin, so she went home almost every weekend to see him. One time, the quarterback of the football team and "big man on campus" Ivan Schottel asked her out. She said, "I don't even know him. Why would he want to go out with me?" She really had no idea how beautiful she was. He persisted and she finally went out with him. She pronounced it the most boring date she had ever had.[1]

I loved sitting up talking to the other three girls in the suite as well as to the other girls at the Holt house. We had two rooms: the desks were in one room and the two double beds were in the other. We talked about everything—school, classes, teachers, the boys we were friends with, clothes, family, books, and other girls. We all talked so much that I never took a bath without someone sitting in the bathroom talking to me.

During my first year I had a course in the humanities with Dr. Blanche Dow. She was a dynamo. It was an overview covering great music, art, and architecture—sort of an overall world culture survey. I wasn't much interested in those things at the time, but I was interested in being like Blanche Dow. She had been everywhere and done everything I wanted to do. She had lived in France for a time and had been to Greece and Italy. She was short—maybe 5'2"—and of medium build, dynamic, and confident. She had black hair, fair skin, and a generous mouth. She had a wonderful face that always appeared to be about to smile.

I got a rude shock my first quarter in school—I received a pink slip in biology at midterm from Dr. Frank Horsfal. I could scarcely believe it. It meant I would fail the course if my class work didn't improve. In contrast, I received an honors slip in gym that midterm. Of course, this led to many jokes among the girls in the Holt house about me being brawny but not brainy. I wrote my parents that I would pass Dr. Horsfal's course. My mom wrote back that she and Dad were sure that I would. Mom was like that—always supportive and encouraging. She never jumped on me when I was down. Instead, she always tried to help lift me up.

It was difficult, however. Dr. Horsfal gave us a vocabulary test of word definitions every day. He would not accept a dictionary definition, the textbook definition, or a contextual definition. I flunked these tests every day. The class was in an uproar as the students argued with Dr. Horsfal over his grading of their definitions. Finally, after much hair-pulling and headaches, it occurred to me that what Dr. Horsfal really wanted was an amalgam of all three. I guess that was it, because I began passing the tests and did pass the course. Years later, I ran across Alfred Korzybski's book *Science and Sanity: An Introduction to Non-Aristotelian Systems and General Semantics* (1933, 1941). I realized that Dr. Horsfal must have just read the book and decided to teach us to define words accurately, neither underdefining nor overdefining them. Korzybski argued that people went insane using two-valued Aristotelian logic when there were many variations in life.

Dr. Horsfal had also worked for the American Agricultural Administration in Arkansas during the Depression. He told of the starving families that received government food through that organization. He claimed that, the next year after getting enough food, the wives had a child by the hand and a child under the belt. He also had the job of teaching us about sex. After going over the biology of it, he set a box on a table outside his office where we could write down our questions on pieces of paper and put them in the box unsigned. (I never had enough chutzpah to put in a question.) He promised to answer every question, and he did. I learned such astounding things as that having sex to determine compatibility with a guy before marriage didn't work, because having sex was like playing the piano and it took practice to get good at it. He also ranted and raved at the way people pruned their trees by just lopping off limbs without treating the wound to keep out insects and rot. He would say things like "I saw a cold-blooded murder of a tree on my way to work." Strange as it may seem, I was crazy about Dr. Horsfal. I mean, I liked him. I really, really, honest-to-goodness liked the man. He was a character, and I loved characters. But then I was a bit of a character myself.

Dr. Joseph Hake was head of the mathematics department and my adviser. I had started college thinking I would be a pre-journalism major. I didn't want to be a math major because I didn't know what I could do with a math degree except teach school, and I didn't want to do that. So the first quarter of school, I had Mattie Dykes as my adviser, who was also the adviser on the school newspaper, the *Northwest Missourian*. She was one of the spinster schoolteachers who had thought my brother Bob was just super. I didn't like the woman at all, because she treated me with disdain and seemed to constantly belittle my writing efforts and abilities in a critical rather than a constructive way. I quickly changed my major from journalism to math.

Near the end of my first quarter of college, on December 7, 1941, I was playing bridge with the girls from the Holt house when someone ran in and said that Pearl Harbor was being bombed by the Japanese. Everyone immediately gathered around a radio and listened in horror as the news of the devastation was broadcast from Hawaii. The following day President Franklin Roosevelt, in his famous "a date which will live in infamy" speech, asked Congress to declare war on Japan. Three days later, on December 11, 1942, Japan's allies, Germany and Italy, declared war on the United States. We realized our lives had changed forever. The next quarter, the whole atmosphere at school was very subdued. Male students who were not 4-F either volunteered for service or were drafted, including Ivan Schottel. Somehow school seemed irrelevant for many in the face of war.

That summer, 1942, my sister Lou and her husband, Harold Jennings—a fifth cousin of ours—were stationed in Pensacola, Florida, while Harold was in flight school. They sent me money for a roundtrip bus ticket to Florida. Because they couldn't take a vacation home, they brought me to them. Until this time, I had never been more than forty miles from home. Although the forty-eight-hour bus trip was pretty horrendous, I enjoyed seeing different parts of the country.

That summer, I worked as a waitress in a Greek restaurant to earn my keep, and we went to see lots of movies on the naval base. All of the newsreels showed the Japanese and Germans as ugly and vicious. There was always a short film on plane recognition to familiarize the sailors with enemy planes.

Pensacola was not a pleasant place in the summer; it was hot and muggy. Still, I enjoyed being with Lou and Harold, although I did not like waitressing. The Greek place specialized in sizzling steaks. A black woman cooked spaghetti and meatballs in a kitchen in the back. And another woman cooked all the steaks in skillets over a number of burners on a platform in sight of the patrons. The aroma from them clung to my clothes, so that my sister didn't even want them in the clothesbasket.

Lou and Harold Jennings (Betty Jean's sister and her husband, also their fifth cousin) on their front porch in Pensacola, Florida, 1942.

The owners, two brothers in their forties with dark, slicked-back hair, bet on the greyhounds at the dog tracks, and their mood each day depended on how well they had picked the winners the night before. The two men never talked to me. They came in and sat at the counter drinking coffee and discussing the dog races with each other and any of their friends who came in. One time a rumor was whispered around that one of them had made five hundred dollars at the track the night before.

My brother Bob had given me his fraternity pin. I wore it so that everyone in the restaurant would think I was pinned to somebody. As the other waitresses and I set up the tables with white tablecloths and salt and pepper shakers, they, and occasionally some customers, would all tease me about the fraternity pin, but I never told anyone that it was my brother's. I chatted with the customers who came in during the morning, because there wasn't much to do. People seemed to like to sit at my tables, and I was tipped very well. Still, that summer convinced me I never wanted to be a waitress again.

When I returned to Missouri from Florida in the fall of 1942, I was seventeen years old, and my school was practically deserted since enrollment was down. That year I primarily took courses in humanities, history, geography, psychology, and foreign language. I chose French and had my beloved Dr. Dow as my teacher. The war was getting scarier, and life on the Northwest campus was somber and quiet. I joined a group organized by Dr. Dow to roll bandages for the Army. We still had football and basketball teams, and there were intramural sports, but at the end of the basketball season, ten men on the team were drafted into the Army and three others joined the Navy Reserve.

While we all enjoyed ourselves at school, we worried a lot about friends and relatives who were fighting overseas. Connie had a friend who had joined the WAVES,[2] and several of my peers seriously considered joining too. I thought about doing so myself because I wanted to help the war effort as well, but ultimately I decided against joining the organization.

In the midst of all that anxiety and awareness of death, our surroundings were never more beautiful. Trees were everywhere and spring was a lovely time with flowers blooming just about anywhere you looked. From 1917 until 1927, Northwest had planted three hundred trees a year, making it almost a campus situated in a forest. In fact, years later in 1993, Northwest's continuing commitment to trees earned them the honor of being named Missouri's official state arboretum. When everything was growing and green at Northwest, one would often see someone out looking for four-leaf clovers on the expansive lawns, sometimes to send to a loved one on the front lines. Some of the girls would collect flowers and leaves and press them into letters to remind their loved ones of home. Despite the war, campus life went on.

Female undergraduates rarely ever wore pants on campus. We always dressed in blouses or sweaters and skirts—short ones, too—and I can still vividly remember my bare legs freezing as the cold winter wind blew up my skirt. Now I can't imagine why we didn't wear pants when temperatures dropped below freezing. But those were the times and that was the fashion, and while pants were sometimes worn by actresses in movies and women in the military, they weren't widely accepted as appropriate everyday attire for respectable young women. In fact a group of Women Airforce Service Pilots (WASPS) was arrested in 1944 for wearing pants at night.[3] Although now I can clearly see the discrimination in society's fashionable dictates, at the time I didn't think too much about wearing a skirt, even in bad weather. In fact, I couldn't imagine wearing anything but a skirt when a boy was anywhere around. That was life on the Northwest Missouri campus in the spring of 1943.

The summer before my junior year, my father asked me to help him on the farm, which I did. I really enjoyed that summer with Kackie, Mom, and Dad. We worked very hard. I never really sat and talked to my father until 1943, when I was eighteen. Then I spent time with him because World War II was on and my brothers were away. He said that if I would help him on the farm, he would pay my college expenses the next year. He told me that he was having a railroad car full of lambs shipped in from Idaho; he planned on making my college tuition and expenses from them.

Betty Jean and a friend walking bare-legged across the wintry Northwest Missouri State campus, ca. 1942–43.

I took care of the horses and the farm animals. We had no tractors, so I plowed, sowed, raked, and planted using a team of horses. I loved it and was amazed at how sentimental my father was and how much he loved all of us. When he worked with me, he called me "Honey Dear." He told me that I was wonderful help and that he was proud of me. He was very worried about my brothers in the service and talked about them. He told me that summer that the ideal world for him would be to draw a circle ten miles in diameter and have all his children living within that circle.

My father certainly never got his wish that we all remain close by. Only three of us stayed in Missouri—William, Erma, and Raymond. Growing up, I knew he loved us, but I never realized he was so proud of us. During World War II, my brothers Raymond and Bob were in the Navy. Raymond was a pilot flying PBY Catalinas, which took off and landed in the water. They provided mainly escort service for ships. Bob was the executive officer of a net-layer, which laid nets in the water surrounding harbors to keep out enemy submarines and mines. Once Bob was in a convoy with a troop ship following him. The Japanese blew up the troop ship and all lives were lost. Bob's ship only escaped being hit because the troop ship was a much bigger and more important target. As you can imagine,

I'm so very proud of Bob and his service to the United States. My sister Lou was married to a Navy flyer, and Erma's husband, Forrest, was in the Army infantry. Only Kackie and I were at home that summer.

Dad would have had a fit if he had known that a neighbor, Jeffer Karr, had given Kackie and me a whiskey bottle with a little bit in the bottom. We took it up to our room and sipped it every once in a while, then giggled and acted drunk. Neither of us had ever tasted anything alcoholic because we were a teetotaling family. My uncles Fred and Roy would go on toots every now and then, and Dad would have to go pick them up and bring them home. So we never had any liquor in our house, except for that bottle Kackie and I smuggled in and nursed that summer.

Lieutenant Commander Robert Jennings (Betty Jean's brother), 1944.

In the spring of 1941, there had been 450 students at Northwest Missouri State Teachers College, including 134 men. According to the 1943 *Tower* (the Northwest yearbook), enrollment for the 1942/43 school year had slumped to 185 students, only eleven of whom were men. All of that was about to change in my junior year. In July 1943, Uel Lamkin, president of Northwest, offered to provide whatever instruction the Navy needed. When I came back to school that fall, we had Navy V-5 and V-12 programs—one was for sailors who had been to sea and the other was for new recruits. There were now four hundred sailors on campus.

The sailors had taken over the girls' dormitory as well as the Quad, so all of us female students lived in houses in Maryville. The sailors all ate at the Quad dining hall, and all of us girls ate at the dorm. I may have been the only student who loved dorm food, compared to eating what I had managed to fix in the Holt house basement with rudimentary facilities and little money or time for cooking. That year I had a job in the bookstore, which contained a coffee shop. The school furnished books for the students, who merely had to check them out at the beginning of term and check them back in at the end of term. At those two times we worked hard in the bookstore part of the operation. During the term, we spent most of our time working in the coffee shop.

I took analytic geometry, trigonometry, and physics with the sailors: I was the only civilian and the only woman in the classes. For the physics lab, I had about a dozen sailors ask to partner with me. Although I didn't know very many sailors, they all knew who I was. Many of them came down and talked to me in the bookstore, and I became friends with many of them. One or another of them always seemed to come by before assemblies or as I was setting out for the library, so I always had company. The sailors seemed very exotic to us Missouri girls, especially those who had been to or seen the sea. Most of us had never seen the ocean except in pictures. Plus, one of the sailors was actually from Brooklyn, New York, a place we knew about only in stories.

The atmosphere of the school had again changed. Football and basketball became an extension of the physical training for the sailors, in that the teams were almost entirely made up of sailors. We could have dates with the sailors, and there were dances held at the college again. When a sailor was on detention, he had to sign in every hour, so dates could be rather hectic, with sailors racing over the campus to check in.

I did find a special sailor at this time, a fellow of Syrian ancestry named Joseph Amad, whom I cared deeply about. Even though the war was always foremost in our minds, Joe added an unexpected and delightful dash of excitement and romance to my life during that grim, but rewarding time. Joe was a Catholic from St. Louis and had originally gone to Washington University. He was a good-looking man, just a little taller than me with gorgeous curly, black hair. I thought he was incredibly sexy and so did many of my girlfriends. Unfortunately, some people had a hard time with my dating Joe because he looked Semitic. You see, I ran around with a group of sailors who were friends of my girlfriends, and these normally nice, young men were nasty to me about my dating Joe because they thought he was a Jew. I ignored them and their disapproval because I liked Joe too much to stop dating him. Besides, my family had always been open-minded and I had been raised to be tolerant and accepting of other religions. So even if Joe had been Jewish, I would still have dated him because he was a great guy, the best.

Joe and I had met one night after I had been out with some girlfriends. Normally we had a ten o'clock curfew every night except dance nights; then we had to be home thirty minutes after the dance ended. But for three nights a term we could get passes to go to midnight movies. That night, a group of us had gone to the midnight show. As we were walking home, a group of sailors joined us. When we reached the Holt house and were saying goodnight, this sailor grabbed me and kissed me. I had never seen him before, but he had seen me in the math classes. I was amazed by his boldness and, yes, flattered. A few days later, Joe called me up to go to the movies. That date led to many more and many more kisses, including a few on what was known as the campus "kissing bridge."

Joe was a wonderful dancer. At dances, he often ended up being the center of attention because he was so good on the dance floor. In fact, he often found himself dancing the jitterbug with Bettie Claire Wallace, the daughter of a couple who lived half a block down High Street from Arlettie Holt. Bettie Claire was a terrific dancer, and the two of them were so good together that everyone stopped dancing to watch them. But I didn't mind, because I enjoyed watching them dance too and encouraged Joe to do so since he was so good at it. You see, I was not all that good a dancer and preferred to watch most of the time rather than participate. Joe never made me feel bad about that fact though and he always made sure that I didn't mind when he took to the floor with Bettie. Consequently, I never felt jealous. Joe was always kind, considerate, and fun, and I enjoyed being with him no matter what we were doing. Joe and I had a lot of things in common too. We were also both very ambitious and we really understood and appreciated this about each other.

Despite my worries about the war, like any young schoolgirl with her first real sweetheart, my world revolved around my boyfriend, my friends, and my class work. In short, my life was pretty good. When not running around with Joe and my friends, I was taking classes surrounded by energetic sailors, the majority of whom flirted outrageously. I was also taking more education-related and physical education courses such as practice teaching and golf. The first time I ever played golf, I nearly killed a girl with a golf ball. I had gone to the Maryville golf course with a friend. This was our very first game, and when we had played a few holes we came to a tee-off at the bottom of a hill. The hole was at the top of the hill, and some girls were on the green. It was my turn to tee off, but I was waiting for the girls to get off the green. My partner asked, "What are you waiting for?" When I said I was afraid I would hit someone on the green, she laughed and said, "There is no way you can hit the ball that far." The green was pretty far away and although I was a bit worried—because of softball I knew I could hit a ball a long distance—I went ahead and teed off against my better judgment. My ball went high in the air and straight as an arrow for the middle of the green. The ball came down right on top of the head of one of the girls standing on the green, and she went down as if she had been shot and didn't get back up! I was terrified—I thought she was dead. My ball had knocked her unconscious and given her a sizeable lump on her head. Fortunately, she healed up just fine and was kind enough to accept my apology. Since then, I have never teed off if anyone is on the green, I don't care how far away it is.

During Christmas holiday, Joe was scheduled to ship out to Albuquerque, New Mexico, for further training. When I found out he was going to Albuquerque, I cried—in private. I never let Joe see how upset I actually was because I didn't want to make him feel bad. While I was a dreamer, I had always been a practical sort too, and I understood that Joe had to go and there was no sense making it harder on either one of us by bemoaning the separation. Besides, I had plans of my own to pursue. I didn't want marriage and babies at the time, I wanted an adventure. I think Joe understood that about me and shared my desire to have an adventure himself. Like I said, we were both pretty ambitious people.

Joe was also a thoughtful, modern thinker and I think he worried about leaving loved ones behind if he went into combat and something happened to him. Rushing to the altar before a soldier shipped out was quite common in those days, but Joe didn't think much of the practice. He once said that he would hate to leave a grieving, possibly pregnant wife behind to fend for herself. Consequently, we never made plans for the future, but just agreed to try and keep in touch as best we could. We also agreed that we could see other people when apart, even though Joe had given me his Navy pin. Back then getting "pinned" was a big deal and implied that you were in a serious relationship and wouldn't date anyone else.

Anyway, before Joe left, I told him that a dear friend of mine, Joyce, whom I had roomed with my first two years at the Holt house, lived in Albuquerque and that she would be a good contact for him. Joyce's family had wanted to get her away from her boyfriend back home, and they had persuaded her to go out to New Mexico to live with her sister. I wrote to Joyce about Joe in hopes that she would be his friend, show him around town, and help him socialize.

The evening Joe was scheduled to depart was terrible—we had no privacy. It was very cold. We went to a movie and sat in the back of the theater, necking. I don't remember what the movie was—we certainly didn't watch the film. Then we came back to the Holt house. It was too cold to sit on the front porch, so we sat in the living room, but Arlettie was eavesdropping on us, listening to every word we said from the dining room a few feet away, where her bed was.

Joe's train left at midnight. We kissed like crazy right there on the platform. I didn't care who might see and comment. I knew I was probably never going to see him again. It was a gut feeling and one that would ultimately prove true. Later, I stood on the platform in the frosty air and watched as the train pulled out. Joe threw his head out a window and waved for as long as I was in sight. I felt terrible. So I stood there, feeling miserable as the train disappeared into the darkness, headed south to Atchison, Kansas, where Joe would board an Atchison, Topeka &

Santa Fe train for New Mexico. I turned and walked back to my room, a distance of several blocks, the packed snow crunching under my galoshes.

After Joe arrived in Albuquerque, he did call up my friend Joyce and go to see her, and in a letter, he told me that she hadn't been very nice to him so he would not be bothering her again. I was surprised, but later I would understand. Joyce wrote to me about Joe's visit and asked me why I had sent her "that Jew." She seemed to think I wanted to fix him up with her as a boyfriend. I was shocked, because the idea of her dating Joe had never crossed my mind. After all, she was a friend of mine. It was one thing to think about Joe dating some other faceless, nameless woman I would most likely never meet, but the idea of him dating a friend was downright hurtful. What if they became serious and I was forced at some point to see them all happy together? The idea made me sick to my stomach. Joyce's obvious prejudice and unkind treatment of Joe, which I'm sure hurt his feelings, soured me on her, and I didn't try to keep up our friendship after that. Joe was a special guy and he didn't deserve to be treated badly.

The next spring, that of 1944, was pretty dull without Joe. We had never made serious plans for the future—with the war going on the future seemed uncertain anyway—but Joe's buddies considered us almost engaged. Since Joe had pinned me, they thought I shouldn't date anyone else and would be marrying Joe one day. So when they saw me arrive at a dance one night with another sailor, they were pretty nasty to me. I tried to explain, but they just didn't understand. After that, I didn't hang around with Joe's buddies anymore. Joe and I communicated on and off after that by letter, but after I graduated and moved to Philadelphia and he shipped out I never heard from him again. I sincerely hope that Joe had a good life and if I could talk to him again, I'd wish him the very best.

Without Joe around, I kept busy by going out with friends, and playing basketball and golf on intramural teams. I took a physical education class each semester, even though I didn't have to. This led to the Physical Education Department trying to persuade me to become a PE teacher. I was not interested. But I did have one memorable course in educational psychology, taught by Miss Margaret Franken. She had a shrill, piercing voice as she prefaced a statement with the words, "Now, don't you know, students—" and then followed that with some remark such as, "two PhDs do not necessarily produce a little PhD." I can hear her to this day, so how could she and her course not have influenced me?

I also took astronomy and calculus that spring with a student from Lima, Peru, named Americas Usandivaras, another math major. He tended to look up to me, probably because I was a little older than he. Americas was about 5'7" and slender, with a very pleasant face. He was bright, but not extraordinarily so. One night Dr. Katherine Helwig, our astronomy teacher, took us out to look at the sky. Dr. Helwig was long past retirement and had been brought back to teach because the male teachers were in the military. She was a little old lady by then, quite feeble and shaky. Americas was very sweet and caring of her. He helped steady her hand as she held up the flashlight to point out the various planets and constellations.

I don't think Dad's plan to pay for my junior year with the sheep hauled in from Idaho worked out too well, because the next summer, 1944, he told me I had to go get a job to earn my tuition and expenses. So that summer Mary Ellen Burr and I went to Kansas City and got jobs at Pratt & Whitney, a manufacturer that employed several hundred workers, most of them union, to build aircraft engines. Mary Ellen was a friend whose father was superintendent of schools for Nodaway County, of which Maryville is the county seat. Mary Ellen lived in an enormous house and her mother rented rooms to college boys. She was obviously a very tolerant lady, for my brother Raymond and my cousin Herschel lived there, and Mary Ellen told me about the raucous wrestling matches they had on the third floor.

At Pratt & Whitney, Mary Ellen and I had to silver-plate a little gear that fit behind the propeller of an airplane. The gear went in a Pratt & Whitney engine that was used in several aircraft. Raymond told me that the PBY Catalina pilots were always glad to have a Pratt & Whitney engine in their planes. We worked from three to eleven o'clock at night, seven days a week. It was a terrible job, and the hours left little time for a social life. Sometimes college boys came down to see us, but by the time we got cleaned up and ready to go out it was about one in the morning, and there wasn't much to do at that hour. We did play golf some mornings, just the two of us.

To plate the gear, we first had to degrease it by hanging it on a cable strung across a big degreasing pit. Fumes rose from the open pit, and we got dizzy if we leaned directly over the pit for very long. I am sure the plant was filled with pollutants, because there were a lot of these huge pits, about ten feet square and several feet deep.

After the gears were degreased, we had to scour them with steel wool to get off any fingernail polish or dirt that might have gotten on them. Workers used fingernail polish to seal the masking tape, which had been applied to the gear to mark which areas to silver-plate. After that, we hung the gears in a silver cyanide plating bath. The steel wool we used earlier in the process scratched our hands. If we got any of the silver cyanide in the scratches, it caused sores to bubble up on the skin.

We did have heavy leather gloves, but we had to take them off to get in the corners of the gear to clean out the nail polish and dirt.

We then had to take the finished gears to inspection, where technicians measured the thickness of the silver plating. It seemed to us that hardly any of the gears passed inspection. Plus, in what further reduced the plant's output, there was a strike. Strikes were generally disallowed during the war, but there was one. Mary Ellen and I were not members of the union so we kept going to work. The union boss threatened us. I developed a physical tic in the right cheek of my face due to the stress.

We did have one exciting night. Our boss, whose name was Charlene, had been a circus performer, but the circus had ceased performing during the war. Charlene had trained and worked with the elephants. Her husband also worked at Pratt & Whitney, and he was a trainer of the big cats. He had a black panther he was training, which he kept in a warehouse in downtown Kansas City. He and Charlene invited Mary Ellen and me to go out to see it. He was planning a circus act in which he would ride around the ring in a convertible with the cat riding beside him. We got to the warehouse, and the panther was pacing back and forth in a ten-by-six-foot cage. Charlene's husband got in the cage, holding a small wooden chair. The panther snarled and struck at him. We were pretty terrified.

At the end of July, my Grandmother Jennings died, and I went home for the funeral. Two weeks later, my Uncle Roy, who had lived with Grandma, died. I felt as if life was pretty precarious, and I wanted out of Pratt & Whitney. Mary Ellen and I quit in late August, two weeks after Uncle Roy had died and two weeks before the semester was to begin. To our surprise, we were told that we had turned out more good gears than anyone else had ever done. I never heard from or saw the circus performers again.

When the Navy program had come to the campus the previous fall, the school changed from the quarter system to the semester system. There were two semesters plus an intersession of six weeks, comprising August and the first part of September. I figured I needed only twenty-two credits to graduate and I could get them all in one semester. I needed two math courses, and the rest were education courses, which I considered very easy.

When I went to register for the classes, the registrar sent me to J. W. Jones, the dean of faculty, to get permission to take twenty-two credits. Dean Jones told me that I couldn't do that because that was too many credits, and the math courses I needed weren't even being offered that semester. I was appalled. Despite slaving that summer at Pratt & Whitney, I had no money to go for more than one semester.

My Aunt Gretchen's monthly stipends had ended after my second year, as was the agreement. I began to cry, and I ran up to Dr. Hake's office. Dr. Hake was sitting there with Dr. Horsfal, who was his office mate. After I sobbed out my story, he and Dr. Horsfal looked at each other. I don't think either one thought much of Dean Jones.

Dr. Hake leaned back and said, "I am head of the Math Department. We can hardly give a degree in math if we don't even give the courses needed to get one. You are the only one needing these courses, so we'll arrange them for your convenience." Dr. Hake had two older retired teachers give the courses I needed. Mr. George Colbert—who had taught my father when he was in college—for Theory of Numbers, and Dr. Katherine Helwig for Modern Geometry. It was from Mr. Colbert that I first learned about the binary number system. Dr. Helwig taught me that parallel lines do indeed meet at infinity. Amazing.

When I had arrived back at school, Arlettie Holt told me I had been kicked out of the Holt house for some unnamed infraction, as had another girl in the house, Eulaine Fox. When Eulaine and I asked Miss Dorothy Truex, the dean of women, what our infraction was, she wouldn't tell us either; she just implied it was too bad to talk about and we should know what it was. Eulaine and I then rented a room at the Wallace house, down the street from the Holt house on the corner of Fourth and High. Mrs. Wallace said Arlettie's problem with us was that we were not going to be there all year. I have never understood why people would rather lie than tell the truth. No one could blame Arlettie Holt for wanting to keep a full house all year. Badmouthing us was tacky, and the way the dean of women acted was just as tacky.

The Wallace family was wonderful. Mrs. Wallace was gracious and kind. Mr. Wallace played an old grump, but we knew he was a pussycat. Their daughter Bettie Claire was a college friend of mine and was delightful. Once, in the middle of the night, Mr. Wallace knocked on our bedroom door. When I opened it, there he stood holding a very frightened young man by the arm. "This young man was climbing up on the roof outside your bedroom," Mr. Wallace said. "Says he needs one of your brassieres for some damn fraternity nonsense." To Mr. Wallace's surprise, I promptly gave the young man one of my bras and he quickly departed. It was a funny moment and I still laugh at the memory.

Another time, the Barkatze, the pep club to which I belonged, was giving a halftime performance at a football game. One formation required every other member to stand on his or her hands, while that person's neighbors held his or her feet up in the air. I was a good athlete but never agile. The day before the performance, Miss Carruth, our sponsor, walked up to me and said that I would have to be one of those doing a handstand. I tried to protest, but she said, "Be quiet. You are doing it." As you can imagine, I was horrified. When Mr. Wallace found out about what I was expected to do, he said, "This is one football game that I am going to." He did, and I did it perfectly. Miracles do happen.

As the end of the semester approached, I became more and more worried about what I was going to do when I graduated. I talked to my calculus teacher, Dr. Ruth Lane, who told me there were many things I could do besides teach school. IBM was looking for what they called Systems Service Girls. One graduate, a year ahead of me, had applied and been hired. But she had written to friends at the college that it was not a very good job: it required long hours of work, she had to dress very well, it was expensive to live in New York City, and the salary was too low to do these things comfortably. Nevertheless, I did apply, but wasn't offered a job. Then, one day, Dr. Lane came in with a recruiting letter issued through a math society, soliciting math majors to be "computers" for Aberdeen Proving Ground in Aberdeen, Maryland, on a project to be located at the University of Pennsylvania in Philadelphia.

The girls' basketball team at Northwest Missouri State Teachers College, ca. 1943. Betty Jean is in the front row on the right.

Dr. Lane had worked at Wright-Patterson Air Force Base in Ohio before coming to Maryville as a teacher. She told me that the base had a differential analyzer. She said there were three in the world—one at Wright-Patterson, one at MIT, where Vannevar Bush had invented it, and one at the University of Pennsylvania. Dr. Lane said, "Go there [University of Pennsylvania], because they have a differential analyzer." Actually, I later learned, there were at least two more—one at Aberdeen, and one in England, the model for which Douglas Hartree had built out of Meccano parts.

I asked Dr. Hake about applying for the job, and he told me to forget it: "You will be just a cog in a wheel, while if you stay here and teach, you will be a respected member of a community," he said. Naturally I ignored his advice and applied. He had no idea how much I wanted to do something other than teach. Besides that, I wanted to see something of the world. I wanted an adventure.

CHAPTER 3
Human "Computer" to ENIAC Programmer

I had dreamed of going to a big city such as New York, Washington, Chicago, Los Angeles, or San Francisco—but I never really considered Philadelphia. I had read about its place in colonial times, when it was at the center of the American Revolution, but then everything had moved on to Washington, D.C. I never heard about anything happening in Philadelphia. Really, all one heard about Philadelphia were the jokes about it. W. C. Fields was supposed to have said, "Philadelphia, wonderful town, spent a week there one night," and made many other jokes about his hometown.

As I began to think about a job in Philadelphia, I did a little research and discovered that it was a city of 2.5 million people and had been a great textile town until the mills moved down South for cheaper labor. It also was the home of Stetson hats and of John Wanamaker's, one of the fine old department stores. And of course, it still had the historic sites: Independence Hall, the Liberty Bell, the Betsy Ross House, Benjamin Franklin's grave, and, outside the city, Valley Forge. It was close to New York City, Atlantic City, and other shore points, not to mention Washington, D.C. I began to think that maybe Philadelphia might not be a bad place to live.

In Maryville, Missouri, the semester was over in January. Although the ceremony wouldn't be until June, I had fulfilled the requirements for graduation, and I went home to Stanberry to wait for my job offer from Aberdeen. But none came. Every few days my father came home with news of another high school that needed a math teacher. I refused to apply for any of the positions. I fiddled around the house, and no offer came. When people asked me what I was going to do, I would say that I was waiting for a job in Philadelphia. The weeks passed and so did the winter, while I was in limbo.

Then one day toward the end of March, the ice dam broke. In true government fashion, when the job offer finally came, it came in a telegram that said, "Report as quickly as possible." The telegram was actually delivered to my sister Erma. Stanberry being a small town, the Western Union man knew Erma was my sister, so he delivered it to her. She called me and told me the news. When I put the receiver back on the hook, I looked out the window at the fields, which were just turning green. It was a pleasant, sunny day, but rather cool. I remember going out and sitting on the wooden platform at the base of our windmill, which pumped water to our house and to a tank for the cows and horses. I remember thinking this was the last time I would probably ever sit there when it was my home. I had a few moments of desolation at the thought that I would only see my family on visits. Dad had told me never to expect him to visit me, but he told me I could come home anytime I wanted—he would be there.

Back in 1879, the Western Improvement Company had developed the town of Stanberry for the Wabash, St. Louis & Pacific Railroad. The Wabash wanted to put a roundhouse there to build and repair locomotive engines, and it needed places for the workers to live. It laid out the town and even built a little hotel, also called the Wabash. We had a midnight Wabash train out of Stanberry to St. Louis. The next midnight, I was on it, on my way to Philadelphia. My fare was thirty-five dollars. Erma loaned me the money to get started—about one hundred dollars. While her husband, Forrest, was in the Army fighting in France, his father was running his feed and seed business for him. Erma was also a good businesswoman, and after I finished college, she had asked me to go into the dry-cleaning business with her: Stanberry had been without one during the war, and Erma felt it would be profitable. The last thing I wanted to do, even after teaching, was to run a store. I turned her down, but Erma was always good to me and she graciously loaned me the money I needed.

Trains were very crowded during the war. Many people stood. I didn't take a sleeping car because of the expense; instead, I sat up all night. I changed trains in St. Louis around breakfast time and rode all that day and the next night, across southern Illinois, Indiana, Ohio, and into the long state of Pennsylvania. I got there on the second day. I arrived in Philadelphia on March 30, 1945. The train came into North Philadelphia Station, and I got off because I didn't even know the main station in Philadelphia was Thirtieth Street Station, a big, beautiful station. I knew very little

Betty Jean Jennings's appointment as a "computer" for Aberdeen Proving Ground in 1945.

about getting around in a big city, so I just took a taxi to the YWCA in downtown Philadelphia, checked in, and took a cab to the University of Pennsylvania. Needless to say, they were shocked that I had gotten there so quickly.

The computing group was located in a beautiful old brick fraternity house on Thirty-Fourth and Walnut. There were very few men on campus, so it had become available. The group had originally been located in one of the houses around Penn but had moved to the frat house later to have more space. They told me they had meant for me to get a physical before I arrived, but since I was here I could go to a doctor around the corner. It was a Friday afternoon. The doctor examined me for a while and was overly familiar, then he said, "I don't have time to finish this. You must come back on Monday afternoon." I said, "Okay," and left. Sunday afternoon, I got a call at the YWCA from the doctor saying that he would finish the physical if I would come to his home. I must say the old farm boys had taught me well to stay out of secluded places such as haylofts with them. I considered that a man's home on a Sunday afternoon qualified as secluded a place as a hayloft, so I declined, and kept my appointment on Monday afternoon. He was "handsy" at that follow-up. When I informed the manager of the project what kind of lecher he was using as a doctor, he was no longer recommended.

I was hired as a "computer" with a job rating of SP-6 (sub-professional 6). Men math majors were given professional ratings, but women were not given professional ratings until later—I got mine in 1946. As an SP-6, I made two thousand dollars a year, plus four hundred dollars a year for working Saturdays. The men made the same as we did for the same job, but there were only two or three men doing that job.

I was given an electric Monroe hand calculator, which did multiplications as a series of additions, and was shown how to calculate a trajectory for a big gun. The operation included several additions, subtractions, and multiplications, as well as doing division and taking the square root. All of this was done to calculate each point on the arc a shell made as it was fired from a gun. Input data for the trajectories were obtained from the firing range in Aberdeen, where the guns were test-fired and the results carefully measured. Only a few firings were done for each gun, and the rest of the trajectories were calculated. The results were put in firing tables that soldiers used to set the angle of elevation for reaching a distant target.

Aberdeen had advertised for women with math majors in the Philadelphia area, but as time went on the Proving Ground began an advertising campaign that reached across the country and to me in Missouri. When I arrived, there were four other women who had gotten there a month or two earlier. Two were from Kansas, one from Ohio, and one from Wisconsin. We became friends and spent Sundays, our day off, running around seeing the sights of the city.

Long before I arrived, Aberdeen had hired Adele Goldstine to teach the newly hired "computers" about computing techniques in a classroom at the Moore School Building. She had come to the university when her husband, Herman Goldstine, was put in charge of the Moore School group at the University of Pennsylvania in September 1942. Shortly thereafter, Herman Goldstine had somehow persuaded the University of Pennsylvania to replace its computing teachers with instructors of his choice, allowing his wife, Adele, to obtain a position at the university. Adele had also been placed in charge of the recruiting and advertisements that had led me to apply.

The first day of class, in walked this woman dressed in a skirt and blouse, with a cigarette dangling from the side of her mouth. She perched on the edge of her desk with her left leg thrown up over the corner and began to lecture in a Brooklyn accent. I sure knew I was in the big city now! The girls at Northwest Missouri State Teachers College had to go down to the school's greenhouse to smoke a cigarette. Adele lectured away. I was impressed. The classes lasted for about an hour a day for a couple of weeks. There were six or so of us in the class. I asked lots of questions, and Adele seemed to like that. She taught us about computing methods on calculators, such as how to do inverse interpolations.

My room at the YWCA was very small and plain with a bed and dresser. There was a toilet and showers down the hall. The room went for two dollars a night, but I could stay at the Y for only a week, so I needed to find permanent housing. Most of the rentals in Philadelphia at that time were horrible. My sister Lou came through Philadelphia the first week I was there. She had gone to Newport, Rhode Island, to be with her husband, Harold, before he shipped out to the Caribbean. Harold flew PBYs, the same as Raymond. Right after she saw him off, Lou took the train from Newport and came through Philadelphia on her way back to Missouri. She was pregnant with her first child, Dianne, at the time, so she was anxious to get home, but she said she wouldn't leave until I found a place. We read the ads in the paper and rode the subway to the houses where rooms were available.

Philadelphia is called the "City of Homes." Most of them are in row houses, which Lou and I considered slums. Finally Lou said, "Come home with me; this is just a city of slums." I decided to go to the housing office on the Penn campus. They sent me to a Mrs. Furlong, who owned a house on Spruce Street, in a neighborhood of large, three-story houses with white cement steps that were kept spotless—a hallmark of the area. Mrs. Furlong rented rooms to students from the Curtis Institute of Music and a technology school. Her son-in-law was Mason Jones, the lead horn player in the Philadelphia Orchestra, one of the finest orchestras in the world. Her rooms had kitchen privileges. She had a room. I moved in, and my sister went back to Missouri.

I had only been in Philadelphia for a few days when President Franklin Delano Roosevelt died on April 12, 1945. I remember walking through Rittenhouse Square as newsboys called out the news that the president was dead. People were openly crying. I ate at a counter in a Horn & Hardart, a cafeteria with an automat section, and people were seated at tables crying and reading newspapers edged in black. It was a sad time.

I had a great time living with the students from Curtis. All the students were on full scholarship, and they were all extraordinary musicians. I was no competition for any of them, so they told me many things they would not have told another musician. I earned their trust by never gossiping about what I was told and trying to give them the best advice I could when asked.

Looking back, I hope I was a good listener and good friend to those who shared their fears and aspirations with me. You see, several of the boys talked to me about whether or not they were gay. Many believed at that time that artistic men tended to be more homosexual than businessmen or athletes. Some were and some weren't, but all were anxious about what the future might hold for them. We also talked about how they felt about their music and they would take me to concerts at the Academy of Music. I have zero musical ability, so I was thrilled to be involved with such talented people. These young men from Curtis would eventually become the top musicians in orchestras around the country.

When Germany surrendered on May 7, 1945, we were glad that part of the war was over, but President Truman and other government officials warned that the war with Japan would probably go on for years. The war in the Pacific had already been a very bloody struggle, with American GIs island-hopping and breaking Japanese control over them. There appeared to be no easy end in sight. By the time Germany surrendered, almost every family in the United States had suffered casualties from the war. However, we were still fighting Japan and more casualties were likely unless something extraordinary could be done to end the conflict. My brothers were still in the South Pacific and I worried about them constantly.

When Curtis let out in the spring, an apartment became available at 2317 Delancey Place. Beatrice Ficaro, a coloratura soprano from Curtis, offered it to me for the summer. She and one of her friends would take it in the fall, so I had it for the summer. Ruth Penny, a young woman from Wisconsin, and I moved into it in June. Ruth was a beautiful woman and a very interesting personality. She looked like Hedy Lamarr, and she talked about philosophy. Ruth and I stayed up almost every night until one or two o'clock in the morning talking and acting silly and just having fun. The next morning, I would always resolve that I would not stay up so late that night, but I always did. Meanwhile, Bea and her other friend had a falling out over a mutual boyfriend over the summer, so she asked me to continue on in the apartment with her. In the meantime, Ruth had decided to go back to the University of Wisconsin in Madison. So from September on, Bea and I shared the apartment.

Lila Todd, who was in charge of the "computers," was a tiny woman, very efficient, with a glass eye. She supervised a group of about two dozen of us. When I joined Lila Todd's group of computers—all of which had the duty to calculate firing trajectories—it included two sisters who had lived in Missouri, Madeline and Mary Jane Crosby. Madeline was slim and sultry-looking. She spoke with a nasal quality to her voice and threw in French phrases all the time. She was haughty and claimed she had as a special friend a Frenchman who was a commandant in the French navy, although no one ever saw him. Men were mesmerized by Madeline—at least the 4-F computers were. Mary Jane, the older sister, was very pretty but, unlike Madeline, she was very personable and utterly likable by all.

Due to our connection to the Show-Me State, Mary Jane and Madeline insisted that I come home with them to meet their mother, whom they called "Mama," and Aunt Bess. When I arrived, Mama met me at the door. Her first question was, "Do you know Truman?" When I told her I didn't, she said, "That's all right; I understand he is a nobody." I was dumbfounded that anyone would say the president of the United States was a nobody. Later, I would briefly meet Truman when he visited the ENIAC and I thought he was a nice man.

The Crosbys were a bizarre family. The four of them lived on the first floor of one of the big old houses on Delancey Place in Philadelphia. They slept on sleeper sofas—they had no bedrooms. They put every-

Beatrice Ficaro and Betty Jean Jennings on the front step of their apartment building at 2317 Delancey Place in Philadelphia, ca. 1945.

thing away in the daytime so one would never know they slept there. They would invite me to tea after church on Sunday. I attended the Presbyterian Church at Twenty-Second and Walnut, and then walked the five or six blocks to their house. We drank tea and they discussed the society column of the *Philadelphia Evening Bulletin*. I had never even looked at the society page and never knew anyone else who did or cared what was in it.

Mama Crosby was an insurance saleswoman, and I soon had a policy to take care of my remains if something bad happened to me in Philadelphia. Although I may have been invited home originally so Mama could sell me insurance, I think they came to like me, for I was invited to their house many times. Mama had a boyfriend who was as tough as nails, but was completely devoted to her. I think he was a lot younger than her, but I'm not sure. I never had the nerve to ask. I do know that the sexual chemistry between them was pretty intense. Mama and her boyfriend would prove to be invaluable friends. The two came to my rescue when a crazy guy I got mixed up with attacked me in my apartment. The guy—I won't say his name—wasn't anything like my sweet-tempered Joe. Initially I was attracted to the man. He was very charismatic. While he wasn't all that handsome, he was built like a bricklayer and had tremendous sex appeal. Unfortunately, he was a bit of an animal with a quick temper who didn't like hearing the word "No." Years later, when I saw the movie *A Streetcar Named Desire*, the dominating Stanley Kowalski reminded me a lot of that man.

Fortunately when the attack was happening, Mary Jane stopped by and her arrival prevented something ugly from turning even uglier. The man who attacked me claimed that I wanted him and was playing "hard to get"; he told Mary Jane to get lost and let us work it out, but Mary Jane didn't believe him. She could see how scared I was, not to mention the fact that I looked like a complete mess, and refused to leave me alone with him. Finally, between the two of us, we managed to convince him to go home, but he told me that he would be back later to finish what "we had started." After he left, Mary Jane called her mother for help. Mama and her boyfriend dropped everything to come to my rescue. In fact, I ended up staying the night with them. One of the first things Mama asked me when she saw me was, "Did he try to kiss you?" I thought, "Yes indeed, after he ripped off my clothes!" But I didn't say that, I simply told her, "Yes, he did." I just couldn't go into details. I was too upset and embarrassed, but Mama somehow understood completely. She said not to worry. She promised that he wouldn't bother me again. At some point, Mama had her boyfriend go "talk" to the man. I'm not sure what happened between them at that talk, but Mama's promise proved true. The man didn't bother me ever again.

I must admit I was shook up for a few weeks after the attack, but with the routine of work to keep me grounded, I soon got over my nerves and went back to feeling normal and good about my life. However, I was actually getting a bit bored and wanted a new challenge. Although I found doing trajectories interesting, it was monotonous work and over time it became dreadfully dull. I knew the feeling would only get worse too. Also, I was the low man on the totem pole; everyone had been there longer than me and some had been there for over two years. I looked around and wondered what I could do to make sure I didn't just become a cog in a wheel, as Dr. Hake, my adviser at Maryville, had said I would. How could I get into a situation where I started out on an even footing with the others in the group? I was highly ambitious and wanted more from work than just getting a paycheck. I also felt strongly that I could compete with anyone if we started out on something new at the same time. I just needed to find something new. Fortunately for me, that "something new" was soon to occur.

In June 1945, a memo came around telling us "computers" that the Aberdeen Proving Ground was looking for math majors to work on a new machine being built at the University of Pennsylvania. It was called the Electronic Numerical Integrator and Computer, or ENIAC. We were invited to interview for the job. What none of us knew was that of the five positions that were said to be available, four had already been filled. Only one position was still open and thirteen of us applied. We were called in one by one to be interviewed by Dr. Leland Cunningham, from Aberdeen's Ballistics Research Laboratory, and Herman Goldstine, who was then an Army colonel and the liaison between Aberdeen and Penn. They didn't know what questions to ask. After we had talked about my background for a while, Goldstine asked, "What do you think of electricity?" I said that I didn't know much about it, but that I had had a course in physics and knew that E equaled IR (Ohm's Law).[1] But Goldstine said, "No, no, I don't care about that, but are you afraid of it?" I said that I wasn't. Then he explained that the job would require me to set switches on equipment and to plug in cables. While he was interviewing me, Adele Goldstine came into the room, looked at me, and then nodded to him as she went into an inner office. I've always felt that this was some kind of signal to Goldstine to select me.

After a few days, the announcement was made that the five programmers had been selected, along with two alternates. I was the second alternate. "Well," I thought, "that's the end of that." However, on the Friday before the programmers were to go to Aberdeen to study punched card equipment, I was called into the office of Lt. Tornheim, the overall manager of the computing group at the fraternity house, and asked if I could be ready to go to Aberdeen on Monday because I had now been selected as an ENIAC programmer. I was delighted and emphatically said, "YES!"

What had happened was that the fifth programmer selected had a very nice apartment in West Philadelphia. Aberdeen Proving Ground, on the other hand, was considered a hellhole. Because housing was very tight in Philadelphia, she decided not to give up her apartment. The first alternate was out of town on vacation. When she was reached and told that she would have to cut her vacation short to come back to Philadelphia and go to Aberdeen on Monday, she too turned the job down.

On Monday morning, when we all met on the railroad platform for the trip to Aberdeen, the other programmers wondered where I had come from. None of them had ever seen me before. We introduced ourselves and speculated on what it might be like at Aberdeen. They were busily asking me who I was and how I had gotten there. Although the four other programmers didn't really know how they had been selected, we worked out this scenario. None of them were interviewed for the job, instead they were just offered the job.

Betty Snyder was the oldest, at twenty-eight. She had been a computer for a long time and had been on special assignments, such as computing trajectories at a site in upstate New York where guns were fired in extremely low temperatures. Kathleen "Kay" McNulty, who was twenty-four, had run the differential analyzer for four years, and she had experience cranking shafts and setting gears, which was somewhat comparable to what we would be doing on the ENIAC. Twenty-three-year-old Marlyn Wescoff was so accurate in her calculations it was said she never made a mistake. Ruth Lichterman, at twenty, was a very bright woman from Hunter College and ready for a bigger challenge. And then there was me—and I was not afraid of electricity!

We were all very excited about this new adventure. It was the second week of June 1945, and we were going to be in Aberdeen until the end of July 1945, learning how to wire up the plugboards to run the punched card equipment we would be using with the ENIAC—a card reader, a card punch, a tabulator, a sorter, and a keypunch. When we got to Aberdeen, we were given rooms in a barracks-like dorm with shared showers. In her account, Kay McNulty Mauchly writes, "We were housed in a one-story women's dormitory with about 30 austere rooms, each shared by two people. It was probably built on a cornfield. It was on the far side of Aberdeen, and we always got there by walking. It had a large lavatory, and it also had a large living room where we could greet and entertain guests from Philadelphia."[2] Marlyn and Ruth roomed together; I roomed with Betty Snyder; and Kay had a roommate who was not part of our group. The barracks had no kitchen, so we had to eat out in the little town of Aberdeen, which was really just a wide spot in the road with a few stores and eating establishments on each side.

The town itself had maybe five hundred people. We generally ate in a diner on the main highway there, just a ready-built steel structure similar to a Quonset hut, which we walked to every night. We sometimes ate breakfast in town, but usually we ate breakfast and lunch on the base. There was a little railroad line that ran from the station in Aberdeen to the Army base on Aberdeen Proving Ground, which consisted of thirty-two thousand acres. It was later combined with the Edgewood

Arsenal (once used for experiments in chemical warfare), which contained fifty-two thousand acres. While there were over twenty thousand GIs on the base, we had no contact with them except at dances on the post. Although none of us had been around very many men recently, we found these masses of men rather intimidating. There were just too many of them to feel entirely comfortable.

The main buildings on the base were the Army Ordnance Laboratory—newly built to house the ENIAC (in preparation for its move there the following year), the differential analyzer, and the other machines we used—and the Wind Tunnel Building. There was also a Stibitz machine, built by Bell Labs researcher George Stibitz (a consultant to Aberdeen in those years) using electromagnetic telephone relays, but we weren't allowed to see it. Since it was wartime and Aberdeen was doing classified work, where we could go was rather restricted. In the latter, the Army tested shells by suspending them and forcing air around them to simulate flight. We were put in a classroom in the Army Ordnance Laboratory and given plugboards for the IBM punched card machines to study. A plugboard was a control panel for a particular punched card unit. The size varied from machine to machine. There were holes in the board that connected to electrical circuits in the machine. We connected these electrical circuits together to perform functions by plugging electric wires from one hole to another. The board for the tabulator was about twelve-by-eighteen inches and had about five hundred to six hundred holes, or connectors. Simpler machines, such as a sorter, had a board that was maybe six-by-ten inches.

Data were entered into the ENIAC on an IBM eighty-column punched card fed through a card reader, which translated the holes in the card into numbers that the ENIAC could use for calculations. The input cards were prepared on an IBM keypunch machine, which had a manually operated keyboard. The output of the ENIAC was through an IBM card punch, which was an output device that translated numbers from the ENIAC into holes in a punched card. The IBM tabulator then read these cards and translated the holes in the card into ordinary text written on paper, which we then could read.

Along with the keypunch to prepare the input cards, we had a sorter to rearrange cards in a different order if needed. We programmed the punched card equipment by connecting wires between holes in a plugboard that carried the signals to the various parts of the machine to tell it what to do. Aberdeen had a very sophisticated punched card installation. Tabulators could add and subtract, but we were going to use this one as the ENIAC's printer. Nevertheless, our teacher, a bright, thorough man, gave us the opportunity to learn the full capabilities of the equipment. For Aberdeen's tabulator, he had devised a fourth-difference plugboard. It was the only one in the country as far as anyone knew. A "fourth difference" looks like this:

Numbers	1st diff.	2nd diff.	3rd diff.	4th diff.
100				
95	5			
82	13	−8		
70	12	1	−9	
65	5	7	−6	−3

The plugboard was so fully packed that we couldn't even see which holes the cables were plugged into. After we had been there a while, our teacher allowed us to document this plugboard by making a drawing of the plugboard showing all the connections. We were so excited, since no one had ever documented a fourth-difference plugboard, and we decided to take out one connector at a time, showing where the two ends were connected on our drawing and, at the same time, plugging in a comparable connector in another plugboard. Thus, when we had all the connectors removed from the fourth-difference board, we would have it documented and a new fourth-difference board wired up ready to be used. We were so careful that we were sure it was perfect. It was not, however, and didn't work quite right—we had evidently gotten at least one of the new connections wrong, if not several.

The person in charge of the IBM punched card installation, Minerva Masoncup, was a thin woman with a shrill voice. She was annoyed to have to be bothered by us and reluctantly let us run the equipment part of the time. To be fair, I'm sure she did have deadlines to meet and we did interrupt her operations. Kay said of Minerva Masoncup, "She was a martinet but very competent."[3] Miss Masoncup had a fit when our new plugboard didn't work, but our teacher calmly told her, "I worked it out before, and I can do it again." And so he did.

We sat in a classroom working on the plugboards in pairs. Ruth and Marlyn worked together, and I always worked with Betty Snyder. Kay had no partner but she hung around with Betty and me, and we discussed various things such as what the circuits meant. In the basement of the building was a small firing range where engineers test-fired small guns. To warn us of a firing, a siren would go off preceding the loud bang so we would expect it and not jump out of our skins when it happened. Strangely enough, these loud bangs throughout the day didn't shatter our nerves or give us shell shock—we were happy to be where people were contributing to the war effort.

The engineers took us out on the firing range so we could see how they took measurements for input to be used in the trajectories we calculated for the larger new guns. They had sensors at various heights and distances along the path of trajectory. These sensors were tripped as the shell passed, and the precise height, distance, and time elapsed since firing was recorded. To obtain the shell's initial velocity, Aberdeen used an RCA "ring of 10" counter. Jack Davis, the engineer who developed the accumulator, says that the RCA counter measured "the velocity of an artillery shell leaving the cannon by having the shell pass through two coils of wire about 10 feet apart. The first coil started the counter and the second stopped it." The counter operated at 100 kilocycles a second. We never saw any demonstrations of them firing guns; all they showed us was the range where it happened. It was swampy out there with very few buildings, just those used for the firings.

As we were working on wiring up plugboards one day, two Marine sergeants and an Army sergeant came in the room and began talking to us. They were stationed at the Army Ordnance Lab, working on some secret project. One of the Marines said he was married. The other did not. Eventually, the second Marine invited Ruth out, and the Army sergeant asked me out. We went to the noncommissioned officers' club, which had booths where we could sit and order food and drinks, and a jukebox so we could dance to records—"A String of Pearls," "Don't Sit Under the Apple Tree," and other Glenn Miller tunes. I drank mainly Cokes or ginger ale—once in a while I had a Tom Collins. It was a very relaxed setting. People came in and out, and we could sit and talk for hours.

We went out with them all summer. My sergeant, Pete Monroe of Biloxi, Mississippi, was about 5'10" tall and of medium build, attractive but not really handsome. Ruth's sergeant, named Greg, was tall and quite handsome. Pete had a rather nice Southern accent and teased me sometimes. He had been in England and Europe and told me about his experiences there. He had been engaged to an Irish girl when he was overseas, but he broke it off when he came back to the United States. I was told that he had another girlfriend, but I knew nothing about her. I didn't take him very seriously. I would never have gotten seriously involved with a Southerner—I was too appalled at the discrimination in the South against blacks. Pete told me once that he would never take me to Biloxi because I was so outspoken in my views on discrimination that I'd be killed.

Pete even came up to see me on weekends after the five of us programmers came back to Philadelphia in late July. Eventually, he was discharged from the Army and went back to Mississippi. His father was so happy that his four sons had all come home from the war alive that he told them they could stay home as long as they liked without working. Several months after being discharged, Pete drove a car to New York for a friend and stopped in Philadelphia to see me on his way back home. He was still loafing around his home. But the magic between us was gone, and I was already going around with my future husband.

But that summer Ruth and I had a good time with the Marine sergeant and the Army sergeant. We went to a few USO dances, but the masses of soldiers were intimidating. The dances were a mess, with all those soldiers hanging around. It was a madhouse, and I hated it. Dating aside, we five women spent most nights sitting in one of our rooms, discussing two things: what we thought we would be doing in our job and religion. Kay was a Catholic, Betty a Quaker, Ruth and Marlyn were Jewish, and I was an ex–Church of Christ Christian. We had a wonderful time with each other, mainly because none of us had ever been in close contact with anyone from one of the others' religions. We had some great arguments about religious truths and beliefs. Despite our differences, or perhaps because of them, we really liked one another. Of course, we had better like one another—we spent almost twenty-four hours a day together. We ate breakfast, lunch, and dinner together, worked all day together, then still wanted to be together in the evenings discussing everything about our lives.

Ruth had grown up in New York City. Her father, Simon Lichterman, was a noted Jewish scholar. The family now lived in Far Rockaway Beach on Long Island. While Ruth had gone to Hunter College, she hadn't graduated; however, she had taken math while she was at college. She was younger than me by two months and was very bright. As an undergraduate, she had seen an ad on a bulletin board at Hunter recruiting math majors for Aberdeen, had applied, and was hired. I think she wanted to get away from her mother, who was very critical of her.

Marlyn was a native Philadelphian. She had gotten her bachelor's degree in education from Temple University in 1942 with a major in sociology and a minor in business education. After graduating, she worked for John Mauchly doing weather-prediction calculations for fifty cents an hour. When Aberdeen set up the satellite computing group at the University of Pennsylvania in 1943, Marlyn moved over to work for the managers there as a computer. Although she had no background in math, Marlyn had taken the three-month-long math training course given by the university for the computers working at Aberdeen who had not had calculus. The course taught them about trajectory equations.

Betty Snyder's father and grandfather were astronomers. Together they taught at Philadelphia's Old Central High School, which had an observatory, for a continuous span of seventy-eight years, their careers overlapping from 1905 to 1920. Her grandfather, Monroe B. Snyder, was one of the founders of the U.S. Bureau of Standards. With her sharp mind for problem-solving, she took after them.

Kay was born in Ireland. Before she was born, her father, James McNulty, had come to the United States and apprenticed as a stonemason with John B. Kelly, the brickwork contractor, famed Olympic rower, and father of Princess Grace—although at the time we were in Aberdeen she wasn't yet a princess. James McNulty had then gone back to Ireland, built himself a frame house, and married Kay's mother, Anne. He was active in the Irish Republican Army (IRA). The night Kay was born, he was arrested, thrown in jail, and kept there for two years in solitary confinement. He had been with a group that had blown up a bridge; everyone else ran and hid, but he went home because he knew Kay was being born, and was arrested there. When he got out of prison, he brought his family back to Philadelphia, where he built houses as an independent contractor for a few years, then worked for John B. Kelly until he retired. Mr. McNulty was a stonemason, but he could do anything that had to do with building. He erected custom homes in the Chestnut Hill section of Philadelphia and supervised lots of workmen. As a young man, he worked on one of the most beautiful buildings in the Philadelphia area, the Bryn Athyn Cathedral, which sits just outside the city. Done in the early Gothic style, it is reminiscent of Gloucester Cathedral in England.

Kay's parents were close friends of the Kellys and went to parties at their house. John B. Kelly was a prominent Philadelphian, active in city Democratic politics, and served as President Franklin Roosevelt's National Physical Fitness Director. His brickwork contracting company built lots of government buildings in Washington, D.C., so he was away from home a lot. John B. Kelly Jr. called Mr. McNulty his surrogate father. During the Depression, people stopped building custom homes and Kay's father went to work for John B. Kelly and worked on the Treasury Building, the Jefferson Memorial, and the Pentagon.

Compared to these Eastern cosmopolitans, I was only twenty at the time and was a red-haired, freckled farm girl from Missouri. None of the other four in the group had ever been around anyone quite like me before. By that I mean someone of my rural, Church of Christ background who was so wide-eyed about the world and so excited about everything we did and everywhere we went. They were absolutely wonderful to me and helped me fulfill my fantasies about seeing and experiencing the big wonderful world.

Ruth took me to New York one weekend. I was so excited as our train pulled into the station and I saw the Empire State Building for the first time. We walked to the Brass Rail Restaurant, which I had read about, put our feet on the brass rail, and had drinks. Then we walked over to the Radio City Music Hall for the show and movie. Knowing what we were about to see, Ruth leaned over in front of me to watch my face as the stage—not the curtain, but the entire stage—arose with the musicians seated on it playing away. She wanted to remember how I looked to tell the others. Needless to say, I found the orchestra rising to the stage astonishing. Then the Rockettes came out and did their synchronized dances. I had read about the Rockettes and knew they were coming, but they were still spectacular. Wow—I knew I was in the big city now!

Then we took the famed New York subway and rode for about an hour to Far Rockaway, in the borough of Queens. I loved Ruth's father. He argued religion with me and offered me "proof" that there was no heaven. As I recall his argument, the dimensions of heaven given in the Bible were so small that the number of people who were supposed to go there just couldn't fit in. Ruth's mother worked in a textile mill in New York and was a member of the famed International Ladies' Garment Workers' Union. Ruth took me around the Far Rockaway area and we went to the beach. What a grand time I had!

One of my fantasies had always been to eat lobster. I had read about the ceremony of getting bibbed and eating lobster using nutcrackers to get at the claw meat and sucking on the little legs to get the tastiest morsels. Determined to give me my fantasy, the other four girls took me to Baltimore, which is about thirty miles from Aberdeen, for a lobster dinner. I had never even seen a lobster until then. It was every bit as exciting as I had thought it would be. I thought it was wonderful to get bibbed and supplied with nutcrackers, tiny forks, and cups of butter. I soon found myself nibbling away on those tiny exotic legs and loving the taste of it. Even today, seeing those Red Lobster ads drives me nuts—I want to run out and eat lobster.

Marlyn said that since Ruth had shown me New York, she got to show me Washington, D.C. Imagine coming in on the train and seeing the Capitol Building in the distance for the first time. We took a taxi over to see it. It was hard to believe that I was standing in the city and the building where our nation's laws were made. We went to Arlington National Cemetery and the Tomb of the Unknown Soldier. The war was still on, and I was overwhelmed by those rows and rows of graves for young men who had died fighting for our country. Each had been men just like my brothers, brothers-in-law, cousins, and friends who were even then fighting for America across the Atlantic and Pacific Oceans. The endless sea of gravestones truly brought the war home to me in a new and very profound way that I had not quite grasped prior to seeing them. "Please don't let them end up here," I prayed as I stood in the midst of the tens of thousands of graves. Unfortunately, my brother-in-law, Harold Jennings, did end up there, but long after World War II ended. Harold's Navy airplane crashed into a mountain along the Gulf of Mexico in 1954 and he was laid to rest at Arlington.

Harold Jennings, ca. 1945–53.

We also went to the Lincoln Memorial. The huge statue of Lincoln is overpowering. The prettiest building was the Jefferson Memorial, and I liked it best of all. It is graceful with clean lines, and a simple grandeur that fits my image of Jefferson. The Washington Monument is big, but it is rather impersonal. At that time, we couldn't go up to the top of it—the top was closed during the war. We didn't go inside the White House, but we walked along Pennsylvania Avenue and admired the outside of that beautiful building. It was quite a day.

One weekend Kay took me to her beautiful home in Chestnut Hill, a posh neighborhood in northwest Philadelphia. When we got there, she slid into an Irish brogue with the rest of her family, and I couldn't understand a word they said. Kay had three brothers and two sisters. At this time, the two oldest brothers were already married and not living at home. Her mother ran the show and was so Catholic that I felt somewhat guilty for not being Catholic myself. I loved Kay and had a good time with her.

Betty took me home with her one weekend and I fell in love with her family. Mrs. Snyder, whose name was Frances, was a wonderful woman, making her home warm and welcoming. She was a great cook, a great seamstress, and a happy person. She and her husband, John Snyder, were crazy about each other. I played badminton with Betty's brother Bob. Betty had four brothers and three sisters. Two of her sisters were in the Navy WAVES and two of her brothers were married. Only Bob and Betty lived at home.

John Snyder, then sixty-one, was a legendary teacher of mathematics at Old Central High, affectionately known as "Professor Johnny" by the boys he taught over a span of forty-six years. I understood why his students held him in such high regard when I heard this story. In the early 1920s, Dr. Snyder had a student named Robert D. Abrahams. One morning "Professor Johnny" was lecturing in front of the entire senior class when Dr. John Haney, the school's president, burst in, clutching a folded paper. He called on Abrahams to stand up, waved the paper at him, and demanded that he withdraw what he had written on it or face expulsion. The document was a ridiculous questionnaire all the boys had been required to fill out as a means of measuring their intelligence. The first question read, "Are you able to keep from asking foolish questions?" To which Abrahams had replied, "Yes, and I do not answer them, either." He had left all the others unanswered. Abrahams refused to retract his words, but he wasn't expelled. Instead, Snyder valiantly took his side, declaring to Dr. Haney, "If he goes, I go, too." Haney turned purple, but he spun on his heel and stormed out, and that was the end of the matter. Robert D. Abrahams went on to become a noted Philadelphia lawyer and a popular author and poet.[4]

When I visited in 1945, Mr. Snyder was at this time of his life interested in sunspots. He felt they had a great influence on the weather on earth. Later on, I spent a couple of nights a week at their house almost every week. I really felt as if I had a home away from home. Our families did have a lot in common. Both of our fathers were schoolteachers; both our mothers were very talented women who spent their time making their homes a good place to live; and we both had big families doing lots of different things.

We were on a per diem of six or seven dollars per day while we were in Aberdeen, and by the end of our seven weeks there I had enough money to pay Aunt Gretchen the four hundred dollars I had borrowed from her to go to college my first two years. I went to the post office and used my per diem money plus some savings to purchase a money order and sent it to her. We were glad that our time in Aberdeen was up because we were eager to get back to Philadelphia to learn about the ENIAC.

When our training in Aberdeen was completed, we came back to Philadelphia, arriving toward the end of July. Imagine—we had no office to sit in, no operator's manuals, and no instructors.[5] Instead, we were given three-by-four-foot block diagrams of the ENIAC circuits and told to study them. During this time, we never even saw the ENIAC, because it was classified and our clearance had not yet come through. We also had not yet met John Mauchly or Pres Eckert or any of the ENIAC engineers.

Betty and I chose to work in a classroom on the second floor of the Moore School—the building in which the ENIAC was being built. I had never read a block diagram in my life. Betty hadn't either, and we assumed it was read from left to right like a book. We sat there staring at the large rolled-out sheets containing the block diagrams of the various units. The Moore School was adding on a third floor and the jackhammers were going full blast. It was hot and humid with no air conditioning. Historic, Penn was; modern, it was not.[6]

This state of affairs went on for several days. Then one day Betty and I were sitting in two classroom chairs—the kind with an armrest that curls around into a small writing desk—trying to figure out how the accumulator worked. The accumulator was the real workhorse of the ENIAC. Each of the twenty accumulators could receive and store a ten-decimal-digit number. Each could add a number it received from another accumulator. Each could either send out its contents to another accumulator for addition or send out the nines complement of its contents to add to the contents of another accumulator for a subtraction. A "1" was added to the unit's position in the receiving accumulator to make it a true tens complement when it was subtracting. Believe me, we understood nothing of this as we sat there looking at this incomprehensible drawing.[7]

Betty Snyder and Kathleen McNulty, fall 1946. Photo by Betty Jean Jennings.

As Betty and I sat there, a man came into the room and walked all around looking up at the ceiling without saying a word. Finally, he came over to us and said, "I'm just checking to see if the ceiling is falling down." (Remember, they were jackhammering above us.) After chatting a bit, he introduced himself. He was John Mauchly. Neither of us had ever seen him before, and we were thrilled to meet the co-inventor of the ENIAC. Plus, we were happy to meet someone who could tell us how the blasted accumulator worked.

John was a born teacher. I believe that, like Socrates, he could teach a slave boy the Pythagorean theorem (or, as Socrates might put it, "help him to remember it"). Mauchly explained the accumulator to us and said his office was next door. He kindly encouraged us to come and ask him questions at any time he was in his office. We began to save up our questions and go in every afternoon to ask them. John Holberton, our manager, shared Mauchly's office, so he sat in on those sessions. Thus began our long association and friendship with John Mauchly.

On an interesting side note, while the ENIAC was being built, Dr. John G. Brainerd, the head of the Moore School of Engineering and the ENIAC project director, was deeply concerned because its construction kept running behind schedule. In hopes of speeding things up, he decided to take John's teaching assignments away from him during the summer of 1944. Up until this time, John had carried a full teaching load while also working on the ENIAC. In fact, John was putting in long hours at the University of Pennsylvania and usually went home around 2 a.m. However, Brainerd wasn't entirely aware of John's workload. You see, Brainerd took the train home at 5 p.m. each day without fail and he wasn't aware of the extent of John's overtime. Taking away John's teaching assignments would have been fine, except Brainerd halved John's salary as well, and John couldn't live on it. He had a wife, Mary, a mother, and two children to support. To make a living wage, he had to take a consulting job as a statistician with the Navy Ordnance Laboratory, where he had to report to John Vincent Atanasoff—a fact that would come to have great significance twenty years later.

Anyway, Mauchly always thought of the ENIAC as a programmable general-purpose computer, although Aberdeen bought it primarily to do trajectories, so its acceptance test was to be the execution of a trajectory.[8] Mauchly compared it to a series of calculators, like those electronic desktop calculators manufactured by Friden, Monroe, or Marchant—the "computers" we had used at Aberdeen to calculate trajectories. The ENIAC allowed these "calculators" to communicate with each other under a master control. Many people have said he thought of it as an electronic differential analyzer, which is totally untrue, although it was sold to Aberdeen to calculate trajectories.

Anyway, we ENIAC women learned about the function tables, which stored the drag function for trajectories (drag was caused by the air surrounding a shell). There were three function tables, each of which could store 102 twelve-decimal-digit numbers. These function tables would later be used to store programs when the ENIAC was turned into a stored-program computer. We also learned about the multiplier, the divider/square rooter, and the master programmer, which was the central control.

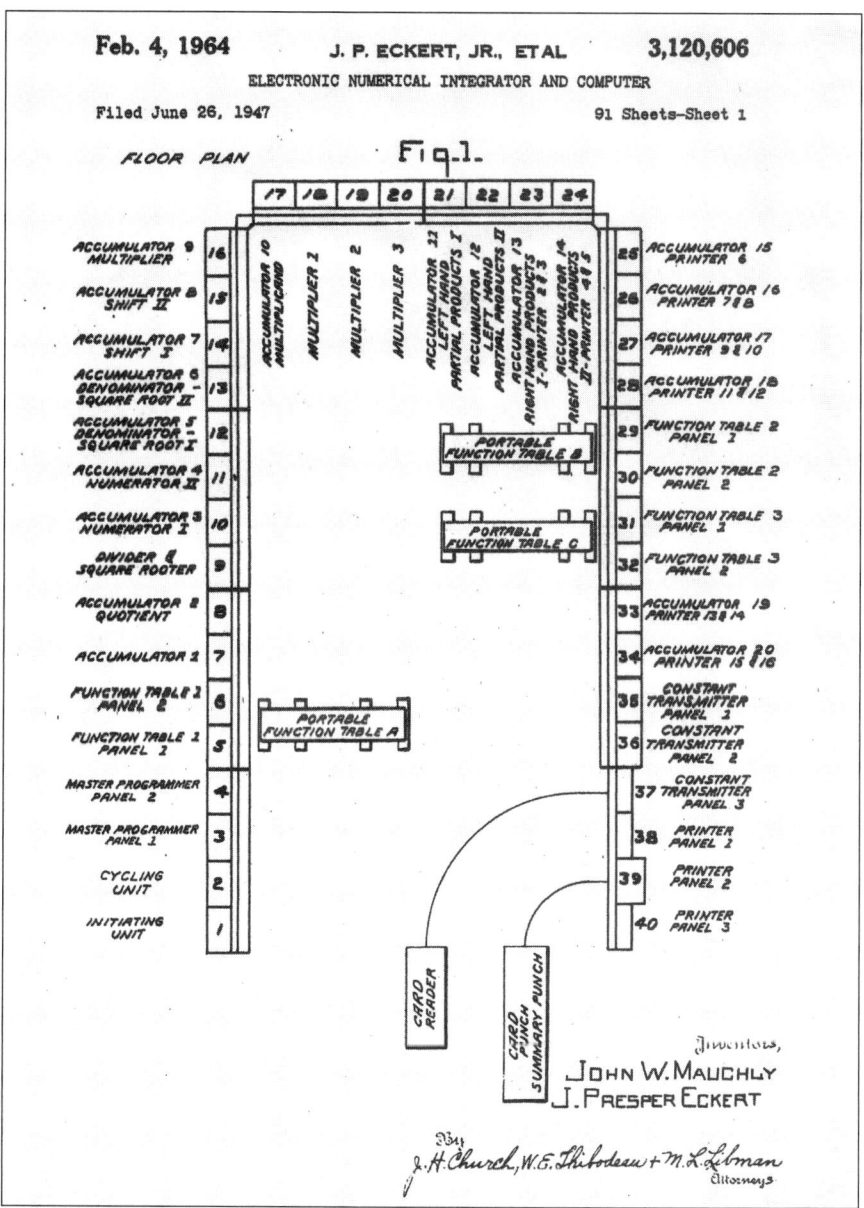

Diagram taken from the ENIAC patent application, showing the units of the ENIAC: initiating unit, cycling unit, master programmer, twenty accumulators, divider/square rooter, multiplier, constant transmitter, card reader, card punch, and three function tables. The power supplies on the fourth wall are not shown.

Senior engineer Arthur Burks and Betty Jean Jennings in front of the ENIAC. The photo was taken in February 1946 by *Science Illustrated* magazine for a May 1946 article. The magazine gave Jean a print; in 2006 Jean and her niece, Diane Passmore, donated the print to the Jean Jennings Bartik Computing Museum.

The multiplier was very cleverly designed. It did not use a series of additions to multiply, as a hand calculator does. It used a hard-wired function table for looking up the two partial products that make up the product of two numbers. For example, nine times five consists of two partial products, a "4" and a "5," which make up the complete product 45.

As the multiplicand in one accumulator was multiplied by each number in the multiplier accumulator, the partial products were summed up in two accumulators—one storing the tens-digit partial products and the other storing the units- (or ones-) digit partial products. After the multiplicand had been multiplied by the number of digits in the multiplier accumulator, the units-digit partial products were added to the tens-digit partial products to complete the multiplication. This had the advantage of being faster than using a series of additions, with the additional benefit that the time of a multiplication could be calculated. The time was independent of the size of the numbers, although it was dependent on the number of significant digits in the multiplier.

The divider did a division the same way it is done by hand. The difference is that instead of multiplying the divisor by the largest digit that would not make the divisor larger than the dividend, the divisor built up that number by a series of subtractions of the divisor from the dividend.

As each subtraction was done, it built up the quotient without turning the dividend into a negative number. When the dividend finally turned negative, the divisor was added back into the dividend once to turn it back to a positive number. The dividend was shifted to the left one decimal position, and the next digit of the quotient was built up. This continued until all significant digits of the quotient were built up. Using this method, the time the ENIAC took to do a division was dependent on the numbers in the dividend and divisor; thus, unlike with multiplications, the time it took could not be calculated.

The signs of the products and quotient were attached depending on the signs of the multiplicand and the multiplier for multiplication and of the dividend and the divisor for division. Like signs produced a plus sign (+) and unlike signs produced a minus sign (−). I have forgotten the algorithm for the square root, but it was based on an iterative process requiring additions and subtractions. The value of a square root is always positive. The time it took to calculate a square root depended on the number in the radicand; thus the time it took to arrive at a square root could not be calculated. Why this is important will later become clear.

Toward the end of August, a room became available on the second floor of the Moore School for the ENIAC programmers, along with a room each for John Holberton and for Dr. L. S. (Louis Serles) Dederick, chief of the computing section of the Ballistic Research Laboratory, who came up from Aberdeen to handle all the details of the ENIAC administration. Dr. Dederick was a very gentle, considerate man, but quite old, and was being eased out. We had very little to do with him, and not much more to do with Holberton, who was our manager but who knew no more about the ENIAC than we did—probably less. Mauchly came into our office and answered our questions.

We five women were together again and began to discuss the ENIAC, how it worked, and how it could do problems. We were now joined by Fran Bilas, who had worked with Kay on the differential analyzer. She became the sixth ENIAC programmer. Fran had grown up in South Philadelphia, the daughter of Joseph Bilas, an Austrian immigrant who worked as a maintenance man, and Anna, from Germany, a schoolteacher. Fran was one of five sisters, all of them pretty and smart as whips. Like Kay McNulty, she was awarded a scholarship to Chestnut Hill College and, like Kay, she graduated in 1942 as a math major (there were only three women math majors in their class). Two weeks after graduation, they together answered an ad for math majors and were told by the recruiter that they were exactly what the Army needed and to report to the Aberdeen Proving Ground group at the Moore School.

All of us knew how to do trajectories and we knew that calculating trajectories was to be the ENIAC's primary purpose. From the start, each of us tried to think of how we could program it to do them. We would study the diagrams and talk about what they meant and try to imagine how to use them to do a trajectory. I am still amazed at how little help, instruction, or supervision we had. Kay remembered Arthur Burks explaining some of the block diagrams, but I don't remember him until later. He may have explained some of them to Kay before we got the office together. Before we were reunited, we didn't even see each other for lunch, or know where the others' offices were. I remember a particular day in September when all of us were sitting in the room discussing how the various units worked and how to program a trajectory on the ENIAC. All of us were working on this problem at that time, but none of us could see how all the trajectory calculations could fit on the ENIAC. Suddenly Kay exclaimed, "I know how! We use the master programmer to reuse code!"

Kay's exclamation was a breakthrough! We quickly began figuring out how to use the master programmer, which was the control unit of the ENIAC. It had stepper switches that allowed the repetition of a program for a fixed number of times before going on to another program. It also allowed the testing of a sign in an accumulator. If the sign was negative, one program could be selected, and if it was positive, a different program could be selected. This feature refutes the oft-repeated lie that the ENIAC had no "if/then" statement. On the contrary, if the sign was negative, then one program sequence was selected. If the sign was positive, then another program path was chosen. Even *Modern Marvels*, a series on The History Channel, repeated the falsehood that ENIAC couldn't make logical decisions in its 1995 episode *The Creation of the Computer*, and WGBH Television never gave credit in its 1992 documentary *The Machine That Changed the World* that the ENIAC was the first stored-program computer.[9]

Early on in the process of programming the ENIAC—around the first of October—we separated. Ruth and Marlyn were given the job of calculating a trajectory exactly the way the ENIAC would do it, add time by add time, only doing it by hand. This turned out to be the smartest thing we did. The ENIAC ran at a

Betty Jean Jennings (left) and Frances Bilas (right) in front of the initiating and cycling unit panels on the left and the two master programmer panels on the right. There are nine program trays stacked underneath the switches that control the units, and part of a function table is visible to the right. Courtesy of the U.S. Army (ARL Technical Library).

100-kilocycle rate, or 100,000 cycles per second. An add time was twenty cycles; thus it could perform five thousand additions per second. Hardly impressive with today's gigacycle rates (a gigacycle is ten thousand times faster than the ENIAC) but in 1945, five thousand additions per second was very impressive.

Kay and Fran were assigned to help Nick Metropolis and Stan Frankel, who had arrived from Los Alamos, to put their problem on the ENIAC. Betty Snyder and I—sometimes helped by Kay—were assigned the task of trying to program the trajectory for the ENIAC's acceptance test. To do that we had to understand the function tables, which stored the drag function. We calculated the argument for the function table.[10] It took into account the height of the shell and various other factors that affect drag: the density of the air, the speed of the shell, and the effects of gravity. The argument selected the line in the function table that translated to the drag on the shell for those conditions.

We had the most fun figuring out how to use the master programmer, which provided the control over the whole operation. All of the units of the ENIAC were interconnected through two sets of buses: the memory bus and the programming trays. The memory bus carried the numbers around to various units inside the computer. The programming bus carried the signals that could be tapped off to start an operation. Once an operation was complete, the unit sent out a signal that could be plugged into the program tray so it could be picked up by other units to do the next operation.

Each accumulator had a switch to select from up to five memory buses to send numbers out on or to receive numbers from. That switch selected the memory bus used for a particular operation, then we had to plug in the buses to the accumulator. I actually never saw an accumulator hooked up to other than two, three, or four memory buses—using all five would have made keeping track of operations too complex.

The memory buses were labeled Alpha, Beta, Gamma, Delta, and Epsilon. A memory bus programming tray was about eight feet long, and we had to connect them together so they could reach all the units that used a particular signal.[11] As part of our programming of a problem, we had to determine how to cable the various units to the memory buses. As for the program buses, we labeled each tray A, B, C, and so on, to H. Each tray had eleven lines, or connection holes, so we would label the lines A-1, A-2, all the way to A-11. The program trays carried the program signals that stimulated an operation and signaled the end of an operation and started the next.[12]

The ENIAC was a parallel machine, meaning that several operations could take place at the same time. If a division was taking place at the same time as several additions, the output signal to start the next operation had to come from the divider because its time of operation could not be calculated. Using that signal kept everything synchronized. If we wanted to repeat a small program or subroutine, we would feed the output signal from it into the master programmer and set a switch telling it how many times we wanted to repeat the program. Each output until the final one would send out a signal to repeat the subroutine. The final output from the master programmer would send out a signal to start the next routine.

The master programmer could also test the sign of an accumulator to determine when it turned negative; thus we could also repeat a subroutine over and over again until a number became a minus value. This feature allowed us to stop the calculation of a trajectory when the shell hit the ground, i.e., when the altitude became negative.

On August 14, 1945, Japan agreed to an unconditional surrender, following the atomic bombing of Hiroshima on August 6 and of Nagasaki on August 9. Final surrender came on September 2, 1945, when a Japanese delegation signed the formal document aboard the battleship *Missouri*. Everyone was glad the war was over, but it was mind-boggling. The devastation caused by those bombs—80,000 to 200,000 casualties for Hiroshima alone—was shocking.[13] We had never heard of such things and couldn't imagine the power of such devices. The reality of the atomic bomb was an unimaginable horror and, although our country was the one that had dropped them, the Philadelphians I knew were afraid of its awesome and horrific power.

Later, reporters asked President Harry S. Truman, who had made the decision to use the bombs, about how hard the decision had been. President Truman replied that he'd slept well the night he made the decision. One reporter went on to say that he'd admired Truman for making such a tough decision, but would have been happier if the president had lost a bit of sleep. I happen to agree with the reporter because the taking of a single human life, even if there is no other choice but to do so, should always cause at the very least a mild form of insomnia; however, I will not reprimand Truman for his blissful sleep—if indeed it was blissful. The war in the Pacific had been long and hard and the bomb stopped the bloodshed. To many that was cause for a good night's sleep. Over 45 million people lost their lives in the horrendous years of World War II. People around the world were so sickened by war that the United Nations Charter was signed in San Francisco on June 26, 1945, well before the Japanese surrender.

In October 1945, Nick Metropolis and Stan Frankel from Los Alamos Laboratory in New Mexico came to put a problem on the ENIAC. It was a secret problem, so we knew nothing about it. They had been in Philadelphia in June or July getting briefed by the engineers on the ENIAC's operation. I guess they were also given block diagrams of it, because they came back with the problem already programmed. We were excited to meet them. The atom bombs had been dropped on Hiroshima and Nagasaki, and Nick and Stan had been at Alamogordo when the atom bomb was tested. Frankel's wife, Mary (who had worked on the project as a human computer), was with him, so we talked to her about the testing of the atom bomb. Like us, the physicists at Los Alamos had been shocked at the power of the atom bomb to devastate a city.

Nick Metropolis and Stan Frankel ran the IBM Punched Card Computing Group in Los Alamos. They were really good. In fact, they caused our eyes to bug out when they had us turn the IBM cards upside down before running them through the sorter. I have no idea what they were doing, but they must have been reading the complement of the numbers for some reason. They were far more sophisticated than we were about the punched card equipment, because we never thought of them as computing devices.

The day in October that Nick and Stan put their problem on the ENIAC was the first time we had ever seen the machine itself or the ENIAC engineers—Bob Shaw, Kite Sharpless, Jeffrey Chuan Chu, John Davis, Harold Husky, and Arthur Burks. We were thrilled to see the ENIAC for the first time and amazed by its size. It was much bigger and more magnificent and intimidating than we had imagined. On that day Herman Goldstine acted like an orchestra conductor. We were all spaced around the ENIAC and assigned various units. Herman would call out a unit, such as, "Accumulator 1, Program Line Input A-0 to Switch 5, set to receive from Alpha!" Whoever was at that accumulator would set the switch and plug in the cables as directed. Then Herman would call out, "Accumulator 2, Program Line Input A-0 to Switch 5, set to add to Alpha, output program pulse to line A-1!" Thus Accumulator 1 would receive the contents of Accumulator 2 from the Alpha memory bus and add it to its own contents. Pulse A-1 would start the next operation.

Of course, the pulse from Accumulator 2 could be attached to any program line to signal the start of an entirely different operation. Care had to be taken that the two different operations did not have conflicts on the memory buses. Also, if the operation was a multiplication or division, the programs would have to be brought back in sync by using the program output from the longest-running program. It was tedious. In fact, my most quoted statement about the ENIAC was that it was a son of a bitch to program. And so it was.[14]

Nick and Stan were in Philadelphia for several months, and Fran and Kay were assigned to help them run their program. The program had been suggested by von Neumann, although (we later learned) its purpose was to enable Edward Teller to evaluate the feasibility of using an atom bomb to trigger an H bomb, or hydrogen bomb. We saw the ENIAC at work during that fall and winter of 1945 when the Los Alamos problem was being done. Dick Lehmer, the number theorist, did some prime number studies on it; he called it a sieve, because it sieved out prime numbers. Then Hans Rademacher, a German number theorist at Penn, and engineer Harry Husky did some calculations on round-off versus truncation errors.

Betty and I continued to work on the trajectory program, getting it ready for the acceptance test. We lived and breathed it. Betty Snyder was my first perfect partner.[15] Betty was bright, logical, and hard-working. The ground rules for the working partnerships we had at the Moore School were very different from most other relationships: as we worked together, each tried to find fault with what the other was doing. Instead of being angry when one partner found a fault, the other was delighted: it meant an error would not be left in the program. I think that this is not only a way to arrive at error-free code, but that it also works well with all design projects. Betty and I had a grand time. We were not only partners, but we were friends and spent as much of our free time together as possible.

I should tell you about Betty Snyder and her amazing brain. Many times, we would have a problem that we couldn't figure out at the end of the day. The next morning, she would come in with the solution. She would say something like, "It occurred to me this morning that this is the problem." And she would be right. I began to wonder if Betty went home and worked on it secretly. She didn't. What she did was think about the problem along with various solutions before she went to bed. Her brain subconsciously worked on the problem through the night and frequently came up with the solution. I now do this and it works, although I've never gotten as good at it as Betty. I have said many times that Betty could do more logic in her sleep than most people can do while they are awake!

Ruth and Marlyn continued to calculate the trajectory, exactly mirroring how the ENIAC would do it, add time by add time. We were going to use it as a test program to make sure the ENIAC was running error-free and, if it wasn't, to diagnose which component was making the error. It succeeded magnificently, and garnered for us instant acceptance by the engineers.

I've always said that engineers are a lazy lot, which is why they design better products—they want to make something that is less trouble! Because of this, they do appreciate anyone who does for them what they do not like to do. Engineers hate to fiddle with products they have already designed. Once a project is done it's done in their minds and they would rather go off and have the fun of building something entirely new that doesn't have any of the bugs in it that the product they just built has. So once the engineers found we could debug the ENIAC better than they could, they let us do it gladly.

The engineers were a wonderful group, with a couple of sexy ones thrown in. Kite Sharpless and Jeffrey Chuan Chu in my opinion were gorgeous men. Kite was a Philadelphia Quaker with grace and charm and prematurely gray hair but a young face. He was the expert on the multiplier. Chuan was mysteriously Asian with beautiful high cheekbones and exotic slanted eyes. When I told Chuan, late in life, how handsome all of us women had thought he was, I was surprised that he apparently had no inkling of what we women had thought of him. Chuan was the expert on the divider/square rooter.

Bob Shaw was an albino, which meant he had very poor eyesight. He was tall and skinny, but what a wonderful person he was. He was a true Renaissance man. He was a great engineer, a good writer, a good talker, and full of a quirky sense of humor. He had a very logical mind, but it didn't follow the usual lines of reasoning. Instead of going from A to B to C, his mind went from A to Z to C. When we were puzzled by some bit of unusual logic from him, Bob would explain it, and it would be entirely logical. We came to call it "Bob Shaw Logic." I think he sometimes thought up weird logic just to tease us. Bob designed the function table.[16] He had infinite patience, was very social, and, despite his fragile physique, he never pampered himself. He was wonderful. Later, at UNIVAC, he drew all the initial logic diagrams for UNIVAC I in a month's time—an amazing feat.

Arthur Burks was a small, unassuming man who had earned a PhD in philosophy from Michigan in 1941 with an emphasis in symbolic logic and then, that next summer, had moved to Philadelphia and enrolled in a national defense electronics course offered at Penn. The U.S. government instituted the course because it was trying to create more engineers to help in the war effort. A number of early computer pioneers also took this course, including John Mauchly, Al Auerbach, and Lou Wilson. The course was taught by Pres Eckert and Brad Sheppard. It was here that Pres and John met and began talking about an electronic computer.

Burks was very bright and courteous, but quiet. We all liked him. I believe Burks did the logical design for the divider/square rooter. When the ENIAC was introduced, it was he who ran the demonstration. Burks's understated presence heightened the dynamic effect of the conclusion of the demonstration. First he quietly did a few simple demonstration problems and explained the various ENIAC units and how they worked. The dramatic climax of the demonstration came when he turned out the lights and ran the trajectory problem with the lights flashing in the ENIAC accumulators as the trajectory was calculated faster than it took a shell to trace it.

Johnny Davis was a large, chunky, affable engineer who worked on the accumulator design. He was always joking around, but he was always helpful when we needed a decade counter replaced because one of the tubes wasn't working. He was a good friend of Shaw's. The two of them, along with Brad Sheppard, played the commodities market, so they spent some time discussing that. I am not sure how well they did, but I don't think their successes were spectacular, because they took quite a bit of kidding about it. At the time, I thought Brad Sheppard was an ENIAC engineer, but he told me later that he was not. He was around because he was working on the mercury delay line memory being tested for use on the

EDVAC (Electronic Discrete Variable Automatic Computer), the successor to the ENIAC. Brad was a taciturn individual who tended to speak in monosyllables. He answered the question you asked but never elaborated on the answer.

Pres Eckert told this story about Brad. One time, he asked Brad whether a particular circuit had seven vacuum tubes in it. Brad said, "Yes." Later, Pres found out that the circuit had thirteen tubes in it. Nevertheless, what Brad had told him was true—it did indeed have seven. Pres said, "You have to know how to ask Brad a question to get the answer you are looking for."

Harry Husky designed the logic for the card reader and card punch. His name was also on most of the logical block diagrams of the ENIAC, meaning he drew the logical diagrams as they had been worked out through meetings with the design engineer and Pres and John. He wasn't around much, so I never knew him very well. He taught at the Moore School.

We never saw Professor J. G. Brainerd, who handled the administrative details for the ENIAC as the University of Pennsylvania's civilian liaison with Aberdeen Proving Ground. The engineers always laughed and said Brainerd didn't even know how the ENIAC worked. We also seldom saw Herman Goldstine, who was the military liaison between Aberdeen and the Moore School. Goldstine was always in a hurry; he was always nervously moving about as he talked. When he talked to me, he never looked me in the eye. He gave the impression that he had many more important things on his mind than talking to me.

In late August or early September 1945, I finally met Pres Eckert when I received a telephone call at my apartment from Hester Eckert, Pres's wife. She said that she and Pres and a friend had been hiking in Fairmount Park, a four-thousand-acre park in the city of Philadelphia, and had decided they wanted to go to a bar in New Jersey, and would I like to go with them? Although it was Sunday, I said that I would be happy to go with them. Pennsylvania had blue laws that forbade the selling of liquor on a Sunday, so on Sundays Pennsylvanians went to bars in Jersey. I got all dolled up in my little black dress. They came by dressed in their hiking clothes and said we would go up to their apartment in Germantown, a neighborhood in northwest Philadelphia, so they could change their clothes.

When we got there, nobody made a move to change. We had a drink, and Pres and the friend, John Sims, wandered around the apartment talking about business. After a while, Sims excused himself and went into a bedroom. The minutes ticked by without Sims reappearing, Press then went into the bedroom to see if Sims was okay. When Pres came out of the bedroom he told us that Sims was sick and needed to go home.

Pres left me with Hester while he took Sims home. Hester and I chatted and drank a little as we waited for Pres to return. When he did, Pres suggested that we call it a night and offered to drive me home. In short, my little black dress went entirely to waste. During the drive home, Pres apologized profusely about the rotten evening. I had never really talked to Pres before this night, especially alone. I found him to be very gracious and we chatted about various things without any uncomfortable silences. Afterward, I more or less forgot about that bad date night. Pres never did.

My relationship with Pres became much closer and friendlier when I was assigned as a logical designer of a backup for the UNIVAC I using cathode-ray tube storage and began working directly for him. Pres and I got along famously and, of course, Hester and I were friends, so we often met outside of work for social gatherings. For years afterward, whenever I found myself in a social situation with Pres he would apologize for that yawn-inducing evening with Sims.[17]

Whenever I worked with Pres, I always felt my IQ went up a few notches. Like Mauchly, he was a superb teacher. He chose to talk to me; I never went up to him to ask him a question—I never even knew where his office was. Nobody ever interrupted when he was talking to me or anyone else. He was focused and gave his undivided attention to me while we talked. No question was too small to ask. Pres also thought with his mouth open. If he talked about something I knew nothing about, I would just ask questions to understand. If I knew something about it, I could ask questions and give opinions about it. Pres listened to every word.

Then, of course, there was John Mauchly. We were all crazy about him. He was gracious and charming and very kind. He was also a fabulous teacher and he taught all of us, in a group and individually. He spent a lot of time with us. He wanted us to use the ENIAC properly and he always wanted us to think of it as a programmable general-purpose computer, not as one that could just do trajectories. He was always trying to get us to think about programming a matrix inversion, which we never did—it was far too daunting a challenge. We just wanted to get a trajectory done right. John was the most responsive person I've ever met. He fell right in with whatever frame of mind you were in and whatever you were doing. If one of us went up to him singing a tune, he would join in. If one of us quoted a line from *Alice in Wonderland*, he would finish the line. He was addicted to puns and was always springing them on people. Some of his puns were terrible, but he enjoyed them anyway, and so did we.

We ENIAC women, now including Frances "Fran" Bilas (Spence), still liked to be together, and we squeezed into a booth to eat lunch at Lido's on Woodland

The only known group picture of the ENIAC women while working at Aberdeen. The picture was taken by Betty Snyder in 1946 outside the Lido Restaurant in Philadelphia. Left to right: unidentified man in uniform, Frances Bilas, Homer Spence (electrical engineer), Jim Cummings (draftsman), Marlyn Wescoff, John Mauchly, Ruth Lichterman, Betty Jean Jennings, and Kay McNulty.

Avenue, an Italian restaurant that was somewhat dark and always crowded at lunchtime. The waiters were always bustling about, and the place had a festive atmosphere. We also often ate dinner at Arthur's Steakhouse at Second and Walnut in Old Philadelphia. At Arthur's, the steaks were carefully prepared and served just right.[18] We always sat at a circular table at Arthur's. We loved going there because it was spacious, well lighted, and not noisy. We weren't rushed. Many times, John went with us, both to Arthur's and Lido's. We would order drinks before dinner, and sometimes we would talk for a short while about something personal, but then we would quickly get back to our first interest, computers. How could they be used? How were we doing with the ENIAC? What was the future going to be like? We realized they would be smaller with fewer vacuum tubes, but none of us ever dreamed of the miniaturization that would occur with integrated circuits. Nor did we conceive of the incredible cost reductions that would make them affordable to almost anyone.

During these conversations, John was already mentioning theories that would go into the making of a new kind of computer, which would be called the UNIVAC. There is a marketing theory that says there are two ways to develop products. One is called the expanding puddle. Using this method, the market widens because a product gets better, faster, more reliable, bigger, or more useful, but it is still basically the same product. This product may last many years, such as Coca-Cola or Gillette razors. The other market theory is the big splash. It is outside the product line and not connected to the expanding puddle. The big splash involves a product that is totally new and can solve problems never solved before or fulfill a need never fulfilled before. It opens up new markets. What we programmers tended to think about was the expanding puddle. Up until this time, everyone thought of computers as handling mathematical computations. It took John and Pres to think up the UNIVAC, which could handle alphanumeric data and the file processing required for the commercial computing market. A big splash.

Before we could get to the UNIVAC, however, or even the EDVAC, we had to prove the efficacy of the ENIAC. A demonstration was set up for February in which we would make history by showing the world a new kind of intelligence, the kind that could calculate a trajectory faster than the time it took a shell fired from a gun to trace it. The ENIAC would, indeed, make a big splash and, like a pebble thrown into a pond, the resulting ripples produced would have far-reaching, history-making impact. Decades later, the *Philadelphia Inquirer* would call the ENIAC "the machine that changed the world" in a February 15, 1976, article. Similarly WGBH Television would also use these same words for the title of their 1992 documentary *The Machine That Changed the World* as would Fritz in his *IEEE: Annals of the History of Computing* article about the ENIAC women.[19] Perhaps it is a vanity, but I like to think of the program Betty and I wrote for the February 15, 1946, demonstration of the ENIAC as the pebble that started it all.

CHAPTER 4

Apricot Brandy and Nighttime Logic

February 15, 1946, was the day we made history—the day we revealed to the world the first computer successfully running a program. But, just as with the Wright brothers' historic flight at Kitty Hawk, there was an earlier attempt that failed to get off the ground. On February 1, there had been a demonstration of the ENIAC to the press, who were asked to hold their stories for release two weeks later, when the formal dedication of the ENIAC would take place for the scientific community. The first demonstration was smaller and according to people who discussed it with us afterwards, was rather dismal. A few simple operations were run to show the rapidity with which the ENIAC could add and multiply—5,000 additions in a second, and 350 multiplications in a second. The ENIAC programmers had nothing to do with this demonstration, so we weren't present. I don't know why the programmers were not part of that first demonstration, but I suspect that Herman Goldstine wanted to say that he and Adele did the programs. In fact, I believe they tried to do the trajectory for it but couldn't.

A day or two later, Herman Goldstine invited Betty and me to their apartment in West Philadelphia. It was a very ordinary apartment, with a large living room, a bedroom, and a small kitchen, but there were few personal touches—no framed photographs, no bric-a-brac, and the bedroom had twin beds, which shocked me at the time. Betty and I had never socialized with Adele and Herman Goldstine; in fact, we had seldom even seen them or talked to them. We were puzzled as to why we were there. To add to Betty's discomfort, their cat kept crawling up on her lap and she was leery of cats. Years later she mentioned how perturbed she had been that the cat kept licking her as she tried to push it away.

Herman dominated the conversation. As Adele served tea or coffee, he told us he had invited us there because he had something important to discuss with us. He understood that we had programmed a trajectory. He told us that Aberdeen wanted to run a trajectory for the public demonstration. Herman asked us if the trajectory program was ready to go. We said it was. He asked if we could put it on the ENIAC and have it debugged and up and running for the demonstration to the public on February 15. We said we sure could. He told us we could start putting it on the ENIAC the next day. We were thrilled—it was like a dream come true.

Herman went on to tell us the types of people who would be at the demonstration—well-known scientists, various dignitaries, many of them men whose names we were familiar with. He stressed that it was very important that it run well. Then he said he was counting on us and had confidence we could do it. All of this time his eyes were nervously darting about the room, as they always did. I don't think he would have asked Betty and me to do it if he and Adele could have done it. It would have been really silly to introduce a computer that Aberdeen had bought to do trajectories and then not to be able to show it doing one, which is what I understood happened at the earlier demonstration for the press.

Betty and I were sure the program was perfect. We had no doubts whatsoever that it would be ready. We knew all the work we had done to finish the program. What we did not fully realize was all the work that lay ahead of us in the next twelve days. Here are the steps Betty and I had followed to program the trajectory in the four months leading up to that February meeting at Herman and Adele's:

First, we developed flowcharts that listed the sequence of steps the ENIAC needed to perform to solve the problem. These steps consisted of the trajectory equations and how they were calculated. We then charted all of these steps on a timeline representing the duration the test would run—about twenty seconds.

Second, we developed programming sheets, which we started calling "pedaling sheets" (perhaps because we had to "pedal" through them to get where we were going, and they showed us what was happening each "pedal stroke" along the way, or add time by add time). These were very large sheets of graph paper with dark-lined one-inch squares further divided into quarter-inch squares. Across these programming sheets, we labeled each one-inch square in the top row with the name of an ENIAC unit, and down the left side, in add times, we charted the timeline in which the process would run. This was important because operations could take place in parallel, and the timing of these operations had to be kept in

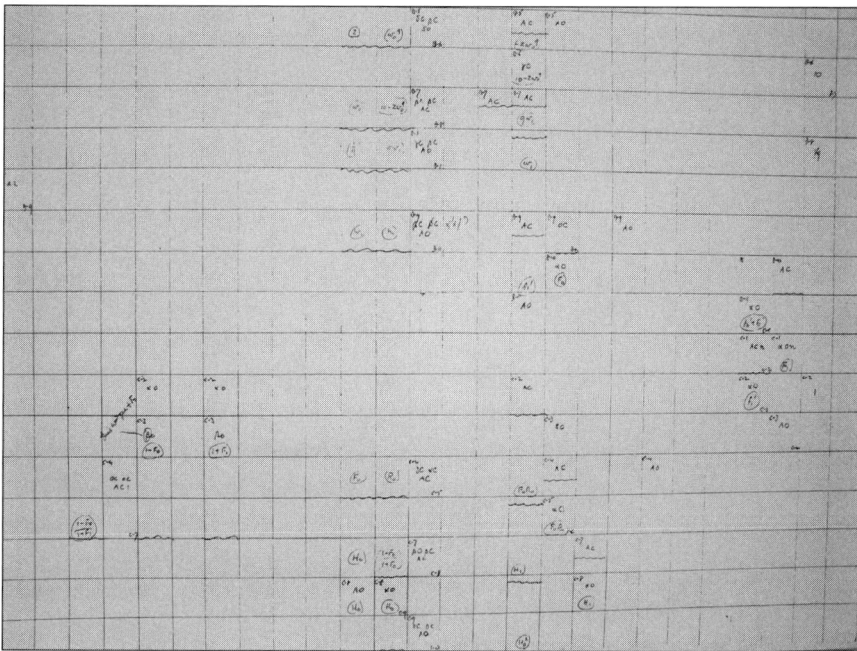

ENIAC Programming Sheet (Pedaling Sheet). © 2002 Jean Jennings Bartik Computing Museum, Northwest Missouri State University.

synchronization so that the different units performing operations would not be using the same memory buses at the same time. For each operation, we filled the one-inch square with the switch settings of each unit used in the operation. We also showed what program pulse stimulated what operation and what output program pulse would trigger the next operation.[1]

Then we made long pieces of cardboard that fitted into a slot on the front of each unit. On these we wrote out the same switch settings as on the pedaling sheet for every operation the unit did to calculate the trajectory, as well as the input and output program pulses.

For an accumulator, which had four receivers (which could only receive) and eight transceivers (which could either receive or send), the switches were operation switches telling which memory bus to receive on or whether the memory bus was to add, subtract, or both add and subtract—that is, whether it was to send out the number, its complement, or both using two memory buses.

A round-off switch told how many significant digits were to be operated on so that the five added for rounding off could be added to the right digit position. There was a switch that could be set to repeat the operation up to nine times (multiply by nine). It also had a little switch telling whether to clear the accumulator before it received or to keep its content and add it to the number being received. And we wrote out the input program pulse for the selector (operation) switch and the output program pulse if it was to be used to trigger the next operation.

All of this had already been done when Herman told us we could put the trajectory program on the ENIAC for the demonstration. Now we had to implement the plans on the pedaling sheets by putting them on the ENIAC—actually wiring up the memory buses, the program trays and lines, and setting the switches. Here is what Betty and I did in the less than two weeks we had in which to get ready for the acceptance test of the ENIAC.

First, we set up memory buses and plugged them into all the units that would use them. Then we set up all the program trays that would carry the control pulses to all the units that would use them. We labeled all of the memory buses and program trays, and we set up all of the switches on the units (the twenty accumulators, the multiplier, the divider/square rooter, the function table control, the master programmer, the card reader, and the card punch).

Second, we plugged in the program pulses that would trigger operations at each step in the trajectory, and we set the drag function in the function tables. (Aberdeen had worked out the values of the drag function in calculations through many years of trial and error.) Then we set up the master programmer, which controlled all of the operations. We also wired up all of the plugboards for the punched card equipment to set the digits needed for the trajectory. And we had to put in all of the headings for the tabulator in order to get a good copy of the printout.

Last, we had to debug the program using the hand-calculated trajectory as the test program. To do this, we read in from the card reader the input for the trajectory Ruth and Marlyn had calculated. The ENIAC had a remote control like the ones we all use now to control our TVs. This control had five buttons, which read "Start," "Stop," "Continuous," "Add time by add time," and "Pulse time by pulse time." For other controls, we could disconnect one of the program-pulse output cables and stop it after a particular operation.

Once we started debugging the program, many times we could not tell whether the ENIAC was making an error or we had a bug in our program. If the ENIAC was making an error, it could be because of a blown tube. Tubes blew all the time until the engineers determined that most of them blew when it was first turned on, because of the power surge that occurred. Once they stopped turning the ENIAC off and on, tube failure was reduced to one every couple of days, but this only happened after several months of operation. We got very good at finding a blown tube because of the test trajectory that Marlyn and Ruth had hand-calculated, which we ran as a test program. To get a reliable answer we ran the test program, then the real program, then the test program again. If the two test programs ran without error, we assumed the real program was accurate. Of course, despite our confidence that we hadn't made any mistakes, we did find some bugs in it, even after the weeks of painstaking checking we had done. The ENIAC managed to humble us all.

Everyone was very interested in how we were doing. Mauchly came in one Saturday with some apricot brandy. He asked us about our progress and gave us a small glass of brandy to drink. It was the first time I had ever tasted it, and it was delicious. From that day forward, I always kept a bottle of apricot brandy in my cupboard because I acquired a taste for the liquor with that single glass. But Mauchly wasn't the only one to offer me and Betty liquid refreshment. Moore School Dean Harold Pender came down and asked us how we were doing. We told him that we were doing fine. He said, "Hop to it," and "Keep up the good work," and left us some liquor—Scotch, if I recall correctly. Betty and I did very little drinking actually—maybe a Tom Collins once in a while—so we never actually got around to drinking Dean Pender's gift. But like Mauchly's gesture, Dean Pender's gesture impressed us and made us understand how much he wanted us to succeed, and how much this event meant to the University of Pennsylvania.

Finally, the night of February 14 arrived, the night before the public dedication and demonstration. It was Valentine's Day, but Betty and I were not out at a fancy restaurant with our significant others (neither one of us had a sweetheart at the time). Instead, we were holed up with that wonderful machine, the ENIAC, busily making the last corrections and checks on the program. We two were by ourselves in the room.

I think it's important to describe once again in detail what occurred on February 14, 1946. Over the years, Herman Goldstine made some false claims about what happened prior to the February 15 demonstration. In *Computers from Pascal to von Neumann*, Herman Goldstine claimed the demonstration program was "solely prepared by my wife [Adele] and me." The statement was false. Other than assigning the demonstration program to Betty and me, Herman and Adele were not involved in programming the demonstration program. He also wrote, "under date of 13 February at 3 am I noted that 'all problems except trajectory are O.K.' and then in an entry which must mean 12:30 pm that same day I jubilantly noted 'Demonstration problems O.K.!!'" But all of the demonstration problems were not okay and the program was not ready for the demonstration, which he would have known if he had checked in on February 14 or had been actively involved in programming the problems for the demonstration. The simulated shell was still burrowing holes in the ground after impact.[2]

The ENIAC was calculating the trajectory perfectly except it didn't stop when it hit the ground; it kept on going, like a hypothetical shell burrowing through the ground at the same rate it had traveled through the air. Betty and I worked late into the evening trying to solve the problem, but we had finally had to leave so Betty could get the last train to Narberth. So we shut off the lights and went home about midnight thinking that we would just have to let it go, that the demonstration would be flawed. But we hadn't reckoned on one thing—Betty's nighttime logic. It was at work as she slept that night, and it was as reliable as ever.

The next morning, Betty came in and knew exactly which switch on the master programmer was set incorrectly. She knew which switch of the three thousand on the ENIAC to reset and which of the ten positions it should be on. She went over, flipped the switch over one position, and we were in business. I must confess that we did dig a little hole (or rather, the hypothetical shell did) because we did a test after doing another iteration before testing a number. In technical jargon, we had a "do loop" iterate one time too many. But once we had corrected that, the shell hit the ground and stopped. We were ecstatic. The program worked perfectly and we were ready to go. It was magnificent, that feeling of seeing the test go just the way it was supposed to: it fulfilled our greatest expectations of what the ENIAC could perform. We had done what we set out to do—we had programmed the ENIAC.

Having a program that would run without a hitch or a glitch was one thing, but you wanted some bells and whistles going off to impress the public. Leave it to Pres and John to provide the extra ingredient for the demonstration—the pizzazz. Picture the tops of the accumulators, which stored the numbers in a ten-by-ten matrix, along with a plus or minus sign. This matrix was formed by the vacuum tubes in the accumulator, which were mounted in the ENIAC chassis with the tips of the tubes showing through round holes drilled in the front panel. Pres and John realized that the faint light from the tips of the neon bulbs, which were indicator lights for the vacuum tubes, would not show up on movie reels or still photos. So they went out and bought white Ping-Pong balls and cut them in half, placing them over the neon bulb tips and painting numbers on them with black paint. Despite having to do this by hand, they painted the numbers very neatly, so that they were easily read. A time-consuming modification that was done for purely theatrical effect, but it did look wonderfully impressive on film. So I suppose the effort was worth it in the end.

Each decade counter of the accumulator—a vertical column of ten tubes—contained all the integers, from 0 to 9. When the program ran, only one number in each decade counter, or column, was lighted, according to which integer was being indicated. As the trajectory was being calculated, numbers built up in the accumulators and were transferred from place to place, and the lights started flashing like the bulbs on the marquees in Las Vegas.

It was quite a distinguished audience that had gathered at Penn that day: many of the best scientists of the United States were there. I understand that Norbert Wiener of MIT was there, but I don't remember seeing him. Kay did, however. She asked him where his coat was so she could hang it up. It was a bitterly cold day, and he was the only one who had not worn a coat. He said he guessed his wife had packed it in his suitcase. Wiener was a brilliant man and the founder of cybernetics, but he could be off in his own world sometimes. He wore bifocals, but he had ordered them specially made with lenses inverted, so the lens for viewing close objects was on the top and the one for viewing objects farther away was on the bottom. Thus, he walked with his head flung back so he could see the things at a distance. I don't recall seeing Dr. Wiener there, but that could have been because I was very excited, and also because I was concerned about making sure that the ENIAC was performing well and that the handouts from the tabulator were accurate. We were worried that a tube would blow and the program wouldn't run.

The demonstration began at about eleven in the morning. There were actually several demonstrations, as the trajectory was run more than once for each group, to show how much more quickly the calculation went without the printing, which only began once the trajectory had reached its summit and ground calculations. The signal for the ENIAC's printer to print the trajectory came when the altitude acceleration changed from positive to negative, which occurred at the zenith of the shell's flight. There were at least two separate groups of about a dozen or so scientists and officials, plus the engineers and Betty and I in the room. The attendees were seated on chairs with Arthur Burks seated before them, narrating the demonstration. Pres stood off to the side.

The task for the ENIAC was to compute the trajectory of a shell that took thirty seconds to reach its target. In the demonstration, the calculation only took twenty seconds—ten seconds less than the flight of the actual shell. Burks explained to the assembled audience that it would take a female computer sitting at a desk with a mechanical calculator thirty to forty hours to do the same calculation.[3]

Betty and I stayed in the room during the demonstrations—we wanted to be ready to swing into action if something went wrong. We were standing in an unobtrusive spot, by the card reader and card punch. I don't recall the outfit I wore, but I'm sure it was a businesslike navy, gray, or dark suit, and shoes with two-inch heels. We took the cards from the punch to have them printed out as a trajectory on the tabulator, which was out in the hallway. We would also take the cards that had been run through and read from the output tray of the reader and put them back in to be read again for the demonstration to be repeated. The punched cards were run again and again through the tabulator to get enough copies of the trajectory to hand out to everyone as souvenirs. I believe that one or two of the other ENIAC women may have come in to help pick up the punched cards and take them out to the tabulator.

For the actual demonstration, one of the engineers in an act of showmanship turned out the lights so that the only illumination came from the ENIAC and the Ping-Pong-covered vacuum tubes. The "bulbs" flashed impressively as the trajectory was traced. The effect was spectacular, and there was lots of oohing and aahing and excited chatter among the guests. For years, when Hollywood wanted to show a computer at work, moviemakers showed the front of an ENIAC-like computer with big, flashing indicator lights.[4] Pres asked audience members to keep their eyes on a particular accumulator that held the calculation of the altitude of the shell. The number grew until it reached the summit, then began to shrink until it reached zero, which meant that the shell had hit the ground.

Pres pointed out that it had taken less time to calculate the trajectory than it took the shell to trace it. That brought down the house. He also slowed down the cycle time of the ENIAC to make a comparison between the ENIAC and the IBM Automatic Sequence Controlled Calculator (ASCC), also known as the Mark I, an electromechanical device at Harvard University.[5] The Mark I was well known to the audience, and its inventor, Howard Aiken, insisted that it was the way to go in the future. By slowing down the ENIAC to compare the cycle times, Pres was demonstrating that the ENIAC was much faster than the Mark I device and was the future.

After the lights were turned back on, the attendees had plenty of questions, and Pres, John, Herman, and some of the engineers fielded these. The letdown came at the end of the day, well after the triumphant demonstrations of the trajectory program, which drew the admiration of each group that saw it. Betty and I were ignored and forgotten following the demonstration. We felt as if we had been playing parts in a fascinating movie that suddenly took a bad turn, in which we had worked like dogs for two weeks to produce something really spectacular and then were written out of the script. When it was over, nobody congratulated us, thanked us, or recognized us in any way—not a single person. Herman and Adele completely ignored us. John Mauchly and Dean Pender, Pres Eckert, and Arthur Burks, who had always been so kind and encouraging to us and appreciative of our efforts, were all caught up in the hubbub of the moment and never looked our way or stopped to shake our hands.

Betty and I took most of this in stride, understanding that Pres and John and the engineers were very busy speaking with all the important scientists, researchers, and dignitaries who had attended. Nevertheless, being ignored was hurtful, especially when we weren't invited to the celebratory dinner, which was held on campus in a banquet room in Houston Hall, the student union.[6]

Afterward, Betty and I trudged home, feeling let down after all the excitement. The night was bitter cold, and we were very tired. On probably no other day of my life have I experienced such thrilling highs and such depressing lows. Betty felt the same way. We said good night and went our own way. It felt as if history had been made that day—and then it had run over us and left us flat in its tracks. But then again, we could still say, "We were there."

The press had not been invited to the big demonstration on February 15, 1946—because, I believe, the officials didn't want them bugging the scientists. Instead, the reporters who had been present for the smaller demonstration two weeks earlier had held their stories. But when those stories about that earlier demonstration appeared the day after the ENIAC's unveiling for the scientific community, it was evident that the press was totally confused by the whole business. "Giant Brain!" screamed the headlines. The reporters never really understood that what the ENIAC could do was add, subtract, multiply, divide, and do square roots very fast. It could also execute different calculations depending upon results from previous calculations. It could do calculations so fast that many problems that had never been done before because of the time required for hand calculations could now be tackled, thus expanding the frontiers of man's knowledge. The ENIAC wasn't a brain in any sense; it couldn't reason, as computers still cannot reason, but it could give people more data to use in reasoning.

The ENIAC, 1946. Left to right: Homer Spence (Maintenance Engineer), J. Presper Eckert, John Mauchly, Betty Jean Jennings, Herman Goldstine, and Ruth Lichterman. Courtesy of the U.S. Army (ARL Technical Library Archives).

Betty was particularly upset with the story that ran in the *New York Times*. You see, the reporter had written it after the February 1 demonstration, which had not included our trajectory; however, the article implied that it was a description of the demonstration on February 15. From the reporter's account, it was obvious that he had not attended the February 15 event. Unfortunately, this *New York Times* article was picked up by other newspapers and its misleading information used by other magazines, as well as for various radio and television broadcasts. Betty, like the rest of us, was dismayed by the media's insistence on calling the ENIAC a "giant brain." MIT mathematician Norbert Wiener's book *Cybernetics*, published two years later in 1948, added to this popular fallacy. In his book, Wiener described the human brain as an analogue of a single run of a computing machine.

In the days after the demonstration, reporters and scientists from around the country came to see the ENIAC. I understand that Russia even wanted to buy one.

We ENIAC women did talk with the photographers and reporters who came to do stories about the ENIAC. Even *Movietone News* showed up and made a newsreel that was shown as a "short." At that time, movies were preceded by these shorts, as well as a cartoon and trailers for coming attractions. When *Movietone News* filmed the ENIAC short, the director posed us like models around the computer pretending to perform tasks. It was exciting, but nobody—not the visiting scientists, not the newspaper reporters, and certainly not the *Movietone* director and his crew—acted as if we women knew anything. We were treated like part of the scenery, doing routine tasks that anyone would do, similar to the "refrigerator girls" of that era—the models who demonstrated the latest line of home appliances at home expos. As far as they were concerned, we might as well have been Vanna White turning letters on *Wheel of Fortune*. No offense to Ms. White, but programming the ENIAC involved so much more than turning switches and looking great as we did it.

About two weeks after the demonstration of the ENIAC, around the first of March, Irven Travis arrived back from the Navy and became director of research at the Moore School. John Mauchly had replaced Travis at the Moore School when Travis, a Navy reservist, was called up to active duty in July 1941. During the war Travis served as a contracting officer, and upon his return one of his first acts was to present John Mauchly and Pres Eckert with a contract stipulating that, to remain at the school, they had to sign over to the University of Pennsylvania their patent rights to the EDVAC, which they had begun working on after the ENIAC's design was frozen. Prior to this, the University of Pennsylvania had given Pres and John commercial patent rights to the ENIAC, with the proviso that the university and the federal government had the right to use their inventions freely. Pres and John had assumed the same agreement would be in effect for EDVAC. They were stunned.

At first, Travis gave them one day to sign the agreement and then he extended it to two weeks. Pres and John declined and left abruptly. Everyone was flabbergasted and thought Travis was crazy. Travis actually thought that he and his engineers could build the EDVAC. He was mistaken, and the Moore School didn't finish it until Sam Lubkin, an engineer working as a consultant for Aberdeen on its computers in its Ballistics Research Laboratory, came along two years later.[7] In my opinion, the Moore School was never again a leader in the computer field. In fact, it never again did any work of consequence on computers. Some people have implied that Pres and John were asking for special treatment, but they were not. All of the professors at the University of Pennsylvania received the commercial rights to patents they developed while at the university. Most of the engineering professors made more money outside the university than from their teaching salaries.

Impressed with the accomplishments of the ENIAC, Travis had every confidence that the EDVAC would also be a tremendous success. Travis also understood the potential financial gains and saw Eckert and Mauchly's new computer as a way to reap big profits for the University of Pennsylvania. Unfortunately, Travis had no engineers of the caliber of Pres and John to finish the EDVAC. Worse, he brought in some of his contract writers from the Navy as managers, and they knew nothing about computers. One seemed to just roam around checking up on people and reporting on who was sitting at his or her desk and who was not. They were hardly the people to push into new computer frontiers.

After the excitement of the ENIAC demonstration and its aftermath—and after Pres and John had been sent packing—things seemed rather dull. Harry Husky and Hans Rademacher, the German mathematician who had settled in Pennsylvania after emigrating from Germany in 1934, did some studies on round-off and truncation errors. Because the ENIAC dealt with fixed-length numbers, it rounded off numbers beyond ten-decimal digits. An example would be numbers with never-ending fractions after the decimal point, such as *pi*, which equals 3.14159...and on and on.

When cutting off the numbers to a manageable length, the ENIAC rounded off by adding a 5 in the last decimal-digit position; thus, *pi* with six digits, 3.14159, would be rounded up by adding a 5 to the 9, causing a carryover so that the number became 3.14164. The user would then shift the number one place to the right, discarding the final 4, and the value of *pi* would thus be rounded up to 3.1416. However, if the value of *pi* had instead been 3.14154, it would have been rounded down to 3.1415. This produced a rather clear-cut decision, but each round-off caused a small error: either the number was slightly bigger than the real number or slightly smaller. When a number like 3.14155 would come along, the ENIAC would round it up to 3.1416 when, in fact, it would have been just as accurate to round it down to 3.1415. This created a slight bias in favor of rounding up. That may seem inconsequential, but when thousands of calculations were done for a particular problem, that slight bias became significant.

Truncation errors came about because numerical integration replaces an arc of a circle with a series of connecting straight lines. The shorter the lines, the closer the numerically integrated arc comes to the actual arc. The longer the lines, the bigger the error in replacing the arc with them (just as a triangle resembles a circle less than an octagon does). Using shorter lines caused the ENIAC to do more calculations, and each calculation caused some round-off error. Using longer lines created fewer round-off errors because fewer calculations were made, but the calculated arc was less accurate. Thus, the studies were done to determine the optimal interval of integration—in other words, the optimal length of the straight lines—to produce a balance between round-off errors and truncation errors.

One interesting thing did happen that summer of 1946: the University of Pennsylvania hired John and Pres, who had left and formed their own company (then called the Electronic Control Co.), to give a computer course at the Moore School, paying each of them $1,200. The course was under the direction of Carl Chambers, the professor at the Moore School whom they most respected. It was popularly known as the Moore School Lectures on Computer Design, but the course's actual title was Theory and Techniques for Design of Electronic Digital Computers. It had been organized in response to the tremendous interest generated by the public demonstration of the ENIAC that February. The course went from the first part of July through the end of August. Eighteen lecturers combined to deliver forty lectures, one each morning for five days a week over eight weeks. The lectures lasted up to three hours; then after lunch the group reconvened for an unstructured seminar.

John and Pres specified the topics of the lectures and decided who gave them. The two of them, plus Herman Goldstine, Kite Sharpless, Arthur Burks, Harry Husky, Calvin Moores, Douglas Hartree, George Stibitz, Howard Aiken, Hans Rademacher, and others, gave lectures that summer. John von Neumann did not give a lecture. He was scheduled to do so but had other commitments and so did not give the ones that had been scheduled for him.[8] The lectures were primarily technical: they dealt with topics such as memory, instructions, the central processor, arithmetic units, and input/output. Mauchly, however, gave one on sorting and collating. Another of his lectures was called Conversions Between Binary and Decimal Number Systems.

Twenty-eight students were invited to attend, each of them a leading engineer or mathematician at an institution working on the development of computing devices. Attendees came from all over: Maurice Wilkes and David Rees from Cambridge and Manchester Universities in England, others from MIT, from firms like Bell or General Electric, from the War Department and the National Bureau of Standards in Washington, and from government armament laboratories such as the Naval Ordnance Testing Station in Pasadena, California. The lectures were wire-recorded, and transcripts were produced. These lectures probably had as significant an impact on future computer development as the EDVAC Report. The course certainly refutes later allegations that Pres and John were secretive about their ideas on computers.

In addition to giving a guest lecture that summer, Dr. Hartree, the mentor of Maurice Wilkes and the main force behind the British computer EDSAC, came from England to do a problem on the ENIAC. Kay was assigned to work with him. Dr. Hartree was a delightful man. He did consulting with many branches of the U.S. government. When he was working with us, he also evaluated us and wrote a report to Aberdeen on what personnel were needed to run the ENIAC. Although he was very complimentary of us and said we knew how to run the ENIAC very well, he wrote that he felt the group also needed a high-level mathematician to translate user problems into the formats needed for calculation—in other words, to turn very complex equations into computable equations. Specifically, he said the group needed a numerical analyst. So what was a numerical analyst? The answer was that nobody knew, except that Douglas Hartree was one. This was 1946 and food was scarce in England, which had strict rationing. Dr. Hartree loved to eat and especially loved to go with us to Arthur's Steakhouse for those wonderful meals we had there. Before he left, he threw a great dinner party for us at a hotel in West Philadelphia. We ate, played games, and joined him with his wife at the piano in singing Gilbert and Sullivan tunes. Dr. Hartree came back the next year to teach summer courses at nearby Haverford College. I later visited him at Cambridge in 1951 when I went to Europe with John and Betty Holberton, who were on their honeymoon.

Meanwhile, I would soon meet the man with whom I would go on my own honeymoon. It happened this way: outside the ENIAC room, in a small room next door, where we kept the punched card equipment—the tabulator along with the hand card punch and verifier and sorter. Bill Bartik was a graduate student at the Moore School at the time, where he worked primarily for the Office of Strategic Services (OSS), which had been formed during the war and was the forerunner of the CIA. He was an expert on electrical noise and how to shield delicate instruments from being affected by it. Bill worked with a classmate named Ted Bonn. If I was at the tabulator when Ted came through, he would stop to talk. Ted liked me but he got engaged, so he told Bill that he should look me over. There weren't very many women at the Moore School, so the bachelors had a habit of putting the rush on new women around the place. In fact, a number of the men did ask me out.

Kay Mauchly had been there on the differential analyzer for over two years, so she was wise to this: she said I was being given the usual rush. I was still just twenty-one years old and considered a man who was twenty-five or older ridiculously old to ask me out, so I turned most of this crowd down. However, taking Ted's advice, Bill asked me out, and, as he was only a year older than me, I said yes. Besides being only twenty-two, Bill was a first-generation American, and I had always been attracted to first-generation Americans. Perhaps as a reaction to the Jennings clan back in Missouri, I disliked the old family traditions and expectations and lack of individual identity attached to those who were long settled in a place. Bill was incredibly smart, and that also caught my interest. I have never considered dumb men or athletes sexy. I also have never considered really handsome men sexy: they are too self-centered. Bill was homely, but he was also strong: the Army tested the engineers at the Moore School once, and he came out the strongman of the school. In fact, he finished tops in all areas of physical fitness. This was because Czechs liked synchronized exercises and there was a Sokol Hall around the corner from the school, so Bill, being of Czech heritage, did gymnastics there. *Sokol* means "falcon" in Czech, and Sokol Halls were set up around the United States after the Civil War as a way to provide physical training, cultural bonds, and family activities for groups of Czechs.

Meanwhile, what was I doing at the Moore School? I was continuing to do programming on the ENIAC. One important problem I worked on was brought to us by Professor Abraham Taub, a mathematician from Princeton University. He had gotten permission to put a problem on the ENIAC, although it was not his own problem but a problem for his Princeton colleague Walker Bleakney, a physicist. The problem had to do with the physics of shock waves and was being conducted for the Office of Naval Research, with whom Princeton had a contract.

Adele Goldstine was the Moore School's liaison with Taub, and I was designated to work with her to do the programming. This was the first time Adele had ever really put a program of any size on the ENIAC. I taught her what we had learned about flowcharting our problems, keeping track of our programs, and doing the programming. She was very bright and wonderful to work with. She knew the ENIAC inside and out because she had written the operator's manual, which was very good but was published too late to help us learn the ENIAC. That next year I was to use the manuals when I set up an ENIAC programming group at the Moore School in 1947. Anyway, Adele and I labored away in that summer of 1946.

After the dustup at the University of Pennsylvania, Herman Goldstine, who had hitched his wagon to the von Neumann star, wanted the Taub shock wave program to be over and done with and for Adele to join him in Princeton. Goldstine took the train to Philly and ate dinner with us many nights. Initially I liked Herman Goldstine, but later his blind (and unethical) support of John von Neumann over Pres Eckert and John Mauchly made me view him in a dim light. He also demonstrated rude behavior on occasion and seemed to enjoy badmouthing Pres and John when they weren't around. I was always confused by his attitude toward them. One time, Goldstine told me that the frontiers of the computer industry had moved to Princeton and had passed John and Pres by. Another time, Goldstine asked me to leave John and Pres to work for him, offering to give Bill, my boyfriend and future husband, a job as well. Although I was flattered by the offer, I never seriously considered leaving John and Pres to work for Herman. For one thing, Goldstine's attitude toward John and Pres seemed disrespectful and that greatly bothered me. Also his support of von Neumann seemed to smack of someone who was both blindly ambitious and unprincipled, a disturbing combination. I did not feel that Goldstine would support me when the chips were down the way John and Pres would and my instincts proved to be right.

Adele Goldstine and I, however, made a great team. She was my second perfect partner, Betty Snyder having been my first. Although Adele and I followed polar opposite ways of solving a problem, we respected each other and the other's method of working. Adele was an active type of programmer, trying things very quickly. I was more laid back and given to attempting to figure out things logically before doing anything. Only one time, early on, did Adele and I clash. We couldn't find a bug in the program, and Adele wanted to keep trying this and that, hoping to run across it. I wanted to figure out logically what could be wrong. She became most annoyed with my seeming inaction, but I did figure it out logically and had to change the setting of only one switch. Adele never criticized me again for my modus operandi.

On the nights when Herman stayed at Princeton, I would spend the night at Adele and Herman's apartment. We worked long hours, until ten o'clock most nights, and I remember that Adele would have a shot of liquor to relax her before she went to bed. I was intrigued by this, for I rarely drank alcohol except on special occasions. Adele and I worked on the Taub problem through all of July and the first half of August—during roughly the same period as the Moore School Lectures were going on. Herman kept nagging Adele and me to get the problem finished so she could join him in Princeton. One time she said to me, "Herman keeps getting me these jobs, then complains when I do them."

Finally, in August, the problem was ready to go. I had plans to take Bill to Missouri to meet my family. Adele agreed that the problem was finished except for the running of it, so I went to Missouri. When I came back two weeks later, it was finished and Adele was gone: she had moved to Princeton. I didn't see Adele again until my wedding, on December 14, 1946. Some years later, Herman Goldstine wrote in his book *Computers from Pascal to von Neumann* (p. 232) that Taub and Adele did Taub's problem, omitting any mention of me. This is obviously wrong, since I have a commendation from Princeton for my work on it. The commendation letter is from Captain W. W. Strohbein of the Navy's Office of Research and Inventions and is dated October 31, 1946.

When Bill and I were in Missouri, Bill asked Dad if he would give his consent for us to be married. They were plucking a chicken at the time, and Dad was surprised by the question. He paused from plucking the bird, looked at Bill, and said, "I don't take care of my children's sparkin.'" Then he asked Bill if I wanted to marry him. When Bill said that I did, Dad said it was okay with him. So we became engaged and began planning our wedding. I asked John Mauchly to give me away since we would be married in Philadelphia with none of my family there. I asked Betty Snyder to be my matron of honor, and Bill asked Al Kozak, a classmate from the Moore School, to be the best man.

Bill was amazed that my parents' farmhouse was a dry household—his own father was a heavy drinker. He had never been around a farm before, so he was pretty much taken with the farms my family members owned. Alanthus Grove, the closest little town, had 104 people in it, along with the town cemetery and the school, both of which were named for the Jennings clan. The smallness of the place really threw him for a loop—it was a totally different world to him.

While we were there, we went on a double date with my sister Kackie and her boyfriend, and as a result of that date Kackie dumped the boyfriend. We had gone to the Frog Hop, a nightclub in St. Joseph where the big bands played when they came through. It had a large dance floor, and everyone in the place danced—everyone except for Kackie's date. He didn't dance and was dumb as a post. I asked her what she was doing with this guy. She said she was going to marry him. "Why?" I asked. She said, "He wants me to." "Do you want to marry him?" I asked. She said, "No." I talked to her about why a person gets married and why you should only marry the person you want to marry. She wised up and dumped him. Kackie could not reject guys even if she wasn't interested in them. You see, as the youngest, Kackie had grown up wanting to be a people pleaser, and a lot of that was our (her older siblings') fault. We all loved Kackie to pieces and we fought over who would sleep with her and who would take her places with them. Whenever she chose one of us, she always disappointed the others. Although she tried so hard to please us all, we really made her feel as though she could please no one. But she was the most wonderful person I've ever met, and was very fetching to boot. She had so many diamond rings that guys had bought for her that when she did finally get married, she wouldn't let her fiancé buy her one. Tragically, her niceness made her ill equipped for the world, and she had a terrible life.

Bill had graduated from the Moore School in 1944 in electrical engineering. The first member of his family to attend college, he was only able to go because he had gotten a Mayor's Scholarship, which fully paid his tuition. His paternal grandparents had emigrated from Czechoslovakia and had homesteaded land in Russia, at which point they had to convert from Catholicism to Russian Orthodoxy. It left Bill's father, William, with a distaste for religion—he said it didn't amount to much if you could just change it when the need arose. In Russia, William had deserted the Czarist army and had been smuggled out of the country by the Jewish underground. Once he arrived in the United States, he became a sheet-metal worker and worked for a company that shipped grain overseas from Girard Point, a port in South Philadelphia. Although he had no formal training as an engineer, he designed many upgrades for the installation. Bill's mother, Helen, was part Czech and part German but had been born in the United States, and his parents met in Philadelphia.

During the war, Bill had been classified as 4-F because of his nearsightedness; however, he volunteered for patrol duty and patrolled the Philadelphia Port on foot, scanning the Delaware River for German submarines. It is hard to believe, but German subs did cruise up and down the Atlantic coastline and sunk many grain-carrying ships as they moved outside the twenty-mile limit.

After I came back from Missouri in September, Aberdeen Proving Ground made plans to move the ENIAC from the first floor of the Moore School to Aberdeen. But the ENIAC was like a ship that had been built in a bottle: once it was finished and ready to be moved, the question was how to get it out of the bottle? Aberdeen solved this by knocking out the side of the wall and moving it out through the hole, panel by panel. Until the ENIAC was reinstalled, there was of course no work to be done on it. After the ENIAC was moved to Aberdeen, it began to have one tube failure after another. John Mauchly learned of these tube failures during one of his visits to check up on the ENIAC's progress. He found out that Aberdeen was turning the electricity off each night. When the ENIAC had been under John and Pres's supervision at the Moore School, it was never turned off after John and Pres discovered that most tube failures resulted from the surge in power when the ENIAC was first turned on. Once the directors of the lab changed their procedures and kept the ENIAC turned on, the rate of tube failure decreased dramatically.

When I returned I learned that Betty, John Holberton, and Kay, who had accumulated months of vacation time because they hadn't been able to take vacations during the war, had taken an extensive trip in the United States, where they had a marvelous time visiting friends. Meanwhile, Ruth and Fran had moved to Aberdeen and had started working at the Proving Ground. Additionally, Marlyn had become engaged to Phil Meltzer, a dentist.

John Mauchly's wife was Mary, a small, slender woman with dark hair who was quick in her movements and terse. I saw her around the Moore School, but I had never taken one of her courses, so I didn't know her; however, Joe Chapline, the differential analyzer's maintenance engineer and John Mauchly's close friend, liked Mary very much. When John had first come to the Moore School from Ursinus College in 1941, he and Mary and their two small children still had a lease on a farmhouse in Chalfont, where they had been living. John had to be in Philadelphia for his new job, but Mary didn't want to live out in the country alone. Joe still worked at Ursinus then, and so John asked Joe to stay with Mary and the children until she could move to Philadelphia, which Joe kindly agreed to do.

In early September 1946, John and Mary were at Wildwood, New Jersey, a popular coastal resort town where they had gone for the Labor Day weekend. They arrived about nine p.m. and decided to go for a swim in the ocean. Of course, the lifeguards had long since gone home and the beach was deserted. That night, there was a strong undertow. Mary got caught in it and was swept away from shore. John frantically looked for her, but he couldn't find her. Finally, he swam back in to shore to get help, but no one could find Mary. Her body washed ashore the next day a couple of blocks down the beach. It was tragic, not only for John but also for their two children—a boy, Jimmy, and a girl, Sidney (fourteen and nine, respectively, at the time).

John walked around like a zombie for weeks, absolutely devastated by her loss. At the time, he had no idea that he would ever be happy again and that the truly great love of his life was waiting just around the corner in the form of my fellow programmer and best friend, Kay. None of us did. All in all, it was a numbingly sorrowful ending to a summer full of changes.

Kay McNulty and John Mauchly, ca. 1946–47. Courtesy of Bill Mauchly.

A couple weeks before my wedding, Kay McNulty gave an engagement party for me at her parents' house in Chestnut Hill. I believe this is the first time John had attended any social function since his wife had died. Pres was not there—I did not get to know him well until I began working for the Eckert-Mauchly Corporation—but the ENIAC women were all there, along with John Holberton, the ENIAC engineers, and the engineers who worked with Bill in the electrical noise lab at the Moore School. It was a wonderful party, except I did have a spat with Bill over his general attitude that I must do things and act the way he thought I should. It was my first inkling that this marriage might not be made in heaven.

John was very sweet to me, but you could see he was sad. He was very thin, and his face looked gaunt. He put on a pleasant face that day but was rather quiet. A few weeks earlier, when I had asked him to give me away, he had teased me by refusing, saying that I was too valuable to be given away. But after fooling around a bit, he had agreed to do it. He came to the party because of that promise. Kay and John always talked to each other—indeed, all of us ENIAC women talked to John, especially Betty Snyder and me. We adored him, because he was so personable and attentive to our questions. John and Kay chatted together briefly at my engagement party and he'd seemed more relaxed and happy when he was with her. Kay told me later that her mother had asked her who the tall man was she'd been speaking to. When Kay told her it was John Mauchly, her mother had reacted quite negatively, warning her to stay away from John and that she didn't "want to see him around her again." Kay's mother was very protective of her daughter. Undoubtedly her mother's reaction stemmed from all the publicity there had been about his wife's death, some of which had been rather nasty, suggesting that John may have been responsible for her death. Kay's mother eventually did warm up to John, but only after he married Kay, and she later admitted that she couldn't even remember exactly why she had been so opposed to John in the first place.

Betty and I had a grand time planning my wedding. Betty really planned the whole thing—I had never even been to a wedding before. My brothers and sisters had just gone off and gotten married by a justice of the peace; I don't think any of them were married by a minister. However, under Betty's guidance, I booked the church, bought the liquor, mailed out the invitations, and purchased the flowers. While Bill and I got the license and met with the minister, Betty and her mother planned the food and arrangements for the reception at the Snyder home in Narberth, a three-story frame house with a big, welcoming porch and a front yard where Betty's brother, Bob, and I had had our badminton battles. It was so wonderful of them to act as my second family.

John Mauchly gave Betty Jean away at her wedding to Bill Bartik on December 14, 1946.

The day of the wedding, Mrs. Snyder prepared the food while Betty and I ran to the church—which was very close to their home—to check on things. Overbrook Presbyterian was a Gothic revival church of cut stone built in 1890 on an estate that had been part of William Penn's liberty lands. It featured a great, square tower with battlements. During my time in Philadelphia I had attended a Presbyterian church close to my apartment in the downtown area, but this church was a beautiful building in a quite wealthy community. So on December 14, 1946, Bill and I were married at that grand church, where the old Lancaster Pike met City Line Avenue, just outside Philadelphia. Betty was my matron of honor and John Mauchly gave me away, with a hint of a smile playing on his lips and a twinkle

Betty Jean and Bill's wedding reception, December 14, 1946. Left to right: Al Kozak (Bill's best man), Betty Snyder (Jean's matron of honor), Bill Bartik, Betty Jean Jennings Bartik, and John Mauchly.

in his eye. During the service, my roommate at the time, Beatrice Ficaro, sang—gloriously, I might add. She was a coloratura soprano studying at Curtis under Madame Gregory, sister of the famed French-American coloratura soprano Lily Pons. Beatrice was an Italian from Detroit and had taken voice lessons all her life. She had a beautiful voice, but it wasn't big enough for opera. Later at the wedding reception, John finally got up the nerve to ask Kay out on a date. She accepted, but hid the fact from her mother, afraid of her disapproval.

Bill and I honeymooned in Aiken, South Carolina, because it was a horse town, and I had convinced Bill that he wanted to spend his honeymoon riding horses. Owners of horse farms in the north stabled their racehorses in Aiken for the winter. It was great for me because I had grown up on horses but had not been around any since I had arrived in Philadelphia twenty-one months before. The horses we rode in Aiken were not nags, but they did not compare to the thoroughbreds wintering there. Growing up in Philadelphia, he had never been around them. Unfortunately, we soon found out that Bill did not like horses.

At that time, Aiken numbered a little over six thousand people, and there wasn't anything to do but ride the horses available for rent and admire the racehorses at pasture—very fine horses with long legs and beautiful conformation. Near the stable where we rented our mounts were riding paths that led through the surrounding countryside, and we would take these paths every morning in the crisp weather. But for kicking off the marriage, it was not the best of choices. Bill made it clear that this was my idea of a honeymoon, not his. I'm sure he suffered a good deal. I know I felt restricted in what I could do because he was so bad at riding. I wanted to gallop away on my horse, but I always had to wait for him. What I had imagined as an exhilarating activity for the two of us became a plodding affair. We did go shopping one day in Augusta, Georgia, giving Bill's saddle sores a rest.

• • •

Now, let's backtrack for a brief moment. I had been working for Aberdeen for only about eighteen months when the ENIAC was shut down for moving to Aberdeen in the fall of '46, and I had taken my allotted vacations. So I had little vacation time left, plus I planned to get married. Since Bill's job was in Philadelphia, I was not going to Aberdeen with the ENIAC. Consequently, there would be no paychecks coming in that fall, and I was looking around for another opportunity.

Dick Clippinger had a group at the Ballistic Research Laboratory's wind tunnel at Aberdeen. Since his problems were too big to go on the ENIAC as it was programmed, Clippinger had the idea to turn the ENIAC into a stored-program computer.[9] That meant it would have its instructions stored in the function tables, which were no longer needed for programs other than trajectories. Dick Clippinger had run his idea by John Mauchly and Pres Eckert, who gave him their thumbs up, since both John (in December 1943) and Pres (in January 1944) had conceived and written about the concept of the stored-program computer.[10]

As the stored-program concept was batted around, many people, including von Neumann, began proposing instruction sets that could handle all the programming needs. Clippinger specifically talked to von Neumann about his idea and Clippinger began working out an instruction set for the ENIAC. Clippinger had initially thought of using a three-address code for the ENIAC, but von Neumann talked him into using a one-address code. At this time, Dick did not know how to program the ENIAC. Clippinger, with the assistance of John and Pres, managed to get me assigned to Clippinger rather than have me leave the employ of Aberdeen. Clippinger worked it out that I would come down to Aberdeen for a few days a week to teach him how to program the ENIAC. The rest of the time, I would work at home, programming the ENIAC to load and execute the proposed stored-program instruction set. Of course, multiple programs using the new instruction set had to be written and tested as the conversion was implemented. I was involved in every aspect of the project. This instruction set that we formulated was called the ENIAC's sixty-order code.

Dick Clippinger was a brilliant man—clever, witty, vivacious, and fun. Sandy-haired and of medium build, he was attractive but not handsome. His attractiveness came from his personality. He also had some interesting habits. If he felt tired, he would just lie down on the desk and keep working. He smoked, even lying down, and always kept the ashes in a little container on his desk for some experiment he was doing. Clippinger had a number of people working for him, but one in particular always needed his help with something. I never paid any attention to him; I would just keep on working. So I thought this guy was pretty dumb if he always had to consult Clippinger about everything he did. He would show up at the lab, wanting to know what to do next. It irritated Clippinger to be interrupted so often because he was eager to learn how the ENIAC worked so he could organize his problems to fit it. So we all played a game of hide-and-seek with this fellow. We would actively hide from him in out-of-the-way places so we wouldn't be interrupted. Unfortunately, our little game rarely worked. The man always managed to find us by ten or eleven o'clock in the morning. One time we hid in the furnace room, but he found us at noon. Sometimes we would work at Clippinger's home. To keep from being distracted by the noise of their four children, he would turn up the hi-fi so it drowned them out. His wife, Dorothy, was imperturbable and went along with whatever he did.

Clippinger had grown up in New Jersey, not far from Atlantic City and its famed Steel Pier, which was a 1,500-foot wooden pier with steel underpinnings that jutted out into the Atlantic. It was known as "an Amusement City at Sea." As a youth, Clippinger would hitchhike to Atlantic City and do everything on the pier—ride all the rides and play all the games and watch the high-diving horse that would jump off a forty-foot diving platform into a tank of water. Clippinger had studied at the Sorbonne in Paris from 1933 to 1935; during that time, Clippinger also traveled in Europe and journeyed across Russia on the Trans-Siberian Railroad, a 5,700-mile route that starts at St. Petersburg and finishes at Vladivostok on the Sea of Japan several days later.

When Clippinger would have to stand for long stretches of time, he learned to lie down in the train aisle and make a pillow out of a handkerchief for his head. He still used this method when he worked at the Aberdeen Proving Ground. He would roll up his handkerchief into a cone, like a little tepee, and put it under the back of his head when he lay down on a desk. I don't know how comfortable it was, but he did indeed have a little pillow. We worked hard, but Clippinger was never dull and so work was never drudgery. He saw the humor in everything, and I found myself laughing my way through the workday.

Clippinger was planning to build a house on a hillside in Havre de Grace, a few miles from Aberdeen on the headwaters of the Chesapeake Bay. The town was home to a horse racetrack in those days and thus was a stop-off for gangsters and gamblers on their way to New York City; they would follow the pony routes up from the South in the spring. Al Capone was rumored to have spent some time at the Crazy Swede, one of the restaurants there. The problem with Clippinger's lot was that the land on which he was going to build was a rock pile. As a change of pace, at the end of the day, we would go out and pick up rocks in his field and take them to a dumpsite. He had a tractor with a little trailer hitched to the back that we would load the rocks into. Many times, I had dinner with him and his family. It was a great experience working with Clippinger, and he was always very appreciative of everything I did.

Clippinger tried to get programming help from Aberdeen's Ordnance Department, which had control over the ENIAC, but he could get no help whatsoever. He knew that I was an available programmer, so he decided to write a contract with the Moore School to set up a group of five ENIAC programmers with me as their leader or manager. When I brought it up with Irven Travis, who was now in charge of all research and development at the Moore School, he was very skeptical of the whole affair. He hemmed and hawed about how the whole thing was dependent on me. I was sure the school had done many projects dependent on one person and I was puzzled by his reluctance until it dawned on me that he was afraid I would get pregnant and leave. I assured him that I did not intend to have children for several years. Once he heard that, he relaxed and agreed to accept the contract.

One other thing did bother him, however. The government in its wisdom could not just contract for programming work; it needed to buy something. Thus, the school set up a contract for Aberdeen to buy twelve programs, one each month of the year. The first three were for turning the ENIAC into a stored-program computer, and the other nine were for wind tunnel problems we would program.

Since I was the project team leader I was responsible for hiring the ENIAC stored-program team members. My team would be primarily comprised of newly graduated college math majors whom I would have to train before they could do anything productive. Clippinger managed to get Travis to structure the contract so that the first three programs were for work I would be doing with Clippinger and von Neumann and others. Clippinger told me that he realized we could not predict how the work would go; thus he promised to accept whatever we got done as fulfilling the contract. In other words, we would be paid every month. Travis wasn't too keen on accepting Clippinger's promise, but he finally did and we met every goal.

I was very lucky in that I hired four wonderful young math majors—actually they were about my age—who were bright, enthusiastic, hard-working, and responsive. Three of them had gone to Temple University and one to Swarthmore College. They were Kathe Jacobi, Sally Spears, Ed Schlain, and Art Gehring. Except for Sally, whom I lost track of when she moved away, we all remained good friends for the rest of our lives, managing to stay in touch even over distances throughout the years. All of them ended up having great careers. I knew nothing about how to pick good programmers, but I had no trouble knowing I wanted these four to work for me. No others appealed to me. What was it that made me pick them? It was their interviewing me about the job rather than my interviewing them about their qualifications. All were eager to learn what the ENIAC was all about. It was their energy, curiosity, and sense of adventure for something new that set them apart. After I selected the ones I wanted, Travis interviewed each of them, then discussed them with me. When it came to Kathe, he said with a smirk, "I don't know if she knows anything, but she certainly is beautiful." I'm sure he intended it to be humorous, but the remark offended me. In fact, Kathe was more brilliant than she was beautiful—a real find.

The group was set up and ready to go by March 1947. I taught the four members about the ENIAC, using the ENIAC manual that Adele Goldstine had written. The manual was very good and contained a clear description of the workings of the ENIAC. I spent the rest of the time programming the instruction code for the ENIAC to turn it into a stored-program computer. The ENIAC had already been dismantled and shipped to Aberdeen the previous fall, but we did not need the ENIAC to do the programming on paper. While I trained my group using the ENIAC manuals, Clippinger and I, along with von Neumann and Adele Goldstine, were defining the instruction set and programming the instructions. We had programming sheets we used to indicate the switch and cable settings.

Each instruction read out two decimal digits from one of the function tables and sent it to the master programmer to be decoded and to send out the signal that started the execution of that instruction. The instruction set was one worked out by von Neumann and Clippinger.[11] We used an architecture built around a central accumulator with a one-address instruction. The address was designated by the next two decimal digits following the instruction in the function table. At this time, there were many different proposals for instruction sets, since a number of people were thinking about what instructions one would need to do the mathematical problems and proposing different solutions. People proposed one-, two-, or three-address instructions. (In computing, an "address" is a number used in information storage or retrieval that has been assigned to a certain memory location.)

In one-address instructions, one operand was always in the central accumulator and the result was always placed in the accumulator. In two-address instructions, the two operands were designated by addresses and the result was placed in the location of one of the operands. In three-address instructions, two of the addresses selected the operands and the third selected the address where the result was placed. The one-address code was by far the simplest to program. There was even one suggestion for a four-address instruction set, with the fourth address picking the address of the next instruction. The others assumed the next instruction would be in the address following the current address.

I would go to Aberdeen to consult with Dick and to work with him on the programming. In the meantime, he had two mathematicians working for him; he wanted them to learn the ENIAC because they would be formulating wind tunnel problems so the problems could be run on the ENIAC. Neither of the two men, A. S. Galbraith and John Giese, particularly wanted to be there. Dr. Galbraith had been a professor at Colby College in Waterville, Maine, and was eager to get back to teaching there. Dr. Giese was a theoretical mathematician and was disdainful of numerical integration and other such inexact mathematics—the kind he was forced to rely on in his wind tunnel problems, which involved air flow around a suspended shell. Giese went on to become a computer expert at Aberdeen. At the fiftieth anniversary of Aberdeen's receiving the ENIAC, his eyes glazed over in total forgetfulness when I mentioned those days. Neither Galbraith nor Giese made any real contributions to the programming.

About every two weeks, the four of us—Clippinger, Galbraith, Giese, and I—would go to Princeton for a couple of days to consult with John von Neumann. While there we worked and slept in some old government housing units that the Institute for Advanced Study (IAS) had bought from the federal government and moved to the site. These unsightly, ramshackle buildings caused quite a ruckus. Princeton is a beautiful town, and the residents were incensed at the sight of the sprawling, one-story prefab units that von Neumann had moved in to house employees who were needed to work on the "Johnniac"—the facetious designation for the IAS computer at Princeton.

The IAS computer was based on the EDVAC design and on ideas von Neumann had gleaned from English mathematician Alan Turing (often considered the father of modern computer science) during the late 1930s when Turing was a graduate student at Princeton. In 1938, von Neumann asked Turing to continue on at the Institute as his assistant, but Turing chose to return to Cambridge. That

Table 1: Multiply Test for Stored-Program ENIAC (March 10, 1948), a procedure program to test the multiply operation of the stored-program ENIAC. A program could have up to twenty-seven columns for accumulators and other storage areas. There were sixty orders (machine instructions) in the sixty-order code. After several hardware upgrades, there were one hundred orders in the one-hundred-order code.

94		01		12		63		05	94
01		00		63		04		00	00
62		95		(alpha)2	0(alpha)	16	74		
81		63		03		80		30	33
03		33		65		63		75	44
01		45		02		34		22	33
61		00		00		00		00	00
95		(alpha)2	3(alpha)	21		74	00		
70		01		34		04		34	75
95		(alpha)2	0(alpha)	16		74	00		
95		(alpha)2	7(alpha)	24		74	00		
70		01		35		05		35	75
94		01		00		63		04	94
0(alpha)	15		73		00		00	00	

SOURCE: Table 5.I: Test Procedure for ENIAC (10 March 1948), from R. F. Clippinger, "A Logical System Applied to the ENIAC," Ballistic Research Laboratories Report No. 673, http://ftp.arl.army.mil/mike/comphist/48eniac-coding/sec5.html (accessed 2/25/2011).

proved fortunate for England, as a year later Turing was working on the code-breaking computer at Bletchley Park that would be used against Nazi Germany.

Whenever we were in Princeton, Adele Goldstine joined us in programming the instruction set.[12] Consequently, when we went to consult with von Neumann, Herman Goldstine went along. When we met with von Neumann, we would tell him about the problems we were having programming the different instructions, and he would suggest alternative ways to go about it. The main problem was that we were having a hard time fitting everything on the ENIAC. Sometimes von Neumann would propose a simpler version of the instruction or a substitution of another instruction. We would meet with von Neumann and Herman Goldstine for about an hour to go over these matters concerning the sixty-order code implementation. Herman Goldstine never made any contributions to the discussion. In fact, I never heard him make a technical contribution anywhere.

One time, von Neumann made a statement—probably in regard to some alternative that he thought would work better than what we were now doing—and everyone but me said, "Yes." I said, "No." Herman Goldstine glared at me as if I had blasphemed God. But von Neumann, realizing his mistake, merely laughed and said, "No, that's not right," and proceeded to correct himself. Goldstine's glare merely showed his uncritical acceptance of anything von Neumann said.

Another time, when we were at Princeton working with Adele, it was late in the afternoon on the day we were to leave. Someone said that it was getting late and we should start walking to the train station at Princeton Junction, which was about a quarter of a mile from where we were working. Adele said that Herman was coming back and would drive us to the train, so we kept working.

When Herman got there, Adele told him he must take us to the train. Goldstine said that he wasn't doing it because he had to take "Johnny" somewhere. (Everyone called von Neumann "Johnny"—but not to his face.) Adele said, "But I promised." Goldstine said, "I don't give a damn what you promised. I'm not doing it!" Adele looked humiliated, and I felt pity for her, married to a man who apparently had no regard for her honor and couldn't take five minutes off from being von Neumann's gofer to allow her to keep her word. Dick shot Adele a sympathetic look and Herman a disapproving one and then said, "Let's get out of here." So Galbraith, Giese, and I grabbed our suitcases and followed Dick out the door, running all the way to the train. We just barely made it. Dick was none too happy with Goldstine, I can tell you.

I had a wonderful year with my group at the Moore School. They were very talented, bright, and lively and we met all our goals. We all loved working for Clippinger; he was a hard worker without ever being critical, and he always had fun with whatever he was doing. He would come up to Philadelphia every few weeks, so everyone in the group got to know him very well. He was no holier-than-thou mathematician, but a great teacher who loved teaching others. He would give us lectures on his problems, explaining what he was trying to do and what he expected from us. We would all have lunch with Dick, either at Lido's on Woodland Avenue, where the ENIAC programmers used to go with John Mauchly, or at the Houston Hall or Sargent Hall cafeteria on the Penn campus, and he would tell us what it was like riding across Russia on the Trans-Siberian Railroad and would recount his adventures on that trip and in Europe and the Orient. He must have been a wonderful young man, full of curiosity and desire for adventure. He always complimented my team and we all adored him.

By the end of March 1948, the contract was up and we had completed the twelve goals it called for. Having completed and executed our test stored-programs successfully, the ENIAC was operating as the world's first stored-program computer. The ENIAC functioned as a full-fledged stored-program computer from April 1, 1948, until October 2, 1955, when the "giant brain" was finally shut down. By completing the project, my team had given birth to a new mode of programming that—like the ENIAC itself—would forever change the world.

Having accomplished everything I could do with the ENIAC, I wanted to get on with doing something new. Pres and John had already set up their own company, the Electronic Control Company, and Betty Snyder had gone to work for them in the early part of 1947, at first working weekends, then full time. I called up John and set up an interview.

When I walked in the building on Twelfth Street in Philadelphia and down the aisle to John's office, whom should I meet but John Sims, my erstwhile blind date of two years earlier! He was bald as a cue ball—turns out he had worn a toupee on that previous occasion. It was quite a shock to realize this, and I almost laughed but was able to keep a straight face. Since I had last met him, Sims had married Hester Eckert's sister. In the interview, John Mauchly offered me a job as a programmer for the UNIVAC, which was going to be a commercial computer that could handle alphabetic data as well as numeric. I accepted and resigned from the Moore School.

Dick Clippinger was very supportive of my decision. He knew it was a great opportunity and was happy for me. Irven Travis didn't care—he had a new contract and a new lead person on it. I had recommended that Art Gehring be given the job of managing the group because Clippinger was extending the contract for a year. Art was given the job and did it very well. The following year Ed Schlain, another member of my group, took it over and ran it for a year. By that time there were more ENIAC programmers at Aberdeen, so Clippinger had no need for the group.

I hated to leave my group, because they were all very good programmers and we got on so well together. However, I was happy to say good-bye to the Moore School. It wasn't the same place after Travis returned from the war and brought his Navy buddies with him to manage the engineers. All of the ENIAC engineers left shortly after Pres and John did, leaving graduate students to work on the EDVAC. Knocking out the wall to remove the ENIAC from the Moore School in the fall of 1946 had been symbolic. By 1947, the place was a mere shell of what it had been, and all the excitement in the burgeoning field of computer engineering had moved on to other places. It was time for me to follow suit.[13]

CHAPTER 5
Surrounded by Brilliance

By the time I joined the Electronic Control Company in April 1948, it had moved to a high-rise building at Broad and Spring Garden Streets. Its name had been changed to the Eckert-Mauchly Computer Corporation (EMCC) when it was incorporated on December 22, 1947. When I arrived, there were maybe thirty to forty people employed at the firm. Most were engineers and technicians working on the components that would be used to build the UNIVAC (Universal Automatic Computer). Of the ENIAC engineers, only Bob Shaw and Jack Davis were there. Brad Sheppard was there from the EDVAC. Betty Snyder and I were the only programmers. Betty was working on the UNIVAC instruction set and on the UNIVAC console as well as on sorting programs. I was programming sort/merge routines, math subroutines, figuring out how to use the input/output (I/O) devices efficiently, and doing general programming problems. Inputs are the signals or data the system receives, and outputs are the signals or data it sends. I/O devices are used by a person or another system to communicate with a computer. Magnetic tape drives served as the UNIVAC's input and output devices.

The UNIVAC used magnetic tape as a mass storage device. The magnetic tape was read and recorded serially—in other words, it did not do random access. Early on, developers recognized that for commercial processing, the main master files of a company would have to be sorted and stored on these tapes. These master files would be updated with transaction or activity data. The master files had to be sorted on an identifying key field—the section of an item in a file of the sorting or merging activity, like a person's name or a policy number—and the activity file, or batch file, needed to be sorted on the same identifying key field. Then the batch activity file would be merged with the master file.

The UNIVAC read and recorded data to and from magnetic tape in blocks of sixty words each. A word was twelve alphanumeric characters long. Each character was composed of seven binary digits; six bits identified the character while the seventh bit was a parity bit that provided for odd/even checking of data as they were transferred in computer memory. To sort, we would begin by sorting blocks of data. Once a block was sorted, it was recorded on one of two output magnetic tapes. The first block would be put on Tape 1, the second block on Tape 2; the third block would be put on Tape 1, and the fourth block on Tape 2. Alternating blocks were put on each tape until all the data had been sorted by blocks.

To continue the sort, the two output tapes were read into the UNIVAC and merged, producing strings of sorted data two blocks long. This time, alternate strings were recorded on the two output tapes, thus making two tapes with sorted data consisting of two blocks. These two tapes would be read back into the UNIVAC and the two-block strings from the two tapes merged into four-block strings. This continued until the string was the size of the master file. Thus, if a file was sixty-four blocks long, it took one sort pass to sort each block of data and six merge passes to get the whole file sorted and merged.

The UNIVAC could read blocks backward or forward from the tapes. The blocks were stored in memory in exactly the same way, whether read forward or backward. What this did was to allow sorts to be done faster than if data could only be read when the tape moved forward. This sorting process was quite tedious, but fortunately the master file was sorted only once, when the application was set up. Thereafter, only the transaction or batch file needed to be sorted before it could be merged with the master file. Batch processing was the usual mode of operation for commercial applications before mass storage devices, such as disks, were developed. A bank or insurance office would collect all the transactions for the day, sort them, and then merge them with the master file daily or at whatever interval the installation chose.

My dear friend Betty Snyder Holberton and I worked on many of these programs—both apart and together—but Betty, who was in my estimation the far better programmer, did far more actual programming than I did due to my other work duties. Moreover, Betty was meticulous at the job. One of Betty's greatest talents, besides her logical mind, was her ability to finish a program with no loose ends dangling. When she was through with a sort, or with any routine, she had the problem done—plus she had the tapes labeled, the ends of the tapes marked, multiple tapes sequenced. The program was finished and ready to run.

Grace Hopper, who among her many accomplishments developed the first compiler for a computer programming language, said that Betty was the best programmer she had ever met. Betty, who was always a modest person, brushed off Grace's comment by saying, "Well, you know Grace...if anyone could do something she couldn't do, that person obviously had to be the best in the world at it, because only the best could outdo Grace!" Betty did admit somewhat sheepishly, however, that she had once debugged one of Grace's programs when Grace hadn't been able to locate the problem. So, I honestly think that Grace truly appreciated and admired Betty's skill as a programmer. I know I certainly did.

While I had been hired as a programmer and logical designer for the UNIVAC, I soon found myself also working on the Binary Automatic Computer (BINAC). You see, to test the mercury delay line memory and other components that would be used in the UNIVAC, in 1949 Pres and John entered into a contract with Northrop Aircraft to build the BINAC (they also needed money to cover some of their development costs for the UNIVAC). The BINAC was originally intended to act as the onboard computer to control and guide the Snark N-25 missile, which Northrop Aircraft was developing for the U.S. Air Force; however, the Snark N-25 missile did not meet performance requirements and was eventually scrapped in favor of a newer version. Plus, Northrop decided not to use the BINAC for the Snark N-25 when they realized the computer was too massive for their purposes. The BINAC measured five feet high, four feet wide, and a foot deep, and weighed three-quarters of a ton. It was also too fragile to be fired in a missile, since it had seven hundred vacuum tubes in each of the twin units that would never

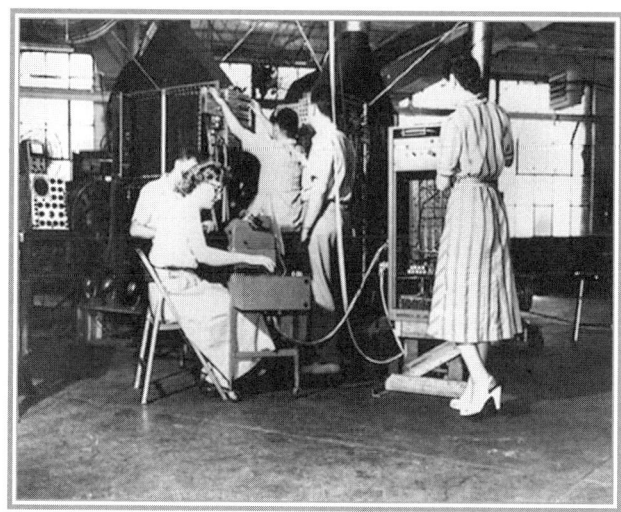

Programming the Binary Automatic Computer (BINAC), ca. 1944. Betty Jean Jennings is seated on the left, John Mauchley is standing in the middle, and Betty Snyder is on the right.

The Eckert-Mauchly BINAC, 1949, that went to Northrop. Photo donated by the UNISYS Blue Bell Retirees Group to the Jean Jennings Bartik Computing Museum, Northwest Missouri State University.

have survived the firing intact. But the BINAC, which operated successfully at Eckert-Mauchly, still had general purpose computing capabilities and Northrop Aircraft decided to use it to solve other problems.

According to Northrop Aircraft's president, John K. Northrop, the defense contractor "intended to use it to reduce preliminary development and test time and to save time and money on research and development projects by doing calculations that had previously been impossible or impractical." The firm "expected to save hundreds of thousands or even millions of dollars that had previously been required for design and development time."[1] Marvin Jacobi, Kathe Jacobi's husband, was hired by Eckert-Mauchly to work out the mathematics of calculating the Snark's trajectory, while I was given the job of programming the BINAC to calculate this trajectory.

The BINAC was a stored-program computer and would use mercury delay line memory as the UNIVAC did. It had 512 thirty-one-bit words of storage for data and instructions and it used binary arithmetic. Like the UNIVAC, it was a serial machine. It was built around a central accumulator architecture and was very fast: it ran at 4 megahertz, or 4 million cycles per second. In comparison, the ENIAC ran at 100 kilocycles—one hundred thousand cycles per second—or one-fortieth the speed of the BINAC. For reliability, the BINAC consisted of twin computers that mirrored each other's operation, so that their outputs were compared pulse time by pulse time.

Al Auerbach, the engineer who got the BINAC to pass Northrop's acceptance test, had said that the BINAC should never have run successfully because the cycle time was just too fast for the mercury delay line memory. Yet it did.

Questions about how much actual use Northrop Aircraft got out of the BINAC have generated a lot of speculation over the years. Unfortunately and unfairly, the BINAC has often been overlooked and even disparaged due to the perception that the computer was somehow faulty or never successfully worked in the first place. Wrong! Here were the two primary issues that resulted in the BINAC's being dismissed by the computing industry. First, the BINAC design, because of the speed at which it ran, was on the edge of what was doable. Second, the attitudes of the officers at Northrop were rather dismissive and downright suspicious from the get-go.

The "missile boys," as everyone at Eckert-Mauchly liked to call them, seemed to have only a superficial interest in electronics, which they apparently considered a technician's problem. Furthermore, they seemed to have little respect for the men who made the electronics successfully work. In short, if you didn't work for Northrop and it didn't go bang, they didn't much care.

On top of that, the missile boys were so paranoid about security that they refused to have any of the Eckert-Mauchly engineers on their premises to help set up the BINAC. More importantly, Northrop refused to consult with the Eckert-Mauchly team afterward about any snags or issues with the BINAC or allow any of the engineers from Eckert-Mauchly on site in California to help with the BINAC's installation and operation. The missile boys' paranoia was exacerbated by an alleged incident that occurred when they visited the Eckert-Mauchly facility in Philadelphia. The Northrop team insisted that someone had searched their hotel room one night. Everyone at Eckert-Mauchly was concerned, but since nothing had been stolen, we really didn't think about it. Later we found out that the Northrop Aircraft team had told the FBI that someone who worked for Eckert and Mauchly must have been responsible for searching their room. Everyone who had worked for Eckert and Mauchly was stunned by the claim. From that

FBI report, we also learned that a hotel employee had entered the room to return some dry-cleaned clothes. In my opinion, the engineers' assertion that someone had been searching their room could have stemmed from nothing more than this employee hanging shirts in their closet.

While the BINAC had worked to perfection in the Eckert-Mauchly laboratory, Northrop claimed that they had all sorts of problems with the BINAC from the beginning. Not surprising really when you consider how Northrop treated the BINAC. They had dismantled the BINAC, put all the pieces into crates, and shipped them from Philadelphia to California. Once the crates got to California, Northrop allowed the BINAC to sit in pieces for months before hiring a recent college graduate in engineering to put it back together and make it work. Due to Northrop security rules, this engineer was not allowed to seek out the assistance and expertise of any of the Eckert-Mauchly team. After all of that, is it really any wonder that the BINAC didn't work as well as it had in Philadelphia? What a difference it would have made to Northrop had they simply allowed Al Auerbach to put it back together.

The BINAC's alleged inability to function properly became an ongoing source of dispute between Northrop and Eckert-Mauchly. According to Northrop, the computer sat idle in a laboratory and worked only sporadically. But this, as I found out later, was not the case at all. Despite its rather less than careful handling and the inexperience of its reconstruction team, the BINAC worked well when it was actually used.[2]

The first UNIVAC to be built was ordered by the U.S. Census Bureau. After their experience with the BINAC, Pres, John, and the Eckert-Mauchly engineers reduced the UNIVAC's cycle time from 4 megahertz to 2.25 megahertz. The reduction in speed caused some problems with the Census Bureau because of the computer's performance specifications in the contract, so the length of the mercury delay line memory tanks was shortened to recapture the speed.

It was at this time, in 1949, that Grace Hopper was hired to work with John on an assembler language for the UNIVAC. Grace had worked on the Mark I, II, and III calculators with Howard Aiken at Harvard. John had been thinking about having this done for a while, but Betty and I were tied up with other work, so he interviewed Grace. Betty also interviewed her. When, after the interview, John asked her for her opinion of Grace, Betty said (as she later recalled), "Fine, as long as I never have to work with her."

My recollection of Grace at that time is that she acted rather silly. She also had, in my opinion, a severe drinking problem. Perhaps the two were related. Grace would rattle on about inconsequential things, giving trivial things more importance than warranted. In fact, she would sometimes begin talking about some insignificant thing as though it had earthshaking importance, when in actuality it had no consequence at all.

Grace was also fond of talking about the Mark calculators as though they were the greatest computers in the world. I considered them rather trivial in comparison to the ENIAC, the BINAC, or the UNIVAC. Of course, I may have been a bit prejudiced. Grace had taught at Vassar (where she had graduated Phi Beta Kappa with a degree in mathematics and physics in 1928) and believed it was the school to end all schools. She talked about her experience in the Navy constantly, and I couldn't see that she had done anything there that we had not done at the Moore School. In the Navy all she did was work on the Mark computers. So how was that different from our experience? I must admit that I found Grace's superior attitude and strong (often unasked for) opinions annoying.

My friend and colleague Milly Koss, whom I greatly liked and respected, had a far different view of Grace. Milly worked for Grace later at Remington Rand and always told me that Grace was very good to her. So undoubtedly there was a side to Grace that I was not privileged to have seen and that can genuinely be admired. When Milly became pregnant and told Grace she would have to leave her position in order to stay home with the baby, Grace told her she didn't need to quit. In fact, Grace was quick to support her in every way, encouraging her to work from her home rather than to leave her position. Milly did that and it worked very well. Learning from her experience with Grace, whenever Milly negotiated a job offer after that, she always insisted that she be allowed to work at home and come into the office as needed. After working for several corporations, Milly went on to Harvard, where she spent twenty-seven years managing a forty-person applications development group and a technology evaluation group for the Office for Information Technology.

When I was told to program the BINAC, I had nothing to work with except the advice of the engineers. I asked Brad Sheppard to show me how it worked. He kept putting me off. Finally, one day, Brad handed me this eight-and-a-half-by-eleven-inch sheet of paper folded in two, with drawings on the top half of it. These drawings were partially erased and overwritten, so that both the drawings and the writing were almost unreadable. This was my programming manual. Brad was very bright, but his communication skills were limited. His wife, a psychiatrist, laughed when I told her the story. But with the help of Bob Shaw and others, I did program the Snark trajectory problem.

Bob contributed to the design of the function table. He was a wonderfully courageous man, universally respected and loved. He was tall and quite thin and fragile. But he asked for no special favors and never talked about his various problems. Bob was an albino and had problems with his eyesight; also, his legs were very unstable, so he sometimes used a cane. His father was a minister, and my husband remembered that when Bob came to the Moore School to get his master's degree, his father would sometimes carry him into the building, he was so weak. When I ate lunch with him, he would order a meal of different things, then mix them all together and eat the mixture. Since Bob couldn't see very well it didn't matter to him that it looked messy; he just didn't want to fumble around with his fork to find the different foods.

The BINAC was the first hardware stored-program computer built and the first computer utilizing the twin-units concept. In April 1949, it ran nonstop for forty-four hours; it was stopped only because the engineers wanted to do some work on it.[3] Generally, the British computer EDSAC (Electronic Delay Storage Automatic Calculator) is given the distinction of being the first stored-program computer built, but EDSAC did not perform a successful demonstration until the following month, May 1949.

I saw the EDSAC at Cambridge in October 1951 on my trip to England with Betty and John Holberton, and it still looked like a lab model; it had wires and cables looped around the floor and little wooden bridges built over them to carry the foot traffic around the room without people tripping over them. All this rather messy wiring was quite a shock to me, since the wiring of the ENIAC had been neat and for the most part hidden. You see, because the ENIAC had been built during the war, telephone installations were at a standstill and telephone company wiremen were available. These experienced wiremen worked on the ENIAC and had given the computer incredibly tidy, unobtrusive wiring.

When the engineers were working on the BINAC, they discovered they could have it play "music" by hooking the output of one of its circuits to a radio. Mind you, this weird music wasn't like anything being broadcast on the radio—it was just a sequence or pattern of sounds emitted from the radio as the BINAC was running. Al Auerbach said he'd quickly discovered that he could tell whether the BINAC was running correctly by the sounds coming out of the radio when he played the test program. They called this test program "Old Faithful." Once, they hooked the

BINAC Engineering Team, 1949. First row, left to right: Presper Eckert (VP of engineering), Frazier Welsh (chief mechanical engineer), Jim Weiner (chief engineer), Brad Sheppard (memory), and John Mauchly (president). Second row, left to right: Al Auerbach (engineer), Betty Jean Jennings (programmer), Marvin Jacobi (engineer and mathematician), John Sims (engineer), Lou Wilson (engineer), Bob Shaw (engineer), and Jerry Smoliar (engineer).

BINAC up to the radio during a demonstration to surprise John Mauchly. To add to the surprise, a jokester rolled an egg out from under the computer, thus showing it could compute, play music, and lay an egg all at the same time. In *ENIAC: The Tragedies and Triumphs of the World's First Computer*, journalist Scott McCartney recounts this incident, then adds, "Fittingly, BINAC laid a big egg. After it was delivered to Northrop in California, it never really worked." I read the proofs of McCartney's book before it was published, and gave him the name and telephone number of the Northrop engineer (a relatively inexperienced recent college graduate) who had put the BINAC together after it was shipped to California. McCartney chose not to call him, and in his book he ignored the reasons why the BINAC didn't work.

Sadly, some of the men I worked for in those years were soon to have their careers entangled with the paranoia of the Red scare and the suspicions of McCarthyism, which caused them to be denied security clearance. Security clearance was absolutely essential for the line of work we were in—companies needed clearance to do business with the federal government, and a company's security clearance depended on the security clearance of its personnel. The McCarthy-era witch hunts, which rampaged from the late 1940s through the mid-1950s, have to be one of the stupidest blots on the body politic in U.S. history. Joe McCarthy, a blowhard, self-serving senator from Wisconsin, along with his unscrupulous assistants, Roy Cohn and G. David Schine, began to accuse people in the entertainment industry, union activists, educators, and government employees of being traitors and Communist sympathizers. Cohn and Schine ran around the country, supposedly investigating traitorous behavior in Hollywood, in the State Department, in private companies, and in government agencies. This far-reaching paranoia even wormed its way into the offices of Eckert-Mauchly in Philadelphia. John Mauchly's security clearance was questioned (and therefore held up), and so was the clearance of a few Eckert-Mauchly employees.

Almost anyone could be accused, and once a person was accused, he or she was assumed to be guilty. It was almost impossible to find out why one's clearance was denied. John initially assumed that he was denied because he had a secretary who had once been a member of the Communist Party. During the Great Depression, many people had flirted with communism as a political remedy for the economic devastation that had leveled so many lives and hopes. Most had given it up. Nevertheless, McCarthy and others played on the public's fear of Soviet infiltration into our free society. John was terribly frustrated by being denied security clearance because he had no way to fight it—the charges were secret. Meanwhile, his company suffered contract cancellations because of it.

Some seventeen years after John began encountering security clearance problems, on July 4, 1966, President Lyndon Johnson signed the Freedom of Information Act. As a result of this act, Kay Mauchly Antonelli was finally able to get a copy of the FBI report on John. It is about 150 pages long and consisted of two basic charges repeated ad infinitum, along with such profoundly incriminating statements as these: he spent all his time thinking about computers, he was eccentric, and the president of Ursinus College didn't like his lectures (because he spiced them up to bring in more students).[4] The first of the two charges was that he had joined Consumers Union, which publishes the monthly magazine *Consumer Reports*, but which the FBI report called a Communist-front organization. The House Un-American Activities Committee had placed it on a list of subversive organizations—in part because a rival, *Consumers Research*, had reported it. The second charge was that he was a member of the Association of Philadelphia Scientists (APS).

John did subscribe to *Consumer Reports*. He maintained that he had never joined the APS, but he may have signed a form to receive literature at some meeting somewhere and the organization put him on its membership list. One entry in the FBI report said that he was denied clearance because of his general demeanor and failure to take proper security precautions, but doesn't give any details to support these charges. Furthermore, the report also said he spent a lot of time with the ENIAC women. I guess hanging out with us women was obviously considered suspicious behavior.

Bob Shaw is also mentioned in the FBI report on John. Bob had joined the United Office and Professional Workers of America, Local No. 2. He received mail from this organization as well as from the Emergency Committee of Atomic Scientists (cofounded by Albert Einstein in 1946 to warn the public of the dangers of nuclear-weaponry development and promote world peace), the Eastern Chapter of the Progressive Citizens of America (a pacifist organization critical of American foreign policy, which gave rise to the Progressive Party of 1948, which he belonged to), and the American Council for a Democratic Greece. According to Bob's father, Bob had gotten interested in Greece because his roommate at Princeton University was Greek.

Bob's security clearance while he was at Eckert-Mauchly was denied. When he finally learned the reasons—again much later—it turned out that his clearance had been denied because his car had been parked on the street in Washington, D.C., along the route of a demonstration, and the police had taken down the license numbers of the parked cars on that street. Bob wasn't even in Washington that day. Because Bob was an albino and he was extremely near-sighted, he couldn't drive a car, but he was social and liked to go places. Cars were not very prevalent after World War II, but Bob bought a car and had people drive him wherever he wanted to go. One of his drivers had borrowed the car to go to Washington to visit a friend—he wasn't there for any demonstration. But so it went with the witch hunt.[5]

To make matters worse, Dick Clippinger was ousted from Aberdeen. After becoming the most knowledgeable manager at Aberdeen on the ENIAC, he was named the director of the Ordnance Laboratory until his security clearance was denied. It took Clippinger two years to get a list of the charges against him because the government, in its infinite wisdom, classified the list of charges. Until Clippinger answered the charges against him, he could not gain security clearance; but without security clearance, he could not get access to the classified charges against him! It was indeed a catch-22. He had at last built and moved into his new house in Havre de Grace, but he had to sell it in 1952 because he was forced to leave Aberdeen that year, and so he had to take a job at Packard Bell in Boston. The first charge against Clippinger came about because Dick taught a class in mathematics at Harvard on Fridays. He would take the overnight sleeper to Boston on Thursday night, teach the class and handle his professorial duties on Friday, then take the overnight sleeper back to Aberdeen on Friday night. A student in one of his classes was a member of the Communist Party. Dick didn't even know anything about it.

The second charge was based on a situation that had happened at Aberdeen Proving Ground. A foreign national had worked at Aberdeen, but he was discharged after being declared a security risk. Nobody protested this action; however, when the government next tried to deport the man, a petition was circulated protesting his deportation. Dick signed it, as did many others. Once the charges were discovered and a hearing held, it took less than half an hour to clear him of them. His security clearance was restored, but no one could restore his life in Aberdeen and Havre de Grace, nor that of his wife and children.

During this era, people grew afraid to talk to others about controversial issues because real security breaches did not have to occur. Someone could just say someone else was a security risk, and the accused had to disprove it. Innocent until proven guilty was seemingly thrown out the window. Our society seemed to have regressed to the year 1692 and was conducting witch trials. While I can see why security might have required special measures, the McCarthy era sure gave people with grudges an easy way to get revenge.

It became so bad that I became apprehensive one day when I was talking on the phone about a controversial subject. That night, I told my husband about my fears. I was pleased when he said, "We will not be intimidated. You say what you want, on the telephone or anywhere." Fortunately, others felt the same; however, it took that magnificent lawyer Joseph Welch at the Army-McCarthy hearings in 1954 to show what a scourge McCarthy had become. It was a memorable moment and a turning point when Welch took umbrage at McCarthy going after a young law clerk. I listened on the radio to the hearings and will never forget the broadcast that aired that eloquent rejoinder by Welch, which was very dramatic and received a rousing ovation from the Senate chamber.

"You've done enough," Welch snapped at McCarthy. "Have you no sense of decency, sir, at long last? Have you left no sense of decency?" And of course, McCarthy didn't have any. He cared nothing about the many people he had ruined. McCarthy was reviled by everyone I knew, and public opinion eventually swung against him. Edward R. Murrow helped to decisively sway the public against McCarthy on his popular *See It Now* television series by pointing out that investigating and persecuting was a very fine line and that McCarthy had crossed that line.[6] Murrow said, "We must remember always that accusation is not proof and that conviction depends upon evidence and due process of law. We will not walk in fear, one of another. We will not be driven by fear into an age of unreason."[7]

Almost everyone respected Murrow and the public wisely listened to him. But not before McCarthy (and others of his narrow mind-set) made life miserable for John Mauchly, Bob Shaw, Dick Clippinger, and thousands of other Americans, forever altering their careers. I do, however, sometimes smile and wink at the Big

The Eckert-Mauchly UNIVAC Crew, 1949. Front row, left to right: Fran Morello, Bob Shaw, Pres Eckert, Brad Sheppard, Frazier Welsh, John Mauchly, Jim Weiner, Al Auerbach, and Betty Snyder. Middle row, left to right: John Sims, Marvin Jacobi, Paul Winsor, Jerry Smoliar, Arthur Gehring, Betty Jay, Ed Blumenthal, Bob Mock, Betty Jean Jennings Bartik, Herman Lukoff, Bernie Gordon, and Ned Shriner. Back row, left to right: George Gingrich, Marvin Gottlieb, Lou Wilson, Doug Wendell, Charlie Michaels, Ben Stad, Seymore Levitt, and Larry Jones. Photograph by B. Victor.

Guy Upstairs when I think about Murrow's insightful March 9, 1954, exposé, that was instrumental in helping to bring McCarthy down, and the fact that it aired on CBS. That network, you see, was first to use John and Pres's UNIVAC to predict the 1952 presidential race.

As the Eckert-Mauchly Computer Corporation began to get more deeply into the development and building of the BINAC and UNIVAC, it hired more people. One of those hired was Art Gehring from the Clippinger project, who came aboard in April 1949. I was delighted, for I thought he was very good, and I liked him. I discovered, however, that John Mauchly had hired him for a higher salary than mine—four hundred dollars more than I was making, which was $4,700 a year.

I had been with Eckert-Mauchly a full year by then. I went to John and told him I would quit if my salary was not adjusted. I said I didn't want to leave, but I would; my husband was quite capable of supporting me. I understood that the company had very little money, but if it could pay Art more, it could pay me more. John's response was very friendly; he understood and didn't really blame me. He had probably never even thought about my concern before I brought it up. He did adjust my salary to two hundred dollars more a year than Art's, and I was happy.[8]

Shortly after that, Art started working, and John said that he would like for us to work with Pres Eckert on a secret project. Pres was concerned that the mercury delay line memory might not work, and he wanted to be prepared with a backup machine if that happened. He had no free engineers to do work on it, so he wanted to borrow Art and me from the programming group to do the logical design of this machine. He undoubtedly believed, as most engineers did at that time, that programming was secondary to engineering. We told John that we knew nothing about doing logical design, but he said that Pres would teach us. Pres envisioned a UNIVAC with exactly the features of the mercury delay line model, but the backup would use cathode-ray tube storage and be micro-coded.[9]

I told John that I was concerned if I was to work directly for Pres, because I had heard him yell abusively at the engineers. I told John that if Pres ever yelled at me, I was out of there. John said that he didn't think Pres would ever yell at me, and John was right, Pres never yelled at me. I aggravated him a couple of times, and he had a right to be upset with me, but he never raised his voice. Years later, when Pres heard somewhere that I had been afraid of him, he was dumbfounded.

One time, Pres had told me to write down how we were implementing a particular instruction that had to do with comparing a selected field in a memory location with another. He said he was afraid that he would forget how he planned to do it. I wrote everything down and put the instructions in my desk drawer. In the meantime, our offices were moved around and somebody else got my desk. Consequently, the day Pres asked me for the instructions, I couldn't find them. He was clearly angry and reminded me that he had told me to save the document for him.

When Pres was talking, he would pace up and down swinging a little penknife that he had on a watch chain around and around with his right hand. When he became agitated, he would pace faster and faster and swing the penknife faster and faster. I could tell in that moment that he wanted to yell at me, but instead he abruptly left the room. In a few moments he came back smiling, saying never mind, he had remembered how to do it. He earned my respect and loyalty for the way he handled the situation. I never wanted to let him down again, and I never did.

Pres was an incredible teacher. He taught us how to do logical design and how to do micro-coding. It is my belief that this was the first computer ever microcoded, but it was never built because the mercury delay line memory worked, so the backup wasn't needed. With Pres, no question was too small. I learned early on never to pretend I understood something when I didn't. Not that I ever considered pretending, since I knew he would remember it if I did. Pres had, I am sure, a photographic mind. One time I said to him that we had to worry about only one delayed carryover going down the line in an addition.[10] He said, "When did you learn that?" I said that I had just thought of it. He said—not in a boastful way, but in an offhand, matter-of-fact way—that he had thought of it on a particular date several years earlier. I believe he did, too.[11]

We had been sworn to secrecy about this project and were told to talk to no one about it except to each other and to Pres. He didn't want anyone to know that he was worried about the mercury delay line memory—not only could it have harmed the company's prospects for contracts, but it would have undermined morale among the engineers. Pres would come in each morning and afternoon to teach us and to answer our questions. Why he thought we could do this is beyond me. He was amazing in the way he used negative information. I was actually scared the first time I had to tell him that one of his ideas wasn't working out. But it didn't phase him. It was just another piece of data to him. Most people would have gotten angry and bent out of shape, but not Pres.

Jean and some of her colleagues from Eckert-Mauchly. Back row, far left: Betty Jean Jennings Bartik. Standing next to Jean is Art Gehring. Back row, far right: Kitty Gehring (Art's wife), ca. 1950.

Art and I loved working with Pres, and we loved working with each other. Art was my third perfect partner—we were equals in IQ, ability, and enthusiasm. We shared the same values, and we wanted to do a good job and were willing to bust our butts doing it. I trusted him completely, since he wasn't the least bit political. He gave me credit, and I gave him credit. Above and beyond that, we knew each other personally, as Bill and I socialized with him and Kitty. With this perfect partnership in place, Art and I discussed, designed, and pulled each other's work apart looking for flaws. When either of us found an error, we were delighted because now we would have one less flaw in our design. We depended on each other and believed we were producing an error-free logical design. If that is possible, I believe it can be done by such a partnership.

One time, Pres gave us an engineering article to read. Art and I couldn't understand it. For some reason, that day Pres did not come in to meet with us, either in the morning or in the afternoon. My husband, who was an engineer, was coming in after work to pick us up and take us downtown to meet Art's girlfriend, Kitty. We were going to dinner then to the opera at the Academy of Music.[12]

We were very frustrated because we were wasting time and spinning our wheels trying to understand this article. Art said, "Let's ask Bill what it means when he comes in." I said, "Pres told us to discuss things with no one but him." Art pointed out that the article was not about what we were doing but just a straightforward engineering paper. We couldn't understand it because we were not engineers.

Bill came in and Art asked him to look at the paper. As Bill bent over to read it, who should walk into the room but Pres! He went into orbit. He said, "I told you not to discuss this with anybody but each other and me. That includes other engineers, husbands, wives, girlfriends, or anybody." Art tried to explain our dilemma. Pres was having none of it. After lecturing us for a while, Pres must have realized we hadn't broken his rules about secrecy because he turned to Bill to ask him some questions. Bill worked for a small company that did consulting on electrical noise.

At that time, Bill's job was to shield the centrifuge at the Johnsville Naval Air Station in Warrington, Pennsylvania, from electrical noise—not audible noise, but electrical impulses. The centrifuge had an arm about twenty feet long with a gondola on the end to hold an animal or a human being. The arm would be swung around at high speeds to simulate the effects of gravity on a live body. It was going to be used in studies with the astronauts for NASA.

The human or animal in the gondola would be hooked up to all kinds of electrical monitors to measure the effect of different g-forces on the body. Electrical signals generated by a human or animal body are very small; thus the centrifuge building had to be shielded against outside electrical noise. This was done by essentially wallpapering the room with large sheets of copper, which is a great conductor of electricity; when spurious electrical pulses ("noise") hit the copper, they were captured by it and grounded.

Pres began to pick Bill's brain. The space program was just getting started, and he really wanted to know about the work at Johnsville. Bill was telling him how the project was going and what was planned. Time passed. It became close to the time we were to meet Kitty. Art and I got up and put on our coats, and I got my pocketbook. We began walking out of the room. Pres went with us and talked on with Bill. We were on the seventh floor. We went to the elevator. Pres went with us. The elevator came and we got on—so did Pres. He talked on. We got to the ground floor and walked out of the elevator into the street. And Pres talked on. Finally, Pres looked up and saw all the cars whizzing up and down Broad Street at rush hour. He said, "I guess you people want to go." He just turned around and walked back into the building.

Pres was so focused on what he was thinking about that he shut everything else out. It was very flattering when he talked to me, because I truly was the most important person in his world at that moment. I always felt that my IQ went up many notches when I talked to Pres, because I became more focused on a task or problem. Some of this ability to concentrate, which Pres was so remarkable at, already came naturally to me. I could read in the middle of chaos, and I worked for a number of years in an open lab or office space without activity bothering my focus on a task. I lost a lot of that ability, however, in later years when I had children. You simply cannot lose yourself in a problem or task with children around unless you want to find muddy footprints on the floor and finger paint handprints on the walls.

Pres worked by going from group to group, talking to group members about their projects, asking questions, listening intently to the answers, and offering his suggestions. Despite this tremendous workload, Pres never seemed hurried. There was always time for questions with him—and for his answers, which were always complete. I was flattered that this truly brilliant man—one of the brightest minds of the century in his field—considered my thoughts and my work for him worthwhile. I never even knew where Pres had his office; I never saw him in it. He was always out among us, working with us and teaching us.

Our design had come a long way after a few months. One day, Pres came in and told us that, because we were doing so well on logical design, there was something he would like for us to do. He was concerned about the debug time that would be required to get the UNIVAC up and running after it was built. To cut down on that debug time, he wanted Art and me to go over the logic diagrams of the mercury delay line in the UNIVAC to make sure there were no logical flaws in it. Of course, we were happy to do so. At the same time, he told the design engineers that before they could make any design changes, they must discuss them with us. There was some grumbling at first. I don't know if it was because I was a woman or because we were programmers. Engineers generally had a low opinion of programmers. This grumbling quickly passed once the engineers learned that if they consulted us on a planned change, we would track its effects around the computer and make all the changes needed to accommodate their changes. Engineers hate to fiddle with the consequences of their changes and we did for them something they were loathe to do themselves. Consequently, we became accepted members of the engineering team, which consisted of three or four lead engineers and six or seven altogether, headed by Bob Shaw.[13]

Bob Shaw drew all the Logical Block Diagrams for the UNIVAC. Because Bob had very poor vision, he had to hold his face very close to the paper to see what he was drawing. His nose almost touched the paper. Plus, he had a very hard time reading any fine print, so he drew the Logical Block Diagrams on 30" x 40" paper. Bob was brilliant and a wonderful person. He was very articulate, wrote well, was a very good and giving teacher, and very witty. He loved to use unusual logic to arrive at a conclusion, just for fun. Art and I were given the job of checking the UNIVAC logic and putting in check circuits. We had questions for Frazier Welsh about the I/O logic. We tried to show him what bothered us on the Logic Diagram that Bob had drawn, but Frazier would never look at it because he said it was too complex. One day, he came to us with his drawing on an 8.5" x 11" page and said, "Look how simple it is." He had drawn exactly the same thing that Bob had drawn except on a smaller piece of paper. By the way, Bob drew all the Logical Block Diagrams for UNIVAC I in about six weeks' time, and Art and I found no major logical error in them.[14]

One day, Pres came to Art and me and told us that he was concerned because the UNIVAC had no check circuits other than the odd/even check on the memory, the input/output units, and the transfers. The odd/even check worked in this way: a UNIVAC "word" consisted of twelve alphanumeric characters and each character consisted of seven bits, six for the character and one for the parity bit. The alphanumeric character always had an odd number of bits in it. When an alphanumeric character was formed, the bits were added up and, if the number was even or zero, a "one" bit was attached so the number would be odd. The bits in a character were counted when a number was read out of memory or transferred. If the number of bits was even, it signaled an error.

Pres wanted check circuits that would check everything. If a circuit was not checked by something else, it was to be duplicated. I had no idea why he thought we could do this. That is another thing about Pres: he had more faith in Art and me than we had in ourselves. I'm sure he did this with others also. It worked: if Pres thought we could do it, we could.

We started putting in check circuits. Again the engineers began to grumble, this time because we were asking them to duplicate circuits. The grumbling became louder and louder until it verged on rebellion. Jim Weiner, the chief engineer, couldn't stop it, so he called a meeting with Pres. It took about ten minutes. Pres said the rule was, "Every circuit must be looked at for errors by at least one other circuit. If it isn't, duplicate the circuit. The assumption is that the probability of two errors occurring simultaneously is so low, we don't need to worry about it or design for it." As an analogy, he said that police forces do not have every policeman looking at all the other policemen for corruption. Instead, every policeman must be looked at by *one* other policeman. The assumption is that two policemen do not become corrupt simultaneously. End of meeting. End of grumbling. Pres was universally respected in the lab, and besides, his explanation made sense.

After we had put in the check circuits, the UNIVAC design was pretty complete, so Art and I went back to designing the backup UNIVAC. While we all were working on the UNIVAC, Wister Brown was out trying to sell it. Potential customers kept asking him about the UNIVAC's printer. He didn't know what it would be, so he asked Pres about it. Pres said he was too busy to discuss it, but there would be a printer. After a while, Wister began to believe that Pres had no real plans for a printer. Finally, in desperation, he confronted Pres and demanded to know about the printer. In rapid-fire succession, Pres described eight different printers he could use, giving the pros and cons of each. Floundering under the weight of all that detail, Wister staggered out of the meeting vowing never to doubt Pres again.

The time Art and I spent working with the UNIVAC design team was indeed one of the most magical periods of my life. Almost all of the engineers were brilliant. To be accepted into this group was a high such as I've never attained anywhere else in my life. I loved it, and I never again felt so alive. We worked constantly. We arrived early. We arranged meetings during coffee breaks and lunch. We worked late. Often, after the official end of the workday at five, Pres would come by to talk to some of the men about an idea he had or a concern. And often he would catch me as I was leaving work to bounce an idea off of me. Pres thought with his mouth open. We thought it highly likely that, if no one else was around, he would stop a janitor from doing his work while he expounded on a subject.

Pres and Frazier Welsh had been friends since they were children. Frazier was also a genius; he was dynamic, talked fast, and was incredibly bright—a brilliant mechanical engineer.[15] He and Pres would get into a conversation and move around the building as they talked, even wandering downstairs to the basement and back up. Other times they would sit on a table. One time, I am told, they even climbed up on a file cabinet without, apparently, even being aware of what they were doing. The words and ideas were the important things, not how idiosyncratic their behavior might appear. We all accepted Pres as he was.

With me, Pres would sometimes talk about things totally outside my area of knowledge. One of his favorite subjects was random-access storage devices, which were so badly needed for commercial processing. Many people were thinking about the problem. Someone came up with the idea of having drawers full of IBM punch cards and a robotic arm that would go back and forth on a track. When it reached the drawer with the data needed, the arm would reach out, open the drawer, and select the appropriate card, making it a rather Rube Goldberg–like device. Perhaps the person who came up with the idea was inspired by Goldberg's cartoons of ridiculously complex machines to perform simple household tasks. Pres said the idea had evidently come from someone who thought IBM punch cards would never go away.

He also talked about the possibility of using rotating drums with data recorded on the surface in tracks going around the drum. An arm would move the reading/recording heads to the correct track, then lower the heads to read the data. Drums preceded disk storage by many years. Pres was talking to me about drums in 1949—relatively early. He had written a paper in which he described a computer using a drum as its internal memory. Additionally, Pres and John had seen the need for automatic regulation or control of electronic calculations, which is an implicit statement for a stored-program computer, in their "ENIAC Progress Report" of December 1943, and most significantly, Pres had written about the concept in January 1944, well before von Neumann came on the scene.[16] With the UNIVAC, Pres was testing drums to be used as auxiliary storage like magnetic tape. Drum storage came about in the next decade.

When I was programming the BINAC and UNIVAC, I was always excited to listen to Pres and John talk about their ideas. In fact, I was extremely flattered that they felt comfortable talking to me about their designs and their work. I also greatly enjoyed talking with Joe Chapline, who taught a course on the BINAC's operation for the team from Northrop Aircraft; his conversations often made me feel like I was listening to a radio personality, he had such a great voice and communication style.

In the meantime, Grace Hopper was working with John Mauchly on an assembler for the UNIVAC. Herb Mitchell, a very bright mathematician who had worked on the Harvard Mark computers, was brought in to manage the programmers at Eckert-Mauchly, whose numbers were swelling as other programmers were hired. Betty Snyder Holberton continued with her sort/merge programs. Yet the financial and security problems of Eckert-Mauchly persisted. Three government contracts for UNIVACs were canceled because of security clearance difficulties. In the nick of time, it seemed, in late 1948 a savior arrived in the form of Harry Straus of the American Totalisator Company, which made an electromechanical system to calculate and display the odds at racetracks.[17]

Harry was an electrical engineer. He and fellow engineer Arthur J. (Johnny) Johnson used a telephone call–routing system that had been developed by Almon Strowger to design the Totalisator Board. Being a good businessman and knowing that computers would affect the future development of his business, Straus invested in Eckert-Mauchly. He was not a distant investor either; he spent time in the plant and set up a committee of employees with whom he met. Betty Snyder represented the programmers and met with him and the committee to discuss various aspects of the business. While I was not on Straus's committee, I did meet him. He was a tall, husky man with a wonderful smile and a charming manner. Betty and the other employees on the committee also came away very impressed with him. Everyone liked and trusted him, including Pres and John. Orders for

UNIVACs were coming in, and Straus invested $500,000 in the company for 40 percent of the stock and became chairman of the board.

Soon after Straus had established himself at Eckert-Mauchly, he attacked the company's problem of security clearance. FBI director J. Edgar Hoover himself assured Straus that the problems were taken care of. Then tragedy struck. On October 25, 1949, Straus and Johnny Johnson were killed in an American Totalisator Company airplane crash in Perryville, Maryland. Industrial sabotage was not suspected, and government investigators attributed the crash's cause to mechanical failure. Unfortunately, no one else at American Totalisator had an interest in Eckert-Mauchly. With their top management suddenly wiped out, the former subordinates of Straus and Johnson were busy handling their own company.

Hardly surprisingly, almost immediately after Straus died, the FBI office in Philadelphia again questioned Eckert-Mauchly's security clearance. Undoubtedly some person acquainted with Eckert-Mauchly's precarious security status sent a letter to that office, someone who wished ill to John Mauchly and Pres Eckert. Most people in the company suspected a certain individual, but these were just suspicions and there was no hard evidence. But it stands to reason that it was someone motivated by jealousy, revenge, or competitive zeal.

Without the Straus investment, the Eckert-Mauchly Computer Corporation was in jeopardy of bankruptcy. Pres and John endeavored to arrange a series of loans, but they were not successful. Both the National Cash Register Company (which later became NCR Computers) and the Remington Rand Corporation were interested. The latter made the first offer on February 1, 1950, and two weeks later Eckert-Mauchly sold out to Remington Rand. The employees at Eckert-Mauchly were philosophical about the buyout. Everyone knew Pres and John had to sell to someone, and we were optimistic that Remington Rand was a good choice. The company had been in the punch card business for years, although it had not had much success competing with IBM. It seemed like a good move.

American Totalisator got $438,000 for its stock, and Pres and John got $100,000 apiece for theirs. The two men had owned their company for less than two years. They would never again work for themselves.

CHAPTER 6
Moving On, and the Glass Ceiling

In May of 1950, my husband took a job with an engineering company and we moved to Alexandria, Virginia. I stayed on working with Pres because he wanted Art and me to finish the logical design of the backup UNIVAC, so for a couple of months I commuted to Philadelphia. I would come up on Monday morning, stay with Bill's parents during the week, and go back to Washington on Friday. Once that was done, I set to work furnishing our apartment on Pitt Street in Alexandria, then applied for a job at Remington Rand's operation in Washington, D.C. I had heard from the Remington Rand people in Philly that the Washington office needed someone to teach a course to Census Bureau programmers, and that was what I applied for in September of that year.

I was interviewed by Mr. Goodman, the sales manager. Goodman fairly reeked of power, possessing total self-confidence and always speaking with an absolute assurance in his opinions. He wasn't the slightest bit interested in my ideas, but he was thrilled that I had a bachelor's degree. He was thrilled by that because he didn't have one himself and there I was, a college graduate, needing to be approved by him for the job. Goodman seemed amused as he bragged that he had only graduated from the eighth grade. He said he was very proud of that fact that he had succeeded with very little formal education. Furthermore, he was happy to inform me that his father-in-law, who had a PhD in botany, had developed the purple onion but despite all his scientific achievements didn't make much money. Goodman told me that his wife was very beautiful, and that they lived in a beautiful house, describing their possessions in some detail.

Later, I was told that before they were married when Goodman's wife had first come to work for Remington Rand, she had immediately begun asking around about who made the most money in the company. According to rumor, when she was told that Goodman made the most money, she promptly set her gold-digging cap for him. I couldn't imagine wanting Goodman as a husband no matter how much money he had.

Goodman also told me that Pres and John were dreamers, unable to handle their business, and it would take the know-how of Remington Rand to make a success of it. He assured me that his sales force could and would sell the UNIVAC successfully.

Goodman, and Remington Rand, hired me to assist the salesmen as a consultant when they had customers who could benefit from having a UNIVAC. I would listen to a customer's problem and describe the UNIVAC to that person. The first thing I was to do, however, was to teach the Census Bureau programmers how to program the UNIVAC, since the Census Bureau had bought the first UNIVAC. My salary was to be $5,500 per year.

The first morning when I came in to work, I lit up a cigarette as I settled down to work. I barely had time to take a puff when Goodman's secretary ran over and tapped me on the shoulder, telling me that I wasn't allowed to smoke in here. I looked around the room and all the men were smoking, so I asked her, "Why not? The men are smoking." The woman told me that the men weren't allowed to smoke cigars or pipes in the room, but could smoke cigarettes. However, the women weren't allowed to smoke at all except in the ladies' restroom. Outraged, I jumped up and hustled into Goodman's office and demanded, "What do you mean I can't smoke?" Herbert Goodman leaned back, smiled, and then said, "Why, Jean, you can come into my office and smoke anytime you want to." The SOB had me, but I never forgave him.

Smoking or not, this was a job from hell. Teaching the course was fine, but going out on calls with salesmen was a waste of time. They took me with them to tantalize their customers with the UNIVAC, and then the salesmen would sell them typewriters and accounting machines. I was just a way for them to get a foot in the door. I would describe the UNIVAC and tell the customer what it could do: file processing, accounting, scientific calculations. Then the salesmen would take over and peddle their familiar wares. There were two salesmen whom I called the Gold Dust Twins, because they were making so much money they fairly glinted.

One time, I was out with one of the Gold Dust Twins on a sales meeting. He had taken me to a customer who had no real use for a UNIVAC. When I told

Walter Cronkite (right) listens as Dr. J. Presper Eckert (center) describes the function of the UNIVAC I computer. The UNIVAC operator (seated) is Harold Sweeney, fall 1956. Photo by AP, courtesy U.S. Census Bureau.

the twin that, he snapped, "Don't say that. I am selling them typewriters." Salesmen had been on commission during WWII and had made lots of money because everything sold that anyone could produce. Also, federal agencies bought products in Washington for their offices all around the country, so that meant hefty commissions. IBM put their salesmen on a salary during the war so they didn't make exorbitant commissions, but Remington Rand did not, and their salesmen raked in the gold dust.

Teaching the month-long course that was one of my job duties was better than making sales calls. However, there were one or two unique challenges such as the fact that one of my "students," a programmer, was totally deaf. It was my first experience teaching a person with a physical disability. I was originally told that the woman in question read lips so well that I didn't need to worry about doing anything special for her, but that wasn't true of course. I had to remember never to turn my back on her as I wrote on the board while talking. It was a challenge because I wasn't used to doing that with anyone else, but I soon got better at communicating with her, and I sincerely hope that she found the experience with me satisfactory.

I later became more interested in equal rights for women in the work place because of what was happening at IBM. One of the women at Remington Rand had previously been a system service girl for IBM during the war. After a system was installed, a system service girl would go out and show the users how it worked. She was the liaison between the users and the computer company. She was married and had been fired to make room for a returning veteran. When the war ended, IBM rehired all of its former employees who had left to join the military, then fired all of the married women with jobs that could be filled by men. She told me that if she had been single, she might have been able to keep her job. But it was assumed that a married woman didn't need a job, because she had a husband who could take care of her. The woman was naturally irate because she had loved her job.

One afternoon I went into a downtown Washington cafeteria for lunch, and who should I see in line but Dr. Blanche Dow, my French professor from Northwest Missouri State Teachers College! I could scarcely believe my eyes. I greeted her, and she, too, was surprised and delighted at the reunion. We had lunch together. Blanche had left Northwest when Dean Jones, my old nemesis, was made president of the college. She felt that it would be degrading to work for him, so she became president of Cottey College, a prestigious two-year women's college in Nevada, Missouri.

When I ran into her that day, Blanche was serving a term as national president of the American Association of University Women (AAUW) and in that capacity was in town for its annual convention. She asked me, "Do you remember the time you brought me a chicken?" I did, of course.

One day, in my college French class, Dr. Dow had said some rather flippant things about farm subsidies. I argued that from my experience farmers got low prices when they had things to sell and high prices when they had little to sell, so they never came out ahead. Dr. Dow said that she sure wished she could have a nice chicken any time she liked, implying that farmers lived off the fat of the land. I pointed out that having food wasn't everything. We still needed money for clothes, cars, machinery, newspapers, education, and other things. So that weekend, I had my mother dress a chicken for Dr. Dow and took it to her so she would have a nice chicken. She appreciated the humor in the gesture, as well as the chicken.

I never saw Dr. Dow again after that chance meeting. However, in the fall of 2007—a full fifty-seven years later—I was back in Maryville to serve as grand marshal of the homecoming parade at Northwest Missouri State University and to celebrate the university's twentieth anniversary of its Electronic Campus Program, which in 1987 placed a networked terminal in every residence hall room, faculty office, and administrative office. The program made Northwest the first public electronic campus in the nation.[1] During my visit, Northwest's archivist, Catherine Palmer, told me about a biography of Dr. Dow written by her nephew—*A World of Love*, by David Harvey—and she sent me a copy, which I treasure.

I really enjoyed my visit with Dr. Dow that day. Sharing remembrances with her of the beautiful and historic campus situated in the northwest corner of Missouri helped me to briefly take my mind off my frustrations at Remington Rand. Northwest was an oasis of beauty and tranquility in the heart of a fertile farm country. More importantly, my Northwest professors, with the rare exception of Mattie Dykes, had always respected my work and opinions and had actively encouraged and appreciated critical and creative thinking from all of their students, just as Pres and John had done at Eckert-Mauchly, and before that at Aberdeen. At Remington Rand, on the other hand, the salesmen called me "Archimedes," and it wasn't meant as a compliment.

After the open, creative, and stimulating atmosphere at Eckert-Mauchly, being surrounded by Luddites was hard to take. Neither Goodman nor anyone else at Remington Rand had made plans to train the sales force; hence, the salesmen

UNIVAC I with console, printer, and four UNISERVOS (tape devices), ca. 1950s.

were totally ignorant of what the UNIVAC could do. The company had nobody to help any customer who bought a UNIVAC and so customer care was nonexistent. I felt sick that Remington Rand wasn't taking care of business and apparently didn't care enough about the UNIVAC to provide its customers with training and support, particularly when IBM came to town in 1950 with its proposed defense calculator. After all, Remington Rand had a deliverable computer and IBM had nothing but an imaginary system. In my opinion, Remington Rand was administered by arrogant, incompetent men, and I feared the company would lose out to IBM. It turned out that my fears were justified.

Once in a while, Luther Harr, a UNIVAC salesman from the old Eckert-Mauchly days who was now selling UNIVACs for Remington Rand in Philly, would come down, and while he was there I would have someone to talk to who could understand my frustrations and fears. One time Luther came down with Grace Hopper to give presentations to some potential customers. Unfortunately, Grace drank too much and could not give her presentation and Luther had to do it on her behalf. I guess the situation had happened before, because Luther was livid at Grace. He told me that Remington Rand needed to do something about Grace or her unprofessional behavior was going to hurt UNIVAC sales.

While I was worried about the future of Remington Rand and feeling less than appreciated, I finally did get a real assignment offered to me that I could feel proud about undertaking. One of Remington Rand's customers, the Naval Aviation Supply Office (ASO), was threatening to throw out its Cardex system—specialized cards that could be sorted and filed to keep track of supplies. The salesmen on the account told the ASO officials about UNIVAC, and I was given the job of setting up an inventory control system for the ASO. As I recall, there were three ASOs in the United States, including one in Philadelphia. They supplied all the Navy installations around each regional office. Using the UNIVAC, I flowcharted the whole thing, from order to shipping to replenishing supplies at the central site. Not all that sophisticated by today's standards, but pretty nifty for 1950.

As the time approached for the meeting with the Navy commanders and lieutenant commanders who really ran the various ASO installations, Remington Rand got nervous about having me make the proposal. They had a man (Paul Chinitz) from Remington Rand in Philadelphia come down to talk about the theory of inventory control, as if these men didn't already know what they had been doing. The vice president of Remington Rand in New York (surprisingly, his name was "Sales") came down to sit in on the meeting.

Sys No	Customer	Ship Date	Site	Director
1	Bureau of Census #1	3/51	Washington DC	Jim McPherson
2	Air Force Comptroller	3/52	Arlington VA	George Danzig
3	Army Map Service	4/52	Bethesda MD	J. W. H. Spencer
4	Atomic Energy Comm., NYU	4/53	New York NY	Eugene Isaacson
5	Atomic Energy Comm., CA	11/52	Livermore CA	Sidney Fernbach
6	Bureau of Ships (DTMB)	5/53	Bethesda MD	Harry Polachek
7	Rem Rand UNIVAC, DPC	10/53	New York NY	Arthur A. Katz
8	General Electric	1/54	Louisville KY	Roddy Osborn
9	Metropolitan Life #1	4/54	New York NY	John Finelli
10	Air Materiel Command, W-P	5/54	Dayton OH	Charles R. Gregg
11	U. S. Steel	7/54	Pittsburgh PA	Bill Murdock
12	E. I. DuPont	9/54	Wilmington DE	Walter Carlson
13	Bureau of Census #2	10/54	Washington DC	Ed Stein
14	U. S. Steel	11/54	Gary IN	Merle John
15	Franklin Life Ins. Co.	1/55	Springfield IL	James Cranwill
16	Rem Rand UNIVAC Plant	1/55	St. Paul MN	G. Ward Lund
17	Pacific Mutual	8/55	Los Angeles CA	Dick Dotts
18	Westinghouse	9/55	Pittsburgh PA	E. Harder/L. Hague
19	Rem Rand UNIVAC, DPC	11/55	Los Angeles CA	Morgan Huff
20	C & O Railroad	12/55	Cleveland OH	Hy Laden*
21	Consolidated Edison #1	1/56	New York NY	Frederick Porter
22	Consolidated Edison #2	2/56	New York NY	Frederick Porter
23	John Hancock Ins. Co.	12/55	Boston MA	R. Slater/G. Wallace
24	Life & Casualty of Tenn.	4/56	Nashville TN	Morgan Huff
25	Bureau of Ships (DTMB)	2/56	Bethesda MD	Harry Polachek
26	Sylvania	3/56	Camillus NY	Edgar G. Dunn*
27	Metropolitan Life #2	5/56	New York NY	John Finelli
28	Metropolitan Life #3	5/56	New York NY	John Finelli
29	Sperry Gyroscope	6/56	Great Neck NY	Phil Toll
30	Electronic Supply Office	7/56	Gentile AFB, Dayton	Ernie Miller
31	Rem Rand Int'l Division	8/56	Battelle Inst, Frankft	Carl Hammer
32	Harvard University	8/56	Cambridge MA	Howard Aiken
33	Carborundum	10/56	Niagara Falls NY	Wm. Ferguson*
34	McClellan AFB	10/56	Sacramento CA	Paul R. Walker
35	Great Northern RR	11/56	St. Paul MN	Bill Zimmerman
36	Arizona Public Service	11/56	Phoenix AZ	Jack Liecty
37	Univ. of Pennsylvania	2/57	Philadelphia PA	Sol Gorn
38	Rem Rand Accounting	4/57	Buffalo NY	George Smith
39	Department of Agriculture	8/57	Kansas City MO	George Reiser
40	Franklin Institute	1/57	Philadelphia PA	Don Houghton
41	Case Institute	10/57	Cleveland OH	Raymond J. Nelson
42	University of Chicago	11/57	Chicago IL	Edward Wallace
43	Pittsburgh Plate Glass	9/58	Pittsburgh PA	Bill Hollis
44	Rem Rand UNIVAC Eng.		19th & Allegheny	Nat Brisgone
45	Rem Rand UNIVAC Eng.		19th & Allegheny	Nat Brisgone
46	Rem Rand UNIVAC Eng.		19th & Allegheny	Nat Brisgone

"UNIVAC I installations." #2011001, Jean Jennings Bartik Papers.

The Cardex salesmen droned on all morning and most of the afternoon, trying to make the case for keeping their old system. Late in the afternoon, Paul said his piece. Paul was a very nice man, both charming and extremely professional, a true gentleman and someone I instantly liked. Finally, at the end of the day, I gave my proposal and it was a tremendous success. When the commanders and lieutenant commanders in attendance saw that the system was completely computerized and how easy it would be to do the whole operation on the UNIVAC, they went wild. They answered each other's objections. They praised the plan. They expanded on it. We had a grand time and for one of the first times in a long time I felt my efforts had value and were appreciated.

The Mayflower Hotel had a dinner for the men, but the organizers wouldn't let me go to it because they said I "would be offended by some of the jokes." I went to dinner with a commander's wife in the bar of the same hotel where the dinner was held for the salesmen and the Navy men. After their dinner, many of the Navy men rushed from the banquet room down to where we were to find out more about the UNIVAC. They were really excited.

Remington Rand never let me give another presentation. I would go out with Mr. Bledsoe, the assistant manager. He would give a presentation, which I would sit through in agony as he came close to telling one whopper after another. He almost implied it had magical qualities, as opposed to programs that accomplished tasks. I was there to answer technical questions, which I did. Mr. Bledsoe had sold pulpits to churches, so of course he was much more qualified than me to give the presentations. Remington Rand thought the enthusiastic response to my first and only presentation had been a fluke. I wasn't a salesperson, so I didn't try to sell the UNIVAC. I simply described it in detail, and the response took care of itself. The company didn't understand that selling a UNIVAC required a technical person with knowledge about applications, software, and hardware.

The next year, Bill took a job with Remington Rand in Philadelphia, necessitating a move back to that city, so I quit Mr. Goodman's employ—not that he cared one way or the other. When I said good-bye to Remington Rand in June of 1951 after ten months with the company, I was never so happy to leave a job in all my life. I knew Remington Rand was giving away the leadership in the computing industry. They lost it and they deserved to lose it. I was heartsick to think how we at Eckert-Mauchly had worked so hard to design and build a wonderful system that was being totally misunderstood and left unsold.

The Remington Rand management was arrogant and obtuse, and its competitor eventually seized advantage. Initially, IBM came out with some systems that were better than punched card equipment but still not impressive. Before long, however, IBM's first really good system hit the market. The IBM 360, which was designed by Gene Amdahl and Fred Brooks, was that system. IBM developed an upwardly compatible line of computers with standard I/O interfaces and provided good customer support. IBM, in my humble opinion, deserved to win the computer wars.

Despite Remington Rand's ineptitude at selling the UNIVAC, the model did eventually catch on, and forty-six were sold. The name "UNIVAC" became synonymous with computer, much as "Mac" is today. But during the months I was there, the greatest computer the world had yet seen was being used by wise-cracking salesmen as a gambit to sell typewriters and adding machines.

Starting in 1951 and continuing until 1967, I was a housewife. Bill was working at Remington Rand in Philadelphia, and the company did not allow husbands and wives to work at the same site. Remington Rand offered me a chance to work offsite with Bob Shaw, whose clearance was clouded so that he was not able to work at the main site either. But I was generally unhappy with the company and its attitude toward women and computers, so I decided to take time off to have a family. Bill and I lived in an apartment at Chew and Wister in Germantown for a year, then we bought a house in Upper Moreland Township at 613 Delft Lane, just outside Hatboro. During that time, I did not follow the computer industry at all.

When I left Remington Rand, I was disenchanted and wanted to do something totally outside the technology field. Bill and I decided not to have children right away and so I had to come up with something to occupy my time. I took flower-arranging courses and did some flower arranging just for myself. I also tried my hand at painting, but I gave it up because I found I had no talent whatsoever. I became a Democratic committee-woman for Upper Moreland Township and then for Jenkintown, as well as active in the League of Women Voters. I also did volunteer work at Children's Hospital, at Nineteenth and Fitzwater Streets in Philadelphia. Weekday mornings, I worked in the plaster clinic, and in the afternoons I did a survey for the director of the hospital. Bill and I eventually bought and redid a very large Victorian house in Jenkintown, Pennsylvania, a suburb of Philadelphia.

I had three children: Tim was born in 1954, Jane in 1959, and Mary in 1961. I loved being a mother. I was twenty-nine years old when I had Tim. I'd

Mary, Tim, and Jane Bartik at the beach in Cape May, New Jersey, ca. 1967–68. Photo by Jean Jennings Bartik.

had a wonderful career, had eaten my way through all the good restaurants in Philadelphia and Bucks County, been to all the new plays, and was now ready to have fun with my children, which I did. I loved watching them play. I always took a nap when they did. I hurried through my housework so I could be outside with my children. When I heard women complain about being tied down with children, I couldn't understand it. Most of the time, it was playtime to me. My children and I loved science fiction and we watched *Star Trek* together on TV—it was Bartik Must-See TV. I remember laughing at the lightweight, wireless, briefcase-like computer they once used on the show, especially when I thought about all the cables involved with the ENIAC and the UNIVAC. A popular gathering place for the neighbor kids was our backyard with its extensive set of playground equipment. One time I counted forty kids in our yard and I had to declare one to three o'clock every afternoon as quiet time. I had no trouble with the kids honoring this rule.

I did not see much of any of the other ENIAC programmers during those years. Marlyn had married her dentist and was living in Trenton, New Jersey. Ruth had married Adolph Teitelbaum and moved to Texas. Fran had married Homer Spence and was living in Syosset, New York. Betty had married John Holberton and they lived in Washington, D.C. Kay McNulty married John Mauchly in 1948. As you can imagine, I was very happy for my two friends. You wouldn't think a logical-minded scientist like John could find passion beyond the laboratory, but John found it with Kay and Kay with him. They were a remarkable couple who were not only lovers but best friends. Kay and John lived in Ambler, Pennsylvania. Even though Kay was close to me, I didn't see her much after she married John.

The main reason we didn't socialize a lot was because my husband wasn't comfortable around John and Kay. I think Bill was jealous of my relationship with John and Kay. Since I sincerely wanted my marriage to work, I never pushed to socialize with them, but I continued to keep in touch.

While Kay and I didn't see each other very often, we had the same obstetrician and pediatrician. Dr. Randall, the pediatrician, was a lifelong friend of Pres Eckert, so that is why we used him. Kay had given me the name of her obstetrician. When Tim, my first child, was born at Abington Hospital in March 1954, Kay was in the hospital also, having Gini, her third child.

My husband was designing core memories for computers, but we never really discussed computer logic. During these

John Mauchly and Kay McNulty on the day they wed in 1948. Courtesy of Bill Mauchly.

years, problems had cropped up in my marriage. From the beginning, I had been very impressed with Bill because he was quite bright. He had an especially good memory and could fix dates to almost any historical event you could name. That intrigued me, because my memory for dates and odd facts was always poor. In addition, he was well read and could talk about almost anything. I was further impressed that he took voice lessons for fun and sang Paul Robeson and Enzio Pinza songs. He sang in a choir and had been an Eagle Scout. But as it turned out, Bill was what was at the time called a manic-depressive (now the condition is called bipolar disorder). Bill had never gone to see a doctor about it until I brought it up to our family doctor in about 1952. This doctor sent him to a psychiatrist, who said his condition could be helped by psychiatric treatment. Bill went to him once or twice a week for four years. Then that doctor switched to child psychology and referred Bill to another psychiatrist, whom he saw from one to six times a week until Bill left Philadelphia in 1968. At that time, there were few medications available to treat manic depression, but when the doctor did prescribe medications, Bill didn't take them. Bill's health insurance paid only half the cost of treatment for mental illness, and there was a ceiling on the amount that it would pay. That limit was reached in 1966, and thereafter his treatment put a strain on the budget as well as the family.

Almost as bad was that he was the only child of a doting mother and a critical father. His mother pronounced him perfect and delighted in waiting on him hand and foot. His father criticized everything he did. After we were married, Bill's father would say such things as, "I don't know how you ever got Jean to marry you. She is smarter than you are." Bill never sat in a room alone with his father. If I was there, he would stay in the room, but if I left and went in the kitchen, Bill was right behind me. I understood a lot of Bill's problems, but his assumption that I liked waiting on him hand and foot was a major source of tension. I grew up in a large family where self-reliance was rewarded. Why would I want anyone doing things for me if I could do them myself? Our family cultures were completely different. The less I wanted to do for him, the less he felt I loved him. The more he expected me to do for him, the less I liked him.

When I was forty years old, I decided I was going to fix my marriage or get a divorce. I discussed it with my husband and gave us two years. During this time, I went to the University of Pennsylvania and got a master's degree in education with a major in English. If we stayed together, I would teach school. If not, I would go back into the computer industry, where I could make enough money to support my children.

The event that finally caused me to leave was that I suddenly lost my hearing. Bill talked to me and it actually sounded like static on a radio. I suppose it was psychosomatic because of the stress I was under, similar to the tic I had briefly developed while working under the stressful environment at the aircraft plant. I realized that if I cracked up, my children would have no one to care for them, so I began going to a marriage counselor, who suggested some things to try to deal with Bill. None worked, so she helped me get myself emotionally strong enough to leave. No one in my family had ever gotten a divorce before. For most of my marriage I had never considered divorce; it was unthinkable. However, the two-year deadline that I had given us was up, and we hadn't fixed the marriage, so I left my husband and took our children with me in February 1968.

I had decided to go back to work after I had completed my master's degree in August 1967. By that time I had made the decision to divorce Bill, and I needed to go back into the computer field to earn enough money to support myself and the children. By that point, Bill had become unreliable. I also had to earn money to build up a nest egg. I had a small savings at one time, but when Bill went into Philadelphia's Albert Einstein Hospital, I had to use it to pay bills. When I made this decision, I didn't know what kind of jobs to apply for, programming or logical design. Sperry UNIVAC (the Sperry Corporation had bought out Remington Rand in 1955) would have hired me except Bill was still employed there, and the company still had a policy of not hiring husbands and wives at the same site. Consequently, I decided to apply for a job at the Auerbach Corporation for Science and Technology. I had worked with its founder, Isaac Auerbach, as well as many of the people at his company, when we were all with Eckert-Mauchly. A handsome, taut-faced man with square features, black plastic-rimmed glasses, and black hair parted on the side and combed neatly back, Isaac had started the Auerbach Corporation as a consulting company, and from there he got into publishing reports on computers.

Not only had I known Isaac Auerbach back in the days of UNIVAC I, but I was in the room with Pres Eckert the day in 1949 when the Burroughs Corporation called Pres for a recommendation on Isaac, who had applied for a job with Burroughs. The conversation was very stiff, with Pres not wanting to badmouth Isaac, but not wanting to recommend him either. You see, Isaac's ego was bigger than Pres's ego, and they had clashed at times. Isaac had felt that he should be made president of Eckert-Mauchly, with John heading up software and Pres heading up engineering. Although Isaac was very competent, the arrangement would never have worked, because Isaac would have wanted total control. Although Isaac, Paul Winsor, and Arnold Shafritz started the Auerbach Corporation together, Isaac truly ran the company. Feeling confident that I knew the key players at Auerbach and that Isaac knew of my abilities and previous position at Mauchly-Eckert, I applied at Auerbach, which had its headquarters in Philadelphia. Lou Wilson interviewed me. I knew Lou Wilson from Eckert-Mauchly, where he had been a physicist, an engineer, and, later, a liaison with customers.[2]

Lou was gracious, charming, and very bright. As manager of Auerbach's consulting group, he said that the company would hire me on the consultant side but that publishing was interested in hiring me. Intrigued, I took the elevator down to the fifth floor and was interviewed by Jack Hillegas, manager of publishing. Jack gave me an editing test and told me about what they did, which was to produce technical reports on computer equipment. Additionally, he showed me a report written on the IBM 360 by Bert Tartaro, an expert on mainframe programming who knew the 360's operating system better than most of IBM's own people.

Bert was one of Auerbach's editor/writers. I was very impressed with his report because it was analytical as well as descriptive.

After I had taken an editing test, Jack offered me a job as a technical editor. In that position, I would read and edit all the reports on new equipment, such as Tartaro's report on the 360.[3] The publishing group felt this was the best way to get me caught up with the computer industry. But I quickly found that conceptually I had no trouble at all because we had been so far advanced at Eckert-Mauchly with the UNIVAC and so I really enjoyed the position. All of the ideas on random-access storage, file processing, and ink jet printers that we had discussed so thoroughly seventeen years earlier were now being implemented.

When I arrived, Auerbach Publishers had three services: Auerbach Standard Electronic Data Processing Reports (ASEDPR) for mainframes, Auerbach Data Handling Reports (ADHR) for small business systems and peripherals, and Auerbach Data Communications Reports (ADCR) for modems, multiplexers, and private branch exchanges (PBXs). Auerbach was starting a new service, Auerbach Small Scientific and Control Computer Reports (ASSCCR). Each service sent out a monthly supplement, which would include reports on new equipment, updates on old equipment, and a sheet on new developments. Soon Jack switched me over to the new publication on Small Scientific and Control Computers. Digital Equipment Corporation (DEC) had just introduced the PDP-9, and that was the first report I wrote.[4]

Over my first two or three years at Auerbach, I became increasingly aware that the firm had no women managers. All the women employed there were either secretaries or technical writers. Even though I had received outstanding performance reviews each year, I was never promoted. In fact, I had been given the responsibility of training one man as an editor, and then he was promoted above me. In 1971, the local office of the EEOC (Equal Employment Opportunity Commission) had posted flyers advertising for women to meet with it on the possibility of filing cases against employers in the Philadelphia area for discriminating against women. Bernedette Everlof and Eleanor Gebremedan, who also worked at Auerbach, joined me to express our concerns about Auerbach with an EEOC representative.

The EEOC representative spoke to us sternly and candidly, telling us that we needed documentation and records. He said, "Do you always produce your reports on time?" We replied, "No, we are always given more work than we can do in the time allotted." He then told us that would be used against us and we would "be declared incompetent" without documentation. He went on to point out that evaluation of our work was subjective and we would be crucified without dates, times, and events. From that day on, I kept records.[5]

In the meantime, more and more small computers were introduced, as companies sprang up everywhere. These small computers were popularly called minicomputers, and by 1970, about fifty were being introduced each year. Many companies had applications that did not require a mainframe computer but could do very well with a minicomputer. The applications included the control of a process or a special-purpose accounting system. The Auerbach Small Scientific and Control Computer Reports (ASSCCR) were not keeping up with the dozens of new products in the field, so I proposed that we change the name to Auerbach Minicomputer Reports and use new report formats to make reports easier to produce. My suggestion was implemented—I made that sound easy, but it wasn't.

I proposed my idea for the minicomputer reports to my manager, Jim Brown, and Jim discussed my suggestion with his boss, Fred Mumma. They turned it down, saying, "If management in its wisdom wanted minicomputer reports, it would create them." As you may imagine, I was crushed. Later, I attended a farewell dinner for Lou Wilson, who was leaving Auerbach, at which I sat next to Arnold Shafritz, who was a vice president of the Auerbach Corporation. I had met him before, although I did not really know him. But he had a fine reputation as a bright, competent leader, and a straight shooter. He probably knew of me through Isaac Auerbach and through Paul Winsor, deputy technical director, who also knew my history as a programmer. Arnold was very cordial and, naturally, he asked me questions about work. I told him about how we were not keeping up with the industry and that I wanted to create minicomputer reports, but that Jim and Fred had squashed the idea. He told me not to let the two men stand in my way, but to send a memo directly to Ed Block, who was vice president of Auerbach Publishers. I took Arnold's advice and, all of a sudden, activity about minicomputer reports became frenzied. I had worked out how the reports would be different from those we were doing: not only would they be shorter, but they would have different categories of data and a very short form for new announcements. This briefer format meant that if a supplement had to go out in only a day or two, I could go to a press conference to learn about a new minicomputer, stay up most of the night, and produce a report on it.

Jim Brown and Fred Mumma punished me, however, for going over their heads by making Peter Wallace, an editor from England, the editor of the minicomputer reports instead of me. My only consolation was that I got to see Jim Brown fired by Isaac Auerbach because of his management style; he had removed himself from the direct writing and editing process, which was the heart of the company.

Before Brown was fired, he assigned me to work under Wallace, who basically ignored me and knew nothing of my plans for the format of the new reports. If it hadn't been so unfair, it would have been funny. People essentially ignored Wallace and went to me to ask questions about service. Finally, Wallace was quietly moved to another job and I was promoted to the position of editor of the Auerbach Minicomputer Reports. I like to think that I put a crack in the glass ceiling so many women found themselves bumping up against—it was a small crack, but a crack nevertheless. Despite that, I was still paid less than my male peers. I was also stuck, having climbed as high as a woman at Auerbach could at that time. A promotion to managing editor was out of the question.

I was at Auerbach for more than eight years, all spent working on small computers. Over the last few years of my time there, the use of contract workers rather than full-time employees had gained popularity. Isaac liked not having to pay employee benefits, plus with contract workers he could use editors on whatever service needed them at the moment. In fact, Isaac promoted Tom Rullo, who managed special projects, to vice president and managing editor for coming up with the idea. The staff for each service became a skeleton, with only a senior editor, an assistant or two, and contract writers. In theory, it worked, but in actuality writers could not be switched from one service to another because they didn't know anything about the equipment. Some just copied manuals for their articles.

Being a senior editor on a service with contract writers was not fun. There was a horrendous amount of work trying to whip manuscripts into publishable condition. One section of each report gave an analysis of the piece of equipment, covering its good points and bad points and where it fit into the overall industry. For most subscribers, this was one of the most valuable parts of a report. These contract writers (or "editors," as they were called) produced very little analysis. In general with these contract writers, I had to write the analysis for most reports, check the data (which were frequently wrong), and offer explanations of why things were done the way they were in the design of the product. Publishing's reshuffling of the services to use contract writers began in 1972, so my last four years at Auerbach were hell. I was determined either to leave Auerbach or file a suit against the company for discrimination against women.

In 1975, I went to the EEOC again, but this time with my records in hand. Everything was documented—my productivity, achievements, conversations with bosses, and others' promotions over me. The EEOC representatives told me that I had a suit and would win. However, I feared that if I sued it would mean the end of my career in the computer field. I felt it would be a public service to women to force the company to reform its practices, but I was divorced and leery of the financial toll a lawsuit might take. So instead of pursuing the lawsuit, I began job hunting. I was disappointed in myself, but I had three children to support and my children always came first.

After I left Auerbach, I was able to get my next job in computing due to the reports I had written on two 32-bit word minicomputers from Interdata, the Model 7/32 and the Model 8/32. I thought they were wonderful and wrote enthusiastic reports about them. One time, Interdata's marketing manager, Bill Sweet, had said to me, "I wish you worked for me." In May 1976, I was going to New York to attend a press conference about the release of a new minicomputer. The offices of Interdata, in Oceanport, New Jersey, happened to be on my way, so I called up Bill and told him that I was considering leaving Auerbach. He asked me to stop by on my way to New York. When I got to Bill Sweet's office, he closed the door and locked it, and said, "You are not leaving until we work out a job for you." Within an hour, I was hired as the product line manager of the Megamini, the company's newest 32-bit processor, and the executive vice president had signed the job contract and the salary offer.

When I resigned from Auerbach a few days later, Isaac Auerbach came into my office, sat down, and said, "I never thought you'd ever leave me." I replied, "Why wouldn't I leave you?" I explained to Auerbach that I hadn't been promoted or assigned anything challenging for the last four years. I also expressed my dismay at having to rewrite so much of the work produced by the contract writers. Later, at my farewell party, I made a little speech: "They say that the two happiest days of a person's life are the day you take a job and the day you leave it. Today is the second happiest day of my life." There was general laughter at this, but Isaac cringed when I said it. I think Isaac knew that I had been treated unfairly and was sorry. But he had done nothing to change the "All-Boys Club" atmosphere at Auerbach and thus, I had little sympathy for his moment of mortification.

Despite my resentment of Auerbach's discriminatory practices, I had a generally good impression of Isaac Auerbach. I thought he was a smart man, and I respected him for his many accomplishments. In 1961, Isaac had helped found the American Federation of Information Processing Societies (AFIPS), which in 1990, two years before his death, was dissolved and superseded by FOCUS, the Federation on Computing in the United States. As president of AFIPS, he was the main force behind that organization's funding of the Smithsonian Institution project to record interviews with the early computer pioneers. These can be found in the Smithsonian's Computer History Collection.

A tireless promoter of the industry, Isaac also tried to get a series of books written from the point of view of each of the early pioneers. While at Harvard, he had written his thesis on the history of computing and the subject had always been of great interest to him. Isaac wanted to have professional writers write the books on the computing pioneers, and he tried to raise the money for this project. All of the leading companies offered to contribute money for the project except Sperry UNIVAC, the successor to Remington Rand. For some reason Sperry's officers didn't recognize that they had the most to gain of any company, since Sperry UNIVAC was descended from Eckert-Mauchly. IBM was being branded a monopoly, so IBM was careful to explain that it would give only its fair share. The project never got off the ground because of Sperry UNIVAC's lack of cooperation. In later years, I talked to Isaac many times about the history of computing. He wanted to leave a legacy as having made a contribution in the preservation of that history and certainly the Smithsonian records are a tribute to him.[6]

When I left Auerbach, I had lunch with the vice president and told him the company was ripe for a lawsuit for its lack of women managers. I said that I had been told by EEOC that I had a legitimate suit and would win if I filed one. I told him that I didn't intend to file one, but I suggested that they change their ways and hire some women managers. Shortly afterward, Auerbach Publishing finally promoted a woman to be managing editor. It was none other than Bernedette Everlof, who only a few years before, along with Eleanor Gebremedan, had met with me at the EEOC to air our grievances. I like to think that my words had some impact on Auerbach's decision.

My new position as the product line manager of the Megamini at Interdata was a mixed blessing. The company's top salesmen ignored the product managers and got what they wanted from the president, executive vice president, and other top management people. I experienced several product problems where the salesmen would bypass me with their solutions. Interdata had started out as a company that produced 16-bit word minicomputers and became quite successful at it. However, the company made the mistake of resting on its laurels. A Japanese company had made a chip that implemented Interdata's 16-bit minicomputer logic, and that company offered to sell it to Interdata. But the higher-ups at Interdata decided they didn't need it, so they continued to produce discrete-element circuit boards. This worked for a while, but more and more minicomputers were coming on the market using integrated circuit microprocessors.

Interdata was still selling a lot of its 16-bit minicomputers, but the profit margins shrank to almost zero as the company had to cut prices to remain competitive. The firm's 32-bit Megamini had only one competitor and its profit margins were high, so most of the company profits came from the Megamini. The marketing manager, Bill Sweet, noted this and came up with a plan to phase out work on the 16-bit mini and put all of the development funds into the Megamini. I supported his plan.

When Bill's plan was presented to top management, the president was livid. He wanted a plan to bring back the 16-bit mini, not phase it out. Bill and I were the only two backing the Megamini as the main product. As a consequence, Bill was forced out the door and I got the sideways arabesque.[7] Bill left to become a marketing manager for National Semiconductor and encouraged me to go with him. Since Bill was leaving and I was concerned for my future at the company, I decided to discreetly look for another job. For Bill's farewell party, the organizers asked me to give a speech. Since I was planning on leaving Interdata, I decided to create a sensation with my speech.

Men are always bragging about how they put their "balls to the wall" for the company—in other words, go all out. The men would toss the expression out like a badge of honor. What could a woman say that would be comparable to balls? I thought and thought and finally considered that "putting my tits in a wringer" might work. Anyway, I wrote a satirical speech that said if another marketing manager (here I gave a knowing nod to Bill, sitting up front) ever asked me to "put my tits in a wringer," I wasn't going to do it. "Our 'stupid' marketing manager," I said with heavy irony, "had it all wrong. He wanted to make a profit, while everyone knew that unit sales were what counted. Never mind if we had to give the minicomputers away, just think of the numbers!" As you can imagine, women just didn't say stuff like that in public, and the scandal of my speech was all over the company the next day. Of course, Bill was delighted by the furor I had caused. I'm sure he was also delighted when, shortly after 1973, Interdata's president was ousted due to his sorry profits on the 16-bit mini.

One of the funniest things that happened while I was with Interdata took place at an off-site three-day marketing and sales meeting. The retreat's purpose was to allow the marketing group to brief the sales force on the company's products, as well as allow the two groups to develop a rapport. One of the sessions had as its speaker John T. Molloy, author of the best-selling book *Dress for Success*. Interdata's president and executive vice president were noticeably absent at the start of this seminar. Molloy told the group how to dress to accomplish a particular purpose. "Wear beige if you want to appear understanding and comforting," he said. "Wear charcoal gray to be intimidating and powerful. Never wear brown. It is a nothing color. And never wear plaids—those are reserved for clowns. The all-purpose color is navy blue: it makes one appear sincere and perfect."

At this moment, in walked the president and executive vice president. They were not wearing beige to appear understanding and comforting, nor were they wearing charcoal gray to be intimidating and powerful. They were not even wearing navy to appear sincere and perfect. Instead, the president had on the most bizarre plaid jacket the room had ever seen, and the executive vice president a slightly more reserved plaid. It was as if two clowns—to use Molloy's term—had walked into the room on cue. We were all beside ourselves, shooting incredulous looks at each other and suppressing our laughter. As you may imagine, Molloy was speechless and chagrined.

Aside from the whole how-to-dress question, the three-day retreat also offered me an insight into how uncomfortable some men were when dealing with a woman in a business setting. I was the only woman present at the retreat. On the last day of the retreat, the organizers held a golf outing. I hadn't played golf since college, but my golf game wasn't bad. I could hit the ball a long way, although my putting left a lot to be desired. During the game, I was paired with a salesman, and he and I were matched against two men in our foursome. My partner played a horrible game of golf that day. As an excuse for his poor performance, he stammered that he was so flustered playing with a woman that he hadn't been able to concentrate on golf. I asked him why he was flustered, and the poor man said that he was afraid he would talk dirty or take a leak on a green or something. I guess that his dilemma just goes to show that women are truly the civilizing force. Little did he know that if I had wanted, I could have out trash-talked him any day of the week.

Having decided to leave Interdata and needing to support my family, I decided to accept a job as a marketing manager with Systems Engineering Laboratories (SEL) whose main offices were in Fort Lauderdale, Florida. However, I continued to look for a position that was more in line with what I wanted to do. Honeywell was setting up a competitive analysis department at its headquarters in Minneapolis, and its new manager asked me to come and be the manager of minicomputer competitive analysis. In August 1978, I accepted and bid farewell to Systems Engineering.

Honeywell used the matrix management system and had positions at the home office on the president's staff to mirror field positions. It had vice presidents of minicomputers and of small, medium-sized, and large systems, as well as a vice president of general administration, which included competitive analysis. The vice president of minicomputers had a man working on product planning for him. This man asked me to help him on planning minicomputer developments, and we worked together for a while. At Honeywell my manager was Bernedette Everlof, the same woman Auerbach had hired to manage the publishers group after I left.

One day the vice president said he was going to Billerica, Massachusetts, where the minis were made. He asked me (and the man I worked with) to create a report for him about what we had planned that he could read on the plane ride. So we put together a report and I presented it to the vice president. At the time, I honestly didn't think my presenting him the report was a big deal, but Bernedette approached me and asked me why I had not given her the report to present to the vice president. I replied, "Why should I? The vice president asked me to create a report for him." As the words left my mouth, I realized Bernedette wasn't pleased with my response. The simple fact of the matter was that the vice president—not Bernedette—had asked us to write the report for him, and my brain for some reason couldn't understand why she would even want a report created specifically for him.

The next day, I was called into the personnel department, where the personnel manager said that my loyalty to the company was in question. Bernedette had told the personnel manager that I had sent a company confidential report up to Billerica, where it could be given to anyone. The personnel department manager was very close-minded and never asked for my side of the story. I knew I was in big trouble because proving loyalty is almost impossible.

Bernedette's manager was out of town, but the vice president of our group was there. I asked to see him, and he granted me a meeting that same day. When I met with him, I asked him if I could communicate with the vice president of minicomputers without going up the line through Bernedette, her manager, then the group vice president, and then over to the vice president of minicomputers. He said that I could. I explained that Bernedette was ticked with me for doing just that. He said he would write a memo clarifying the chain of command. In the meantime, he kept trying to get me to bad-mouth Bernedette, saying, "Are you sure this is not just a hen fight?"

The question was a bit condescending in light of the seriousness of my situation, but I didn't want to anger him, so I made sure to focus on the report and not complain to him or say anything negative about Bernedette. I told him the report, chain of command structure, and the question of my loyalty were the only things I was concerned about. The vice president did send the memo as promised, so that I wasn't in violation of the chain of command. In the end, Bernedette's manager and the vice president sided with me, and Bernedette disliked me after that, and I knew I had inadvertently created an enemy.

Meanwhile, Elizabeth McKeoun, who had been a saleswoman at Auerbach when I was there, had gone on to work for DataPro, a competitor of Auerbach. With the backing of Ziff-Davis Publishing, she set up another competitor of Auerbach called Data Decisions. Data Decisions claimed to produce coverage on all computer equipment in one service—from mainframes to minis to peripherals to communications and to software. As time passed, this all-encompassing range became impossible to deliver, so the company began to produce other products. Fonnie Reagan, who like Liz McKeoun had also worked at Auerbach before joining Data Decisions, called me to help him develop a communications product. I had been involved with local area networks because minicomputers were the first computers to be interconnected using networks. A number of minicomputer companies had local area networks, such as Xerox with its Ethernet and Wang with its Wangnet. Feeling uncomfortable at Honeywell since my clash with Bernedette, I accepted the job offer.

In July 1980, I left Minneapolis and Honeywell behind and joined Data Decisions in Cherry Hill, New Jersey, which was just over the Delaware River from Philadelphia. I must admit it was fun developing the communications reports at Data Decisions. I wrote on the large communications networks that the major mainframe manufacturers developed to connect all their equipment together. IBM had Systems Network Architecture (SNA), UNIVAC had Distributed Communication Architecture (DCA), and Honeywell had Distributed System Architecture (DSA). Besides these networks, the military connected various university projects together using ARPANET (Advanced Research Projects Agency Network).

At this time, *ComputerWorld* was the most popular newspaper for computers, and I went to lots of press conferences with its reporters. In fact, one of my assistants at Auerbach had become a reporter for *ComputerWorld*. I noticed that there was no comparable magazine or newspaper for communications. There was *Data Communications* magazine, an elegant and well-done monthly, but nothing quick and dirty. Consequently, I proposed a weekly newspaper to be called

CommunicationsWorld. My idea for *CommunicationsWorld* was turned down by Ziff-Davis's vice president, who said that Ziff-Davis liked to buy a rundown publication and build it up rather than start a new publication. I was very disappointed at hearing this, for there *was* no rundown publication on communications, and I was convinced that my proposed publication would have been successful.

On November 13, 1985, I arrived at work to be told, along with everyone else in the company, that as of nine a.m. we were out of business. We had been sold to McGraw-Hill, and they had killed the company. McGraw-Hill apparently only wanted the Data Decisions subscriber list. I enjoyed working at Data Decisions and was disappointed that it was forced to close its doors. I was now sixty-one years old. I had bumped my head repeatedly on the glass ceiling over the years and now had another thing besides my gender against me—my age. No one knew who I was, history had forgotten about the contributions of the ENIAC women, and job offers from big computer-related corporations had dried up.

CHAPTER 7
The Trial to Overturn the ENIAC Patent

Several months before I took the position with Data Decisions, my dear friend and mentor John Mauchly died in Abington, Pennsylvania, on January 8, 1980. I cried at his loss and ached for Kay. When John Mauchly died, the world lost a truly great man—a man to be respected and admired for his brilliance, his integrity, his kindness, and his contributions to the world. You see, John Mauchly didn't just launch a single computer, he launched the entire computer industry. No one can take that away from him. I dare anyone to even try.

I was greatly saddened by John Mauchly's loss, and upset by the unfair treatment that he had received from the legal system and the computer industry in the decades before and after his death. In 1973, the controversial U.S. federal court case *Honeywell v. Sperry Rand* invalidated Mauchly and Eckert's 1964 patent on the ENIAC and placed the electronic digital computer into the public domain. The case pitted two industry giants against each other, the Sperry Rand Corporation and the Honeywell Corporation. Sperry Rand, which had come to hold the patent through a series of acquisitions and mergers, charged Honeywell with patent infringement and demanded royalties. Honeywell, who filed a counter suit, charged Sperry Rand with monopoly and fraud, and sought to invalidate the ENIAC patent. The trial began on June 1, 1971, and was presided over by U.S. District Court Judge Earl R. Larson in Minneapolis, Minnesota. I was deposed by both sides; however, neither contacted me after the depositions, and I was not asked to testify at the trial. I think all of the ENIAC women should have at least testified as character witnesses on John's behalf.

First, let me say that I thought it was absurd that anyone would think that Honeywell, of all companies, could overturn the ENIAC patent. Honeywell wasn't even very competitive in the mainframe market. I was at Auerbach and based in Philadelphia when Honeywell brought the suit and geared up for its onslaught. Paul Winsor, who had been at Eckert-Mauchly while I was there, was at Auerbach with me, and it seemed to me that he turned into a full-time consultant for Honeywell as the case prepared to go to trial.

Winsor had been a young hotshot from MIT, where he had won a National Science Award. Pres Eckert had wanted to go there, but his mother didn't want him to be that far away from home, so she told him that his family couldn't afford to send him there. Believing his mother's financial claims, Pres agreed to go to the Moore School of Electrical Engineering at the University of Pennsylvania and remain close to home. In later years, after he found out that his mother's story wasn't true, he said he was lucky his mother had kept him at home, because the Moore School was the best place for him to be at that time.

Paul Winsor was very bright, and he had gone from Eckert-Mauchly to Burroughs. From there he joined Isaac Auerbach and Arnold Safritz in founding the Auerbach Corporation for Science and Technology to do consulting and build computers. The consulting business took off quickly because the computer industry was expanding. Companies wanted to buy computers and use them, but most did not know how. The Auerbach Corporation showed them how. The consultants for Auerbach made so many comparison charts of different computers' characteristics that the company decided to sell them, giving birth to the Auerbach Reports and to Auerbach Publishing.

Paul had wanted to build computers, and he knew early on that many applications did not require a mainframe computer; customers could solve some of their application problems with a small, inexpensive computer. He wanted to design and build such a computer, which would have been a forerunner of the minicomputer. Unfortunately for Paul, the Auerbach Corporation had so much consulting business that nobody else in the firm saw a need to build any hardware.

As Paul continued to consult with Honeywell on the lawsuit, I began to argue with him about the merits of the case. Paul told me that he had done crucial work on the UNIVAC cycling unit but that when, after he left the company, Eckert-Mauchly applied for the patent on it, his name was not included on the patent application. Paul reasoned that if Eckert-Mauchly would cheat him out of his patent, why wouldn't Mauchly cheat Atanasoff out of his? Paul was very angry about the fact that his name had not been on the Eckert-Mauchly patent for the

UNIVAC cycling unit and seemed pleased at the prospect of getting even with both men. Paul did have a valid point—his name should have been on the patent application even though he had left the company. In later years, Paul softened his view considerably, saying that he supposed Eckert and Mauchly's patent attorney had just provided them with bad counsel. Paul also admitted to Kay that at the time, he had initially thought of the UNIVAC as a single device, the design of which belonged to John and Pres, and so had not insisted on having his name included in the patent. Both Kay and I had agreed with Paul that John and Pres should still have put his name on the patent regardless of any insistence on his part; however, by the time of this softer attitude and admission from Paul, the damage had long ago been done. Paul, you see, was Honeywell's expert witness. Unfortunately, the Sperry Rand/Honeywell trial was about big company lawyers working for their respective companies and not the individual employees.

In this big business versus another big business patent trial, John Vincent Atanasoff, who had previously been a professor at Iowa State University, was proclaimed by the judge to be the inventor of the first automatic electronic digital computer. John Mauchly and Atanasoff had met, but according to Kay and ENIAC co-inventor Pres Eckert, John had thought up the idea for his electronic computer prior to ever meeting Atanasoff. If anything, that meeting may have simply helped John to cement his own separate designs and plans. The latter, of course, is just my opinion, but it is grounded in the knowledge of the many conversations and working experiences I had with John, which were long before the issue of patents was ever raised.

Overturning the 1947 ENIAC patent was based on two major points that tested the rights of Eckert and Mauchly to the original patent. While John and Pres were acknowledged as the co-inventors of the ENIAC, the first point dealt with the origin of ENIAC's design. The second point dealt with the U.S. Patent Office's One-Year-Rule, that a patent application must be filed within one year of the first public disclosure.

The first point that the ENIAC was based on the Atanasoff-Berry Computer (ABC) machine was hard for anyone to believe because of the drastic differences in design. For instance, the ENIAC used ring counters to perform decimal arithmetic while the ABC was designed around binary adders. Of course, the ENIAC was programmable and could be reconfigured to solve a multitude of different problems, whereas the single purpose ABC machine was designed to only solve linear equations. In fact, the ENIAC could be configured, and was configured, to be a stored-program computer. Additionally, the ENIAC used vacuum tubes for memory in its accumulators, while the ABC machine used a worm-gear-driven drum with capacitors.[1] The last difference permitted the ENIAC to operate at full electronic speeds, while the design of the ABC device was throttled to the speed of a mechanical rotating drum.

The second point dealing with the One-Year-Rule was unfair because the U.S. Patent Office had considered the ENIAC eligible for patent and, after the U.S. Patent Office had taken many years to deliberate the matter, they had granted the patent to Eckert and Mauchly in 1964 (U.S. Patent 3,120,606). John and Pres had applied for the patent in June 1947 once they felt the ENIAC was declassified and they were eligible to file without violating security restrictions.

Since lawyers played such a big role in the ENIAC patent trial, it is interesting to note that the University of Pennsylvania attorneys thought the work of Mauchly and Eckert had such tremendous monetary value that they essentially fired Mauchly and Eckert to protect the university's claim to that work. In contrast, the Iowa State University attorneys didn't feel that Atanasoff's ABC machine was worth the effort to acquire a patent nor did they acknowledge that it had any monetary value. Furthermore, the ENIAC was observed by a multitude of scientific experts, the media, and, through the media, the entire world, to be a working, successful electronic computer. In contrast, the ABC only had a few people, if any, observe even pieces of the ABC in operation. The ENIAC spawned a series of successful computers, whereas the ABC ended up being abandoned by its creator and Iowa State University.

Being in another part of the country, I did not follow the trial, but when Judge Larson rendered his verdict in 1973 I was shocked. He ruled that the 1964 Eckert-Mauchly patent on the ENIAC was invalid and put the invention of the electronic digital computer into the public domain.

I didn't understand how a judge could rule that the original ENIAC patent was invalid. The U.S. Patent Office had taken years to examine the case before issuing the patent, and they had apparently originally found that the ENIAC had not been in public use for a year before June 26, 1947, when John and Pres had applied for a patent on a "general-purpose" electronic computer. John and Pres did not believe running classified programs such as the Los Alamos calculations or demonstration programs constituted "public use." Also, it was their understanding that the ENIAC was not eligible for patent until it was officially delivered to Aberdeen in 1947. The ENIAC arrived in Aberdeen in January, but wasn't operational until August 1947.

Honeywell's lawyers, however, argued that the original problem Nick and Stan had run on the ENIAC in December 1945 was when the machine's public use began. I don't understand their reasoning, because Nick and Stan's problem was a classified, high-priority project for the U.S. government. It was totally secret, and I hardly think top-secret government projects fall into the category of "public use." How could that problem have been public use when even the ENIAC programmers themselves had not been told what the problem being run was about?

Could the demonstration of the ENIAC's capabilities to the scientific community on February 15, 1946, be considered public use? I don't think so, and the Patent Office had already decided on that question by issuing the patent in the first place. Judge Larson, however, thought otherwise and used that demonstration as the date when the ENIAC went into public use.

During the trial, the judge didn't only overturn the Patent Office's decision. He also made the decision to assert that the ENIAC was based on the prior technology of John Atanasoff.[2] John Vincent Atanasoff had come to Philadelphia in December 1940 to hear John Mauchly speak about a harmonic analyzer that Mauchly had built. Atanasoff in a letter dated March 7, 1941, invited Mauchly to visit him in Ames, Iowa, which he did. Later, Mauchly visited Atanasoff in Washington, D.C. in 1943, after Atanasoff left Iowa State to take a wartime assignment as Acoustic Division Chief with the Naval Ordnance Laboratory.[3] Mauchly and Atanasoff did communicate professionally, but that was true of everyone involved in the very small, tight-knit scientific community of individuals working in the pioneering field of computer technology at that time, particularly those involved with the military. Despite the small size of that professional community, few people had ever heard of Atanasoff before the ENIAC patent trial, except perhaps, ironically, John von Neumann. In 1945 the U.S. Navy had decided to try its hand at building a large-scale computer, apparently on the advice of von Neumann. Atanasoff had been assigned to head the project. According to journalist and author Clark R. Mollenhoff, Atanasoff asked Mauchly to help him with job descriptions for the necessary staff to assist him with the project.[4] Besides the computer project, Atanasoff was also assigned to design acoustic systems for monitoring atomic bomb tests, and that responsibility was made the priority. When Atanasoff returned from atomic bomb testing at Bikini Atoll in July 1946, the Navy's computer project had officially been shut down due to its lack of progress; and ironically, the project had been shut down on the advice of von Neumann.[5]

Before the trial, as far as I know, Atanasoff had never claimed to be the inventor of the electronic computer in the quarter century that had passed since the highly successful ENIAC was presented to the world. Atanasoff first got involved in the whole ENIAC patent issue around 1954 when one of IBM's attorneys sought out his help with a legal case. IBM wanted to break the Eckert-Mauchly patent on a revolving magnetic memory drum because IBM had been told that Atanasoff's machine had a revolving capacitor memory drum and thus, the Eckert-Mauchly revolving drum may have been prior art.[6] Astanasoff agreed to support IBM in their case, but after IBM entered a patent-sharing agreement with Sperry Rand (Sperry Corporation had acquired Remington Rand), they dropped the patent case and Astanasoff disappeared back into the woodwork.[7]

Honeywell filed its lawsuit against Sperry Rand in 1967, challenging the ENIAC patent, and once again Astanasoff's help was sought. According to rumors that were floating around the computer industry at the time of the patent trial, Atanasoff was offered $300,000 in royalties by Honeywell if the ENIAC patent was overturned. During the trial, Atanasoff's ABC device was introduced as prior art and Judge Larson agreed, ruling that the ENIAC had gotten many of its basic ideas from Atanasoff.[8] In the ruling, Judge Larson said, "Eckert and Mauchly did not themselves first invent the automatic electronic computer, but instead derived that subject matter from one Dr. John Vincent Atanasoff."[9] As you can imagine, everyone in the computer industry who had known John and Pres were outraged by the ruling.

When I went to work for Honeywell in 1978, I was told that Honeywell's legal guns had won the suit by pointing out inconsistencies in John Mauchly's testimony. The company's engineers had programmed a computer to scan his testimony to find places where he contradicted himself. I thought the idea extremely ironic since they had used the very technology John had invented to take him down!

I have no doubt that John most likely contradicted himself. He had aged considerably due to his battle with Hereditary Hemorrhagic Telangiectasia (HHT), which causes holes to form in the lungs and tumors to form in the brain. John's terrible illness had impacted him both physically and mentally by the time of the trial. He was in pain and tired easily. According to Kay, John's mental capacity was diminished and he wasn't as alert as he needed to be during the trial. Kay told me later that she felt Judge Larson had treated John shabbily and should have made allowances for his ill health. The judge had seemed to be biased against him, even calling into question John's lifelong interest in electrical engineering. I don't understand that at all. How could Judge Larson claim to know what John had been interested in from an early age? John had entered Johns Hopkins with the intention of studying electrical engineering. Only after he was there for a bit did he switch from engineering to physics.

Despite the outcome of the trial, I didn't think anyone would take the verdict seriously. In fact, the people in the computer industry with whom I discussed the trial always laughed at the idea that anyone but John Mauchly and Presper Eckert had invented the electronic computer. Everyone I spoke with thought the verdict was an aberration that would no doubt be overturned at some point. Consequently, it wasn't until years later that I began to realize the opposite had happened.

With that realization, I began whenever possible to speak out on John and Pres's behalf. As a former employee of Honeywell, I also had an insider's view of the power the company had wielded and the politics that may have been in play to influence the outcome of the trial. At the time of the patent trial, Honeywell was the largest employer in Minnesota. Honeywell, along with Dayton Hudson (now Target), Pillsbury, 3M, and Control Data Corporation, pretty much ran Minneapolis and the state. Honeywell fought hard to have the trial moved from Washington, D.C., to Minneapolis, and its fight was successful. While there is no proof of wrongdoing by Honeywell—and I'm not suggesting that they did anything legally wrong—I do believe the company wanted a friendly judge. In Minneapolis, where Honeywell was king, they could assure themselves of that very thing.

In the years after the ENIAC patent case, Arthur and Alice Burks wrote two books about John Mauchly and John Atanasoff. I never met Alice Burks, so I know nothing about her except what is in the book she wrote with her husband, Arthur. As for Arthur, when I knew him, he was quiet, unassuming, soft-spoken, and helpful. In 1988, Alice and Arthur Burks published *The First Electronic Computer: The Atanasoff Story* and in 2003, Alice (with Douglas R. Hofstadter) published *Who Invented the Computer? The Legal Battle That Changed Computing History*. In *The First Electronic Computer*, Arthur and Alice allege that John Mauchly and Presper Eckert were self-serving and wanted to keep all the glory that was ENIAC to themselves. They write,

> We think [Eckert and Mauchly] both were impressed with how far beyond the principles of the ABC their own devices went, and they [thought that they] were safe in appropriating these basic concepts because Atanasoff was showing no interest. We think, further, that they were greedy for fame and fortune and did not want to acknowledge any prior inventor.[10]

The Burkses do, however, say that von Neumann should have given credit to Pres Eckert in the EDVAC Report: "In our opinion, the First Draft Report should have carried the name of Eckert, at least, in addition to that of von Neumann (or acknowledged his contribution in some other way)."[11]

You bet von Neumann should have credited Pres! After all, Eckert developed the mercury delay line memory and the stored-program concept that von Neumann had described in the first draft of the report on the EDVAC. But the Burkses made no mention of Mauchly in connection with the "First Draft EDVAC Report," even though everyone involved in the creation of the EDVAC, including Pres Eckert, knew that Mauchly had contributed to the EDVAC architecture. In fact, John and Pres stated many times and in many articles that von Neumann merely restated their ideas in his "First Draft EDVAC Report" and Pres bluntly stated in 1977 that "Von Neumann was stealing ideas and trying to pretend work done at the Moore School was work he had done."[12] With his EDVAC report, von Neumann made a strong statement about not sharing credit for intellectual creativity. In my opinion, John von Neumann, with his June 30, 1945 report, set an unfortunate trend with regard to acknowledging the sources of original ideas.

The trouble with the Burkses' theme that Mauchly got his ideas from Atanasoff is twofold. First, everyone who knew Mauchly knew that he had always been interested in computers, and he was always thinking about computers and coming up with new ideas. Pres and John had a well-deserved reputation for being very helpful and very open in sharing their knowledge and expertise, and encouraging an atmosphere of free-flowing ideas among colleagues. Their colleagues, who benefited from Eckert and Mauchly's superb teaching skills, had noted how many people Eckert and Mauchly had inspired to do things they didn't even believe they could do. The fact that John and Pres freely shared their ideas does not mean that they would freely use someone else's ideas without acknowledging the other person. And I don't think John and Pres, who were in my opinion both ethical men, needed other peoples' ideas to complete their design for the ENIAC.

Second, and most importantly, Eckert and Mauchly's design for the ENIAC was fundamentally different from Atanasoff's design for the ABC—a design that, incidentally, didn't work. Any knowledge Eckert and Mauchly had of Atanasoff's work could only have reinforced their conviction that they needed to use a different design—and they did. And so all those who knew Eckert and Mauchly and their work thought that Justice Larson's pronouncing that the builder of the first electronic computer was Atanasoff was absurd. Adding to everyone's frustration was the fact that Judge Larson declared in his Finding 4 that Eckert and Mauchly were "the inventors" of the ENIAC, "the true and actual inventors" as named in their patent.

How could Judge Larson consider Atanasoff the inventor of the first electronic, general-purpose computer when the design for the ABC single-purpose calculator was not programmable, then declare Mauchly and Eckert to be the "true and actual inventors" of the ENIAC, which was the first electronic general-purpose, programmable computer? The ruling didn't make sense to anyone who understood what the ENIAC's capabilities were.

It is true that Mauchly had visited Atanasoff in Ames, Iowa, for five days in June 1941. This was after they had met when Atanasoff came to hear a December 1940 talk Mauchly gave on his harmonic analyzer and weather predictions. At that December meeting (as John told me later), John Mauchly told Atanasoff that he had made and was using what he called a "harmonic analyzer." John then went on to talk about his ideas for an electronic "programmable" computer. Atanasoff countered by saying he had an electronic computing machine that cost only two dollars per digit. He was reluctant to tell John much about it but invited John to come see it in Iowa.

John later took him up on that invitation and visited Atanasoff the following June, when he was driving to Ohio on personal business. From there, John went on to Iowa with his son, Jimmy. When he met with Atanasoff and saw the Atanasoff-Berry Computer, he found out that it was not electronic but electrical-mechanical, and that explained why it was so cheap. And it is interesting to note that one of the first press releases out of Ames, Iowa, on April 7, 1942, about the ABC machine, described Atanasoff's computing device as a "high speed calculator."[13] John said that the ABC did not run while he was there. In fact, he questioned whether the ABC ever really ran. After Atanasoff left in 1942 to work in Washington, D.C., Iowa State College dismantled and discarded the ABC, since it had little value to the university. The ABC was only rebuilt (allegedly to specification) well after the ENIAC patent trial and then it was not built by Atanasoff.[14] I find it funny and rather misleading that the picture on Alice Burks's 2003 book gives the false impression that it is the original ABC machine. Actually, the image is of the replica, which was built in 1997 at Iowa State University by a team of researchers led by John Gustafson. Obviously the materials, parts, and technical knowledge were far different and perhaps far superior to what had been available and known nearly sixty years earlier.

In any case, John Mauchly was interested in an all-electronic "programmable" general-purpose computer. The ABC was single-purpose, meant to solve linear simultaneous equations. Despite their different purposes, Mauchly and Atanasoff corresponded about computers for some time.

When I first knew Arthur, back when we were working on the ENIAC, we all liked him. But by the time of the trial and the Burkses' 1988 book, I was suspicious of Arthur's motives in working against John and Pres. With good reason. You see, John and Kay had told me about a late-night meeting between the two men. Later Arthur Burks flatly denied the meeting had ever happened, but John and Kay had told me about it at the time and John also testified about the incident in his deposition for the ENIAC patent trial. Kay and John conveyed to me that when they were attending the Association for Computing Machinery (ACM) conference in Washington, D.C., in August 1967, they returned to their hotel suite one evening and found a message for them saying Arthur Burks wanted to talk to John. This was shortly after Honeywell had filed its lawsuit against Sperry Rand, challenging the ENIAC patent. John rang Burks up and he came to the hotel. When Burks arrived, he said he wanted to talk privately to John, so Kay went into the bedroom. About five minutes later, John came roaring into the bedroom, furious, saying he would not be blackmailed. Burks had told John that a lawyer, who also had approached Bob Shaw and Kite Sharpless in 1964, had advised him that he could collect money from the royalties paid for use of the ENIAC patent if his name was on it.[15] By this time, 1967, Bob and Kite had died, so their names could not be added to the patent. Burks told John that if John put his name on the patent that he would testify for Sperry Rand in support of the ENIAC patent; if he didn't add Burks's name to the patent, then he would testify for Honeywell in support of their challenge to the patent.[16] The Patent Office had issued the ENIAC patent on February 4, 1964, more than two years before Arthur Burks met with John, and nearly seventeen years after John and Pres had applied for the patent on June 26, 1947.

After I told about this meeting and Arthur's offer in an online review of the Burkses' 1988 book, Arthur Burks responded by saying the meeting had never taken place (suggesting that Kay had invented it in a misguided attempt to defend her husband) and that John had never testified about it at the patent trial. Whether the meeting took place is a question of whose story one believes, but since John and Kay told me about it shortly after the meeting happened and I never had any reason to believe it wasn't true, I believe their story. I can also understand why Arthur Burks would deny having made this offer, since blackmail doesn't exactly enhance his reputation. As far as Arthur's statement that John did not testify about this, that simply is not true. John reports this incident on pages 1,426 through 1,430 of his deposition for the trial, saying that Arthur indicated that if he (John) could be persuaded that there was "propriety in these claims on his [Arthur's] part and on the part of others, that it would be very helpful if I [John Mauchly] would join with them, announce my help [in adding their names to the patent]; and that, on the other hand, if I [John Mauchly] did not, he [Arthur] thought that things would go very badly and my reputation would suffer, indeed."

One thing the Burkses mention in their book is how alert and articulate Atanasoff was when he testified at the ENIAC patent trial, and how tentative John was. What they neglect to mention is that John was very ill at the time of the trial. Because of his illness, he suffered horrendous nosebleeds every morning, which left him weak.

Even before the Burkses' 1988 *The First Electronic Computer*, they had made some claims about Eckert and Mauchly's role in the development of the computer. In an October 1981 article in *Annals of the History of Computing* titled "The First General-Purpose Electronic Computer," they credited Atanasoff with inventing the computer and discounted Eckert and Mauchly's work as being derived from the ABC. In response, Kay Mauchly wrote an article titled "John Mauchly's Early Years," published in the April 1983 *Annals of the History of Computing*, countering the Burkses' claims in their article and explaining that the invention of the ENIAC followed in a logical way from John's earlier interests and work. In their 1988 book, the Burkses state that only Mauchly's widow came forward to present his side of the story and that Eckert had not responded to their charges.[17] But Kay wrote her article with Pres Eckert's help; he came over to her house every day as she worked on it. Eckert knew everything in the article and concurred with every word.

Pres Eckert addressed the Atanasoff claims a number of times in other venues. In a 1986 speech at the Computer History Museum, he said,

> The best way to dismiss Atanasoff is to say the machine never really worked and he didn't have a system. That's the big thing about an invention—it's that you have a whole system that works. De la Rue tried to build a lamp in 1820, Starr in 1845, Swan in 1880, and Edison built a whole system that related to the generator that was only built five years before. Every one of Edison's ideas had been used before. Edison was a systems engineer and made it work.

"The ENIAC was built as a system that has led directly to today's computers," Pres also said. "I look back at the scenario and ask you to consider the following question: How would you like to see your life's work end up on a tenth of a square inch of silicon?"[18] Even though in his statement Pres was indicating that miniaturization in some way denigrated his work, today we know how important it is that the technology Mauchly and he conceived could be reduced in size and has facilitated a whole new industry of mobile digital computing and telecommunications.

Pres would occasionally say to Kay, "Let them tell their lies about what happened; then you and I will write a book telling what really happened." He also made a statement to that effect in an interview in *ComputerWorld* magazine. In that article, Pres stated,

> In the course of a patent fight, the other side brought up Atanasoff and tried to show that he built an electronic computer ahead of us. It's true he had a lab bench tabletop kind of thing and John [Mauchly] went out to look at it and wrote a memo, but we never used any of it. His [Atanasoff's] thing didn't really work. He didn't have a whole system. That's a big thing with an invention: You have to have a whole system that works.[19]

The last time Pres and Kay discussed writing their own book was in 1992. One night on a trip by limousine from New York to Ambler, Pennsylvania, they talked about what would be in the book, conversing while their spouses, Judith Eckert and Severo Antonelli (Kay's second husband) slept. Unfortunately, the next year Pres contracted leukemia, and the book was never written.

One additional detail added to the reaction of the trial verdict was that before applying for the ENIAC patent, Pres and John had asked the engineers (Arthur Burks, Harry Husky, Chuan Chu, Bob Shaw, and Kite Sharpless) if they had anything they wanted to patent. They said that they did not. At that time the engineers believed that the ENIAC was more than the sum of its parts and that the whole machine was entirely John and Pres's invention. Curiously, as previously stated, Judge Larson ruled that the ENIAC was the invention of Pres and John, which made it impossible for Burks and the other engineers to file any lawsuits. One of the judge's other rulings that seems unaccountable was his ruling that the two-accumulator demonstration model was an "automatic electronic digital computer" and that it was operational in July 1944. Many of the judge's rulings went against Remington Rand, and the aggregate of all these negative rulings seemed like overkill to me.

As Kay had said, the "curse of von Neumann" had a far reach. John von Neumann had essentially purloined the EDVAC design and, with Herman Goldstine's help, published the EDVAC report without giving credit to anyone else, thus making it impossible to obtain an EDVAC patent. On top of that, Arthur Burks made sure that Mauchly's reputation suffered after John turned down his nighttime offer of a deal. The Burkses even portrayed John as being very tentative in his testimony at the ENIAC patent trial, compared to Atanasoff, whom they described as alert and articulate, thereby suggesting that Atanasoff was a more truthful witness than John. What they neglect to mention is that John was very ill at the time of the trial. Because of his illness, John suffered horrendous nosebleeds every morning, which left him very weak. This and other details make me feel the Burkses were strongly biased against Mauchly and Eckert and that their book reflects, rather than a scholarly assessment of the historical fact, their personal animosity not only over Arthur's failed blackmail attempt, but also over Judge Larson's decision regarding the original ENIAC patent. Judge Larson ruled that Arthur Burks, Harry Husky, Jeffrey Chuan Chu, Bob Shaw, and Kite Sharpless were not co-inventors of the ENIAC—which the Burks probably considered yet another slap in Arthur's face.

CHAPTER 8
The ENIAC Women in the Spotlight

In November 1985, just three months shy of the fortieth anniversary of the introduction of the ENIAC, the six ENIAC programmers—Kay, Betty, Ruth, Marlyn, Fran, and I—had a reunion in Philadelphia. Joining us were Homer Spence, the maintenance engineer on the ENIAC, who was Fran's husband; John Holberton, manager for the ENIAC project, Betty's husband; and Adolf Teitelbaum and Phil Meltzer, Ruth and Marlyn's husbands. Kay also attended with her fiancé. Kay was indeed lucky in love. After John's death, she felt that she would never find someone else to love, but fate had different plans. Severo Antonelli, a famed Italian-American photographer, fell head over heels in love with Kay and began courting her. Kay eventually returned his affections and they were married in 1985. Kay and Severo had a very happy partnership until Severo died in 1996 after a struggle with Parkinson's disease.

Kay had arranged for us all to spend Saturday night at the Four Seasons, an elegant and modern hotel with dazzling views over the city. In these regal surroundings we felt as if we had come a long way indeed from our Spartan Army-barracks quarters at Aberdeen forty years earlier. It was the first time we had all been together since the early days, and we had a wonderful time catching up and reminiscing. We talked about our children, and I shared old memories with Ruth about her parents, who were by then deceased. We were all interested in Severo, who had enjoyed international acclaim since the 1920s for his work, and we were excited for Kay that she was getting married. Sadly, that 1985 reunion was also to be the last time all six of

Final picture of all six ENIAC female programmers together, November 1985. Back row, left to right: Ruth Lichterman Teitelbaum, John Holberton (Betty's husband), Betty Snyder Holberton, Homer Spence (Fran's husband), Jean Jennings Bartik. Front row, left to right: Fran Bilas Spence, Marlyn Wescoff Meltzer, and Kathleen (Kay) McNulty Mauchly Antonelli.

us ENIAC programmers would be together. The following March, Ruth became ill and learned that she had pancreatic cancer. She died that August.

In February 1986, the University of Pennsylvania's Moore School hosted a luncheon to mark ENIAC's fortieth anniversary. Kay addressed the gathering at the luncheon, speaking not as an ENIAC programmer but as the widow of John Mauchly. I sat beside Pres Eckert, who was no longer chief engineer at Sperry UNIVAC but instead now served as vice president, performing ceremonial tasks and forming liaisons with other countries. At that time, the Internal Revenue Service office in Philadelphia was having trouble with its new UNIVAC computers, which were making errors. I asked Pres how on earth UNIVACs could be making errors. Pres said that once he'd stepped aside as chief engineer, his successor had begun to loosen standards. The new chief engineer allowed engineers to design circuits for which the components had to work at 80 to 85 percent of their specified operating range instead of merely in the 50 to 55 percent range, as Pres had specified. Thus, when below-par components began to interact with each other, errors occurred. That chief engineer could never have built the ENIAC.

Pres gave speeches all over the world. He gave one titled "List of ENIAC Firsts" on April 15, 1991, to the Eckert Research International Corporation in Japan. In that address, Pres said that he felt that John Mauchly's concept of subroutines was his biggest contribution, while his [Pres's] biggest contribution was using a single memory system for a computer to hold both data and instructions.[1]

At that 1986 luncheon, I met Kathryn Kleiman for the first time.[2] She was then an undergraduate at Harvard University and writing her thesis on women in computing. After speaking with me and the other living ENIAC women programmers, Kleiman realized the historical significance of our contributions to early computing and wanted to get the word out about us to the public. Several years later, Kleiman would be responsible for getting Tom Petzinger, a columnist for the *Wall Street Journal*, interested in writing about the forgotten women of the ENIAC. In January 1996, as the fiftieth anniversary approached, Petzinger contacted me and said he would like to interview me. He came to my house and spent the entire day with me. He used no tape recorder; he just wrote notes. He also interviewed several of the other programmers and made plans to come to the fiftieth anniversary banquet on February 14, 1996. On that occasion, Kleiman had a separate reception for us with Petzinger. It was fortunate that Kathryn made a fuss over us, because the ENIAC programmers—there were four of us in attendance—were given no recognition at the banquet held at the Philadelphia Marriott. The theme was "A Celebration Honoring the Creation of Modern Computing." The program was rather slick, without much substantive content, but I did get to see Betty and Marlyn again; Kay, in her role as John's widow, sat with the dignitaries.

Earlier in the day, Vice President Al Gore (who was one of the few senators who actually understood what the Internet was about and was very supportive in its early funding) had given a speech at Irvine Auditorium and, an hour later at the Moore School, had taken part in a demonstration that reactivated a part of the original ENIAC. The demonstration was a bit ridiculous. The dignitaries performed a two-accumulator test with just a one-decade counter. Gore pushed a button and added something like 5 to 4 to get 9. He sure looked unimpressed.

Over the next several months, I heard from Tom Petzinger once in a while and from Kathryn Kleiman, who was helping him to gather data. Petzinger couldn't decide what to do with the information he had. Finally, he put it into two columns, which ran in the *Wall Street Journal* on successive weeks.[3] Petzinger featured Betty and me, primarily because we had stayed pretty much in the technology business for most of our adult working lives.[4] Betty had a very distinguished career. After leaving Remington Rand, she was in on the development of COBOL. She said that when her girls were little, she and her husband talked about COBOL so much in the car and at the dinner table that the girls went around the house chanting, "Snowball, COBOL, meatball!" In fact, Betty felt she had had as much to do with its development as Grace Hopper, whom Jean Sammet called "the grandmother of COBOL."[5] Betty also thought that Jean Sammet, the primary developer of the FORMAC language at IBM, which eventually became FORTRAN, did more work on COBOL than Grace, but it is hard to overcome popular perception, and for twenty years Grace ran around with her hunk of wire (a visual aid she used to explain the concept of nanoseconds) promoting the field of computing and herself.[6] Betty spent much of her time on the standardizing of FORTRAN. She considered it very important to have FORTRAN programs that were transportable from one system to another. This could only happen if everyone was rigorous in developing standard FORTRAN compilers that would be complete enough to handle all applications for which they would be used.

I called Tom Petzinger the night before the first article was to be printed to verify some small, last-minute detail. I called him again the next morning after reading the article in the *Wall Street Journal*, to tell him that I thought it was very good. He confided that he had wanted to tell me the night before of the trouble he was having with his editor, but could not. Petzinger had quoted me as saying the ENIAC was a "son of a bitch" to program. His editor said that they couldn't print that in the *Wall Street Journal*. Petzinger told him, "If that seventy-one-year-old woman can say it, we can damn well print it." And so they did.

After Petzinger's articles appeared in the *Wall Street Journal* that November, suddenly everyone was interested in the ENIAC women! At that time, the Women in Technology International (WITI) were soliciting nominations for women to be inducted into its Hall of Fame for 1997. My son, Tim, and Kathryn Kleiman nominated the six of us ENIAC women, and we were voted in unanimously. It was wonderful to be recognized by other talented women. Nine other women were inducted into the WITI Hall of Fame that year: Fran Allen, an IBM Fellow; Carol Bartz, chief executive officer of Autodesk; Pamela Meyer Lopker, founder and president of QAD, Inc.; Marcia Neugebauer, a distinguished visiting scientist at the Jet Propulsion Laboratory in Pasadena, California; Donna Shirley, director of the Mars Exploration Program at the Jet Propulsion Laboratory; Shaunna Sowell, vice president of Worldwide Environmental Safety and Health Programs for Texas Instruments; Patty Stonesifer, management adviser for Dreamworks and former vice president of Microsoft; Patricia Wallington, corporate vice president and chief information officer for the Document Company of Xerox; and Rosalyn S. Yalow, a Nobel Laureate in medicine.

Of this distinguished group, I was most taken with the following three women: Donna Shirley, who managed the Mars Rover that explored Mars for NASA; Rosalyn Yalow, a medical physicist who won the 1977 Nobel Prize in Physiology of Medicine for her development of the Radioimmunoassay (RIA) Technique; and Fran Allen, the first woman to receive the A. M. Turing Award from the Association for Computing Machinery (ACM). Allen had been a high school mathematics teacher who loved teaching so much that she only went to work for IBM to pay off her school loans. She intended to go right back to teaching after they were paid off, but, fortunately for IBM, she found out she liked doing mathematics even more than she liked teaching it. ACM honored Fran for her work at IBM in optimizing compilers; her innovations were instrumental in code optimizing and parallelization. Together, we fifteen formed the second class of inductees. The ceremony was held in early June in Silicon Valley, California. I was very proud and honored to be inducted with such wonderful women.

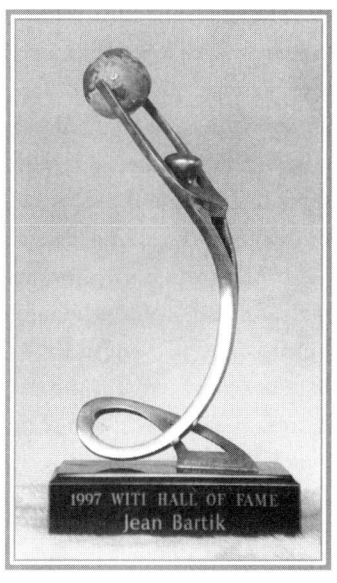

Jean's Women in Technology International (WITI) Hall of Fame award. The statuette is part of the Jean Jennings Bartik Collection at the Jean Jennings Bartik Computing Museum.

The evening was one of the highlights of my life. Although we honorees didn't get our bronze statuettes of a woman leaning back holding up the world until the next year, they were worth waiting for. I love that statuette. It now sits in the technology museum named after me on the campus of Northwest Missouri State University, my beloved alma mater. By this time, Betty had suffered a stroke, and she attended the ceremony in a wheelchair. But she was almost as logical as ever. When accepting the honor at the podium, she reiterated the advice someone had once given to her, which neatly summed up her life philosophy: "Look like a girl. Act like a lady. Think like a man. Work like a dog." That drew a big laugh from the audience, but from our experience it contained a lot of truth.

Betty had learned early on that men paid little attention to women's opinions; many of her ideas were shot down when she personally presented them, but if a male presented her idea, the idea was usually applauded and implemented. So Betty quickly learned to pick out a likely male to approach who would be receptive to presenting her idea whenever she wanted an idea to be accepted. I too had been in meetings where I presented an idea that nobody supported. Then, a few minutes later, a male would present the same idea and everyone would jump on board, lauding it as the greatest thing since sliced bread. Apparently, this is due to some male hearing impairment that only operates when women speak. Of course, not all men have such a hearing impairment thankfully, and certainly, the problem is not as prevalent today as it was back when Betty and I were struggling to make our place in a very much male-dominated computer industry. Today, the Auerbach Corporation couldn't have gotten away with the kind of crap they pulled back then and I like to think that Betty and I, along with the other ENIAC women, helped pave the way for the women who followed in our footsteps.

All of the ENIAC women were sensitive and caring, but they were also as logical as any group of people I've ever worked with. They were lovable and kind, but also hard working, reliable, scrupulously honest, and creative. I am so proud to have been one of them and to have counted them my friends. Betty received many honors in her lifetime, but the capper may have been the Ada Lovelace Award, which she received on March 15, 1997, at a gala affair in Washington, D.C. It is the highest award given by the Association for Women in Computing (AWC) and is bestowed on recipients for "outstanding scientific and technical achievement and extraordinary service to the computing community through their accomplishments and contributions on behalf of women in computing."

In November 1996, nine months after the Moore School held its anniversary, the Aberdeen Proving Ground also celebrated its fifty years in computing. I found the celebration to be farcical; it was full of elaborate pomp and circumstance, with soldiers marching on parade in front of Herman Goldstine, the hero of the hour. During the event, Herman Goldstine inspected the troops, and Kay Mauchly and Judy Eckert, Pres Eckert's second wife, as widows of John and Pres, were invited to cut the celebratory cake.

Herman Goldstine spoke, as did Harry Husky during the program. From listening to the two speak, you would have thought Herman Goldstine was the greatest inventor the computing world had ever known, along with his collaborator, John von Neumann. In truth, all of the people being honored that night owed a great debt to Pres Eckert and John Mauchly; however, the organizers managed to have the whole celebration without significantly mentioning John or Pres, which seemed shockingly wrong, especially in light of Eckert's recent death.

The celebration featured a panel discussion at which one of the panel members said that Harold Pender, John Grist Brainerd, Col. Paul Gillon of Aberdeen, and others had gotten together and said, "There will be an ENIAC. And there was an ENIAC." When he said that, I was immediately reminded of Michelangelo's fresco depicting God extending his forefinger and touching the outstretched forefinger of man, giving life to creation.[7] I said to a man standing beside me near the door, "Who is that idiot?" It turned out that the man beside me had arranged the whole program.

Most everything about the event had the Army's slant, emphasizing their role in development of the ENIAC; however, the organizers did have one seminar with presentations by ENIAC programmers. It included Kay and me, as two of the original programmers, as well as some of those who worked on the ENIAC after it moved to Aberdeen. But throughout the entire celebration, no one mentioned Eckert and Mauchly. On top of this slight, the keynote speaker was the daughter of John von Neumann, who had nothing to do with designing or building the ENIAC. He saw the two-accumulator test in September 1944 and later suggested the Los Alamos problem as a test for the ENIAC; then in 1947, von Neumann was involved in defining the instruction set when it was turned into a stored-program computer. But John von Neumann was a consultant to Aberdeen, so he was included, whereas John Mauchly and Pres Eckert, who had worked for the University of Pennsylvania, were left out.

The handouts all lauded Herman Goldstine and John von Neumann. There was a reprint distributed of a Jayne Lecture that Goldstine had given at the Moore School in 1991, in which, as per his custom, he told his own peculiar version of events. Noting that Dean Harold Pender had assigned Dr. Brainerd to be the University of Pennsylvania's liaison with Army Ordnance, Goldstine wrote that "Brainerd was perhaps the best qualified member of the faculty for this purpose. He combined a considerable interest in computation with substantial ability as a leader of men and a manager of affairs."

Wrong again. Brainerd had such an interest in computation that when he received Mauchly's proposal for the ENIAC, he promptly lost the memo. John's secretary, Dorothy Shisler, had to reproduce for John and Herman

Resume

March-June 1945	Ballistics Research Labs at University of Pennsylvania	Calculated trajectories using electro-mechanical calculators
June-August 1945	Ballistics Research Labs at Aberdeen, Maryland	Selected as ENIAC Programmer. Studied punch card equipment as ENIAC I/O
August 1945-December 1946	Ballistics Research Labs at Moore School at University of Pennsylvania	Began learning to program ENIAC. Developed notation and programmed trajectory and ran it at demonstration
March 1947-March 1948	Moore School under contract to Aberdeen under Dick Clippinger (John von Neumann was consultant)	Set up Programming group, programmed ENIAC to be a stored program computer and programmed Dick's jobs
March 1948-April 1949	Eckert-Mauchly (under Mauchly)	Programmer of BINAC and UNIVAC 1
April 1949-September 1950	Eckert-Mauchly (under Pres Eckert)	Logical Designer for UNIVAC 1 and Electrostatic UNIVAC 1 as backup if mercury delay line memory didn't work
September 1950-June 1951	Remington Rand	Trainer and programmer for Washington sales office. Did flow chart for Navy ASO inventory control
June 1951-October 1967	Housewife; earned master's degree at University of Pennsylvania	Had three children
October 1967-May 1975	Auerbach Publishers in Philadelphia and New Jersey	Developed Auerbach Minicomputer Reports and ran it
May 1976-June 1977	Interdata (Perkin-Elmer subsidiary at Oceanport, N.J.)	Product manager of Mega-mini
June 1977-August 1978	Systems Engineering Laboratories (Ft. Lauderdale, Fla.)	Market Support Manager (Publications, Users Group, Competitive, Software Lib)
August 1978-July 1980	Honeywell, Inc., Minneapolis, Minn.	Manager of Minicomputer Competitive Analysis
July 1980-November 1985	Data Decisions, Cherry Hill, N.J.	Senior Editor (developed communications reports)
November 1985-present	Self Employed	Real Estate Rep

The last official resume of Jean Jennings Bartik, 1996.

Goldstine from her stenographic notes. The engineers used to laugh about how little Brainerd knew about the ENIAC. He was so disliked by the ENIAC crew that he was eventually ousted and Reed Warren was put in charge of the project as liaison. Yet Herman Goldstine found that "it was a distinct pleasure for me to deal with this honest, kindly, and well-meaning gentleman." This gentleman is the same man who took John's teaching assignment away from him so he could spend full time working on the ENIAC, then cut his salary in half. How kindly was that?[8]

No administrator ever raised the standard of living one iota or led the way to a better tomorrow. Instead, the skill and ingenuity of scientists, mathematicians, and engineers have been responsible for enriching the world we live in by increasing productivity and developing products that make life easier, allowing for more leisure time and critical and creative thinking by all. Administrators have their place and deserve credit for recognizing good ideas, but their arrogance more often than not oversteps their actual talent. Herman Goldstine was an administrator, not a scientist or engineer. While he may have been a good mathematician (John Mauchly had once informed me that Goldstine was probably among the top 500 mathematicians in the United States), he certainly never displayed any great mathematical talent or technical skill when I was around him. What Goldstine seemed to be good at was managing—and manipulating—people to his advantage. And he always seemed to be more concerned with how people could help him, not how he could help people.

As you can imagine, Kay, Judy, and I were disconcerted by the notable lack of meaningful recognition of John and Pres, although we understood to some degree why they weren't mentioned more significantly. The event was organized by the U.S. Army and John and Pres hadn't been directly affiliated with Aberdeen and the U.S. Army, whereas Goldstine and von Neumann had been. Since the U.S. Army had funded the ENIAC project, the organizers of the celebration had apparently been far more focused on heralding Aberdeen's part in the construction of the ENIAC than in honoring the inventors. Still, we all felt that it wasn't particularly well done of the event planners.

One of the other handouts at this fiftieth anniversary celebration was a paperback copy of Herman Goldstine's 1972 book, *The Computer from Pascal to von Neumann*. This was the first time that I had seen the book or read any of its contents and I was dismayed by much of its content. Reading Goldstine's book that night, I could not believe how many inaccuracies there were in the book, particularly a book published by Princeton Press and financed by IBM. IBM had given Goldstine a paid fellowship to write his book. Goldstine's book is about as accurate as my name is Elizabeth. I was born Betty Jean, not Elizabeth. But you wouldn't know that from Goldstine's book. In the book, Goldstine called me "Elizabeth" Jennings. Elizabeth! My given name was Betty Jean Jennings, not Elizabeth. I came from the Midwest, where two names were used almost as one:

Betty Jean, Lula May, Cindy Lou. Now, if my name had been the only inaccurate information in the book, I wouldn't have a problem. Unfortunately, the book has a lot of incorrect information and dare I say it, yes—untruths.

Kay told me that Princeton University Press had sent John a copy of Goldstine's manuscript to be reviewed. John had carefully read the manuscript and then thoroughly critiqued the work, paying significant attention to part 2, "The Wartime Developments: ENIAC and EDVAC," which he'd felt was highly inaccurate. According to Kay, John remarked at the time that "Goldstine was about 95 percent correct—but oh! that other 5 percent makes all the difference!" Once he finished editing, John had then sent his copy to the Princeton University Press. When the editor received John's review, he called to tell him that although referees were usually anonymous, John's changes to the book were so extensive that he would have to tell Goldstine who had critiqued the work. Apparently, once Goldstine was informed that John had critiqued the manuscript, he refused to make any of John's changes. Thus, the book was published without any of John's edits.

How could a reputable institution like Princeton Press disregard the co-inventor of the ENIAC? I admire and respect the Princeton University Press, but I'm genuinely confused about why their editors went ahead and published a work that was disputed by John Mauchly himself. If they had doubts about John's version of events, they could easily have consulted with Pres Eckert for confirmation, or even Bob Sheppard or John Brainerd. Instead, they went ahead and published Goldstine's work apparently without any hesitation. One thing I wasn't really all that surprised about was that Goldstine hardly mentioned the ENIAC women programmers, other than to say whom we ended up marrying. However, I really can't hold this against Goldstine, since the majority of publications about early computing prior to 1996 never mentioned our contributions.

Once the *Wall Street Journal* columns appeared in 1996, however, the ENIAC programmers were suddenly in the spotlight and in great demand. However, Betty was in a nursing home, Fran wasn't interested, and Marlyn felt that her involvement had been so short that she really didn't want to speak at the various functions. Thus, it was left to Kay and me to be the spokespersons on most occasions. We were the keynote speakers at the Association for Computing Machinery's awards banquet on May 6, 2000. One of the honorees was Fred Brooks of IBM 360 fame, who received the A. M. Turing Award.[9] Although Brooks slept through our words of wisdom, he apologized later. He had just gotten off an airplane from England before coming to the banquet and had jet lag. I was thrilled to meet him, and he answered a question I had long wondered about. Who had come up with the eight-bit byte for the IBM 360? Brooks said that he had. Apparently, he and Gene Amdahl had worked on the IBM 7030 Stretch Computer, which used an eight-bit byte. Brooks wanted to adopt the eight-bit byte for the 360 as well, while Amdahl wanted the more common six-bit byte. It was an important decision because in the early 1950s memory was very expensive, and nobody could see the need for eight bits. Going with eight bits proved to be a wise decision, however, since those bits came in handy for Asian alphabets and other things. But I can remember how we thought it was bizarre at the time.

In giving talks to various groups, Kay and I went to many places together and enjoyed all of them and being with each other. It was great to share our experiences in the field of computing with others. We complemented each other very well, and over the sixty-one years that we knew each other, we shared an implicit trust and respect for each other. Kay and I spoke at events at IBM and Microsoft as well as to a number of universities, not only in the United States but overseas, including a fun-filled three-university speaking engagement in Ireland. Kay and I always had fun whenever we traveled together. Over the years, we shared many great experiences and made many great memories.

Dinner at Bunratty Castle in Ireland during a three-university speaking tour, 1998. Front row, left to right: Pat Sharky, Kay McNulty Mauchly Antonelli, and Jean Jennings Bartik. Back row: two of the serving staff at Bunratty Castle.

One such experience was when the Jean Jennings Bartik Computing Museum was established. The museum, which was founded by Dr. Jon T. Rickman and Kim D. Todd, is located on the campus of my alma mater, Northwest Missouri State University. Kay was with me in Maryville, Missouri, for the grand opening of the museum in April 2002, and having her with me made the event truly special. All my nieces and nephews were also able to attend the 2002 grand opening, as well as my daughter Jane and my son, Tim, and his family. Following the grand opening, Northwest further honored me with an honorary doctor of

Jean cuts the ribbon at the grand opening of the Jean Jennings Bartik Computing Museum in April 2002. To the left, Kay McNulty Mauchly Antonelli holds the end of the ribbon. Helping Jean cut the ribbon is Dr. Jon T. Rickman, vice president of Information Systems at Northwest.

science degree. Presented to me at the spring 2002 commencement, when I was asked back to be the keynote speaker, I was very proud and happy to receive this great honor from my beloved school. I was also stunned and thrilled to receive a standing ovation for my speech from over two thousand students, parents, and faculty. Later in 2007, I was proud to be made grand marshal of Northwest's Homecoming Parade for the twentieth anniversary of the Electronic Campus.

In 2009, a team of talented Northwest students and staff created a wonderful online computing museum (also named in my honor), which highlights my life in pictures, video, and words.[10] That project was also spearheaded by Jon Rickman and Kim Todd. Dr. Rickman was responsible for turning Northwest Missouri State University into the nation's first electronic campus in 1987 with the help and support of Northwest's president, Dr. Dean Hubbard. Prior to the electronic campus program's being initiated, enrollment was down at Northwest, but providing networked terminals and then later networked computers with standardized software in all the residence halls and faculty and staff offices dramatically increased enrollment and put my alma mater on the map and in many newspapers such as the *Washington Post* and *USA Today*. Later, the Electronic Campus program was expanded to place a university-owned notebook computer with standardized software in the hands of all of Northwest's 7,000-plus students.

I should also mention that Jon Rickman and Kim D. Todd were also responsible for putting together two award-winning videos about me called *Jean Jennings Bartik, Computing Pioneer* and *Jean Jennings Bartik—ENIAC: The First Stored Program Computer*. The latter video, produced in 2008, helped spotlight my accomplishment of turning the ENIAC into the first stored-program computer. Following Northwest's 2008 video release, I was inducted into the distinguished Hall of Fellows at the Computer History Museum in Mountain View, California, along with Bob Metcalfe and Linus Torvalds. Metcalfe was responsible for the invention of Ethernet and Linus Torvalds created the Linux kernel. I had written about Ethernet many times in my years as the editor for the Auerbach Minicomputer Reports, and I knew the Linux Operating System as an open source alternative to Microsoft's Windows, and a group who were translating documentation into different languages so that other countries could use Linux had once visited with me. What a thrill to meet and speak to such wonderful men! Torvalds was quite shy and when asked to become a "Fellow" said he would only accept it if he didn't have to give a speech. To add to my joy of the evening, I was seated beside Gene Amdahl, who is a delightful man. I had the chance to ask him the same question I had asked Fred Brooks several years earlier, "Who came up with the eight-bit byte for the IBM 360?" Amdahl said that Fred had but that he (Gene) had wanted it for most things, but for other things, six bits was sufficient. Gene was told to "either accept the eight-bit byte or say good-bye." Gene also told me about how he kept his systems 360-compatible through the years by making sure the instruction sets were the same.

In 2008, the IEEE Computer Society Board of Governors honored me with their Computer Pioneer award. I was thrilled to receive an award that had been given to Dick Clippinger and Betty Snyder Holberton in 1997. The next year, in 2009, the Multinational Development of Women in Technology (MDWIT) bestowed on me the prestigious Joan S. Korenman Award at its March conference in Baltimore, Maryland.

Another exciting moment came in September 2006 when the Commonwealth of Pennsylvania declared 3747 Ridge Avenue, the site of the Eckert-Mauchly Computer Corporation, to be a historic site. Many people attended the celebration, including many UNIVAC retirees. Also in attendance were Milly Koss, Joe Chapline, Bill Schmitt, Paul Chinitz, Bill Mauchly (John and Kay's son), Chris Eckert (Pres and Hester Eckert's second son), Tom Sharpless (Kite Sharpless's son), and Kathy Kleiman (discoverer and biographer of the ENIAC women programmers). I was happy to attend and speak with everyone, especially Bill Mauchly

Jean Jennings Bartik receives the 2008 Fellow Award, October 21, 2008, in Mountain View, California. Left to right: Tim Bartik (Jean's son), Jean Jennings Bartik, and John Hollar (CEO of the Computer History Museum).

The inductees into the Computer Museum of History's Hall of Fellows, Mountain View, California, October 21, 2008. Left to right: Linus Torvalds, Jean Jennings Bartik, and Bob Metcalfe. Photo by Dr. Jon T. Rickman.

and Chris Eckert. At the event, I gave a speech titled "Eckert-Mauchly: The Technical Camelot," where I compared working for Pres and John to that "one, brief, shining moment that was known as Camelot."

> There was once a congenial spot, / Where ideas flowed so free-i-ly, / And designs were done so speed-i-ly, / Where all of them forgot, Frontiers weren't pierced so eas-i-ly, / No one believed in Not, in Technical Camelot.

Also, during that speech I shared that after "working for Pres and John, no one could ever make me believe that I wasn't an important person. I knew I was because they had told me so in so many ways."[11]

As previously mentioned, Milly Koss had worked for Grace Hopper. Joe Chapline had been the maintenance engineer of the differential analyzer at the Moore School. Joe had also been Pres Eckert's speechwriter, the teacher of the

Group at the Hall of Fellows awards ceremony at the Computer History Museum in Mountain View, California, October 21, 2008. Back row, left to right: Dr. Jon T. Rickman, Kathryn Kleiman, Wendy and Bill Mauchly. Front row, center: Jean Jennings Bartik.

Marker designating the Eckert-Mauchly building as a historic site. The BINAC and UNIVAC were designed and built in the building at 3747 Ridge Avenue in Pennsylvania. Photo by Jon Rickman.

Northrop engineers, and the technical writer for the BINAC. The original BINAC manual, which Joe created, was never distributed because the BINAC patent attorney felt that the manual contained too much technical information. Joe kept that first and very detailed manual safe over the years, and kindly gifted it to the Jean Jennings Bartik Computing Museum at Northwest around 2003. Bill Schmitt, along with John Mauchly, produced the Short Code higher-level language for BINAC. The code could compile a program from inputting just the equations to be solved.

Jean Jennings Bartik with Bill Mauchly (son of John Mauchly) and Chris Eckert (son of Presper Eckert) on the steps of the Eckert-Mauchly building located at 3747 Ridge Avenue in Pennsylvania, 2006. Picture taken during the ceremony dedicating the building as a historic site.

Paul Chinitz was a teacher who was sent by Remington Rand to tell the Navy ASO officers how to do inventory control. Paul donated an original salesman's pot metal model of the UNIVAC I to the Jean Jennings Bartik Computing Museum.

While I've received many honors since 1996, I think the event that moves me the most was the opening of the Jean Jennings Bartik Computing Museum, primarily because Kay was with me to enjoy all the hoopla. The event was a fitting culmination to my enduring friendship with Kay and the six decades that we had spent in the computer field and around the men who made them. When I think of that day, I think of Kay and all that she meant to me and to the field of computing. She was truly one of a kind. Kay died April 20, 2006, after a short battle with cancer. She was eighty-five. I lost my best friend that day and took one step closer to becoming the last living original ENIAC programmer.

Epilogue
Looking Back

In 1996, at the fiftieth anniversary celebration of the ENIAC at the University of Pennsylvania, we old-timers were recognized as computer science "pioneers," and each of us was given a student escort around the campus. My daughter Jane and I were escorted to the exhibit of ENIAC parts at the Moore School. There was a platform with accumulators on it and other units—part of what remained from the original machine, what hadn't been junked out. I was showing my daughter and the guide how we set up the switches on the accumulator, connected the accumulator to the memory bus, and plugged in the control signals. As Jane and the guide continued to examine the accumulator, I stepped off the platform and stood beside two men who were talking. They were decades younger than me. One said, "Since it was wartime, the programmers were women." Then he added, "Of course, they didn't know what they were doing." I couldn't believe I was hearing this in 1996. I asked my daughter if I could go over and punch him out. Jane said, "Please, Mom, don't make a scene."

I made plenty of scenes during my career, ruffled plenty of feathers, and if I had it to do over again I suppose I would have made more scenes, not fewer. It's too bad I ever had to step onto that corporate merry-go-round in the first place. I believe I would have been happy to work for Pres and John forever. That job was my Camelot. Sixty years later, it remains incredible to me how satisfying it was to program the ENIAC and be a part of designing the UNIVAC. Pres and John were not only brilliant men, but were also truly good men and appreciative of what others could and did do. Together they fostered a work environment that was stimulating, fun, and freewheeling. Even though I loved working with John Mauchly and Pres Eckert, Dick Clippinger was perhaps the best manager I ever had. Clippinger was brilliant, clever, fun, fair, loyal, and appreciative. Not only did I never have a cross word with him, I never had a negative thought about him. Dick Clippinger died in 1997 and I greatly mourned his loss. I am so thankful to have worked with all of these extraordinary men.

Back in 1985, I thought my days in computing were over and that my contributions to the early days of computing had been relegated to a handful of Army photographs that didn't have any names of the women in the captions. After 1996 when I (along with the other ENIAC women) were rediscovered, I was so honored to receive so many awards and give speeches to audiences all over the United States and Europe about the ENIAC and the extraordinary men and women I had worked with. One of the most prestigious honors I received was to be inducted in the Hall of Fellows at the Computing History Museum in Mountain View. All three of my children were fortunately able to attend. Jane, who graduated from Rutgers University, is a senior technical staff member for IBM in Poughkeepsie. I am really appreciative of Jane, who was always so willing to accompany me on many of my trips. Her assistance was invaluable. My son, Tim, who graduated from Yale University and is a PhD economist, has worked for two decades now at the W. E. Upjohn Institute for Employment Research in Kalamazoo, Michigan, a nonprofit think tank that employs a dozen or so economists to study employment problems. Tim's focus is on how public policy affects economic development, and he has written several books on his research. He and his wife, Debra Wickman, have two sons, Alex and Jonathan, both fine, strapping lads. My grandsons differ in that Alex is gregarious and charming and seeks adventure, while Jonathan keeps his own counsel, but I am quite sure his thoughts are deep and relevant to the world around him. He is currently an undergraduate at the University of Michigan in Ann Arbor.

My grandson, Alex, is living in Lima, Peru, where he works for the Innovations for Poverty Actions, a private, not-for-profit organization. Its goal is to spend development money and effort on evaluating programs that make a difference in the lives of the native population. Alex oversees a microfinance project in a small village in the mountains outside of Lima. I have Skype, so I can talk to him through my computer. He has a camera mounted on his computer, and I can see him while we converse. Unfortunately, my grandsons, Alex and Jonathan, were unable to attend the awards ceremony at Mountain View.

I was so pleased that my youngest daughter, Mary, and her husband were able to attend and see me inducted into the Hall of Fellows also. Mary was the sweetest baby and grew into the sweetest child I had ever seen—always happy and helpful. Mary, who is an accountant, is married to a wonderful man named Chris

Williams, and they have three children: Christopher, Jamie, and Jesse. Jamie, who is a nuclear engineer with the Navy, gave me a beautiful great-grandson named Jacob. Jamie and Jacob were able to attend the 2008 awards ceremony, much to my delight.

Wireless computing and streaming media were things I never in my wildest dreams thought would be a possibility when programming the ENIAC back in 1946. In fact, at the time, Pres, John, and I would have thought a floppy disk with 1.35 MB of storage would be all the storage people could ever possibly need. I have certainly lived to see some incredible inventions in my lifetime, and I am even prouder to know that I played a small part in helping John Mauchly start a technological revolution with the invention of the ENIAC and later the UNIVAC. Because whatever anyone can say about John and the invention of the first electronic computer, he was absolutely responsible for launching the computer industry.

My biggest thrill in recent years came, surprisingly enough, from addressing the residents of a nursing home one morning during Women's History Month in March 2004 in the Germantown section of Philadelphia. I served on the board of the nursing home (though barely younger than some of its residents), and my only contact with the residents before that talk had been during "sherry hour"—a cocktail hour that we board members would spend with them after a board meeting. During these times, the residents, some of whom were in poor health, kept to themselves and seemed uninterested in us. So I expected my presentation to be a drag and to have to struggle to keep my energy up. Far from it. From my opening sentence, "We all grew up in a male chauvinist pig environment," everyone pricked their ears up and listened to every word. There were about twenty-five in attendance, but only a couple of them were men, one of whom was stretched out on a gurney. Well, all of those women remembered how it had been during their lifetimes—the sexism and chauvinism they had encountered—and were still incensed by it.

When I speak about my experiences, which I still am called on to do occasionally, I always point out (I hope modestly) that "I was just in the right place at the right time." Then I slyly add, "I believe even a man could have done what I did." But all kidding aside, I really do believe that I was just fortunate to find myself where I did, at a moment when history was in the making. My contributions were small, practically nothing in comparison to those of John and Pres and the ENIAC engineers. I would even say in comparison to Herman Goldstine, but the difference is that I don't go around claiming things that aren't true. I can't think of a thing that he really did while I knew him other than talk Aberdeen into funding the ENIAC. But I do have to credit Herman with one thing. I would never have gotten so incensed as to write this book if it weren't for his dismissive attitude toward me and the other ENIAC women.

At an Association of Women in Computing (AWC) meeting in California in September 1997, I participated in a panel discussion on "Women in the History of Computing." I arrived the afternoon before I was to speak, so I walked down a hall and saw a room that was overflowing with women standing outside the door, unable to fit in the room. That session was on the "glass ceiling"—the same glass ceiling Hillary Clinton, in her address to the 2008 Democratic Convention, said she put 18 million tiny cracks in (that being the number of votes she got during her unsuccessful campaign for the Democratic presidential nomination). The sheer number of women present in the room for the panel discussion, compared to our numbers a half century earlier, testified that we had come a long, long way, and that there was a lot more headroom under that glass ceiling than there used to be.

The following morning, our panel appeared before a similarly attentive audience, if not quite as large. Other women on the panel with me were Judy Clapp of the Whirlwind computer at MIT; Thelma Estrin, an engineer who had gone to Israel to build the first computer outside the United States; Milly Koss, who had worked on the UNIVAC under Grace Hopper; and Ethel Marsden, who had programmed IBM's SEAC machine, built in 1950. These women pretty much made it in the business by not asking permission but just doing it: "Act as if you have the job. Act as if you have permission." That was their approach and their advice for blazing a path.

How lucky I was to have those years working for Pres and John and Dick Clippinger! From growing up in rural Missouri, where most men appreciated strong women, I knew how men should and could act—with openness, letting you prove yourself—and these men embodied that standard. Pres, John, and Dick were all problem-solvers. If I could solve a problem, the problem was mine. Even if I couldn't, they believed in their own ability to teach me to solve the problem. All three men were superb teachers, and they taught me a lot. I was indeed in the right place at the right time.

In early 2002, I was invited to visit the Kalamazoo Area Math and Science Center (KAMSC), where my grandson, Alex, was a tenth-grader that year and where his brother, Jonathan, three years younger, would soon attend. I gave two talks, one in the morning and one in the afternoon; each was attended by about fifty boys and girls who were taking a course in computer science. The girls were thrilled with my visit, the boys, not so much. When I started to describe how the

ENIAC programmers had been ignored for forty years before the *Wall Street Journal* articles appeared, and then how we were lauded afterward, one boy piped up, remembering the self-effacing bromide I had used earlier about being in the right place at the right time.

"Since you were just in the right place at the right time," he said, "I guess they now make too much of a fuss over you." "Young man," I replied, leveling my gaze at him, "you are exactly right. They do make far too much of a fuss over me. The truth is, I was indeed merely in the right place, at the right time." But what a place! And what a time!

As a young girl on my family's farm in northwest Missouri, lying out in the east pasture gazing up at the clouds drifting overhead or lying on the haymow in the barn loft idly looking at the dark rafters illuminated by slivers of light filtering in through the barn boards or, at night, walking out to the windmill and sitting down on the platform surrounding it and seeing all the vast, incalculable numbers of stars in the sky, I dreamed of the wonderful things I would do in my life. Beyond the lane to the highway lay Stanberry and the nearby farm towns, which encompassed all I knew of the world. But my dreams flew beyond. Those dreams were of doing something like Aunt Gretchen had done, of living in the city, living with a sense of style and accomplishment, a sense of grace, and of helping others while helping out the family, too.

One thing I *never* dreamed of was being caught up in the excitement of the beginnings of the computer field. I had never even heard the word "computer"—no one had. But I did dream of the big city and of meeting all of those people out there who were doing wonderful things. As I lay in the haymows of my childhood, staring up into the musty dimness of the barn's interior, I could divine no details of my future years, but I knew I was going to do something exciting and rewarding. I had no idea at the time that my life would surpass my dreams.

I truly believe that in many ways "luck beats brains." When I had the chance to volunteer for a job running the ENIAC, I eagerly applied, not knowing my chances were almost nil because the Moore School was looking for only one operator, not five as the administrators had said, and thirteen of us had applied for that one spot, and the others were much more experienced than I. But I had luck on my side. I was only the second alternate, but when the fifth programmer chosen and the first alternate both turned it down, opportunity knocked, and I had enough sense to open the door. Of course, I didn't know it was opportunity—I just knew it wasn't what I had been doing: a job pounding away on a hand calculator, doing the same calculations of a trajectory every day.

What was the calculus that took me from the hayloft to the Moore School? A greater connection than one might think at first glance. My farm life prepared me for the work ahead, not by giving me any of the technical skills, but by giving me my work habits. I truly believe I was successful in my jobs because I was a "finisher." Many people will do the easy, fun parts of a job, but they tend to neglect the nitty-gritty, drudgery parts that finish it and make it work. I didn't do that. I finished my jobs. From the time I was a little girl, I was given chores to do and I was expected to handle those responsibilities. I had to milk cows, pump water, feed animals, and wash the cream separator. I also worked out in the field, plowing the ground, all alone, behind a gangplow pulled by five horses. Neglecting any of my chores had consequences, and I had to handle any problems that arose. Consequently, I learned to think on my feet and to be careful to do everything right the first time so as not to make mistakes that could cost me much more than just time later. But more than that, my family respected learning and education. So when I was suddenly presented with a career opportunity, I jumped at the chance, and set about learning how the ENIAC worked and what it could do. I had no idea that what it ultimately could do was change my life.

Well, now you know my life story, one that overlapped for a period of time with the stories of many others involved with the ENIAC, before we all took divergent paths. Even so, for the rest of our lives, the ENIAC was a force that surrounded me and the other ENIAC women. But then the ENIAC was the central, defining force in many lives—not just of Pres Eckert and John Mauchly, but also for Herman and Adele Goldstine, John von Neumann, Arthur Burks, and others. But what if there had been no ENIAC? What if Pres had been allowed to follow his heart's desire and attend MIT, instead of abiding by his mother's wishes and staying home to enroll at the Moore School, where he met Mauchly?

Who can say where Herman Goldstine would have wound up without the lucky circumstance of his being at the Moore School in 1942. Perhaps, he would have ended up a professor of math somewhere. Without the ENIAC, would John von Neumann merely be remembered as the world's most famous mathematician? After all, he would never have met Mauchly, Eckert, and Clippinger and thus, could not have acquired their ideas to release for any report on computing.

Would Arthur Burks be a modest and unassuming philosopher? Burks had a PhD in philosophy, and if not for an engineering course given by Moore School during World War II, might have ended up teaching philosophy at a university. Would John Vincent Atanasoff have ever been named the inventor of the automatic digital computer without John Mauchly? It's highly doubtful. Without

Mauchly's brilliant work on the ENIAC, Atanasoff's ABC machine would have more than likely never been thought of again after it ended up a tangled mass of wires and dusty mechanical parts in some forgotten Iowa basement storage bin.

Even without the ENIAC, I have no doubt that Pres and John (assuming they had still met and collaborated together) would have gone on to do great things in the field of computing. After all, John had been dreaming his whole life about creating mechanical brains to help mankind, and Pres was a truly brilliant engineer. If not the ENIAC, they would have built another computer at some point, most probably the first successful commercial computer. I like to think that they still would have called it the UNIVAC. I am also positive that Bob Shaw, Chuan Chu, Kite Sharpless, and Jack Davis would have designed many wonderful machines because it was the era of electronics and they were good at it. No doubt they would still have built computers, because the time was right for them to be built. The technology was there, the need was there, and there was someone to pay for it. In fact, Charles Babbage could have built his analytical engine if he had lived in the 1940s. Babbage was simply too far ahead of his time. Likewise, if Lady Lovelace had been alive in the 1940s, she could have been a friend and colleague of us ENIAC gals. Like Babbage, she was simply ahead of her time.

So what about the six of us ENIAC women? Where would we have been without the ENIAC? Although I do believe I was just in the right place at the right time, I also think I would have done something new and exciting regardless because I had two characteristics: (1) the sense to open the door when opportunity knocked, and (2) the determination to have an adventure.

Kay would probably have married a nice, brainy Catholic boy who would have made her mother happy, although, I don't think that Kay herself would have been as ecstatic as she was married to John. She most certainly would always have been gracious and charming and curious about each new day. Kay was just that way—a truly special person. Betty would have done some other important work. She was too good not to. And she wanted to live up to the heritage of her father and grandfather. Ruth, Marlyn, and Fran would doubtless still have found love and happiness, as they did. But all of us would have been the poorer for having missed such a wonderful experience. We were proud to have been there at the dawn of an age, and we loved every minute of it.

Of course, all of this is idle speculation, and the questions generated from such speculation are unanswerable assuredly, but they are interesting ones to think and talk about. Kay and I often had long conversations that began with, "What if...?" Such conversations were fruitless in the sense that the past could not be altered, but they were fun conversations and yes, often emotionally fulfilling. Since the past cannot be changed no matter how hard you might wish otherwise, all I can do is tell my story as honestly as possible and hope my efforts will help to set the record straight so that future generations better know the men and women behind the marvelous machine known as the ENIAC. Someone once said that it is almost an accident if history tells any truth. It was certainly an accident that I became a writer. Therefore, consider this book then, the merest accident.

So this is my story and my truth; one about six women who had the guts to pursue their dreams and in doing so made a small, but important mark in the pages of history. If my life has proven anything, it is that women should never be afraid to take risks and try new things. Women should pursue their dreams no matter where those dreams may lead them and push into frontiers where women aren't necessarily welcome to shape their own destinies. As one of my favorite Rodgers and Hammerstein songs goes, "Climb every mountain, / Ford every stream, / Follow every rainbow, / Till you find your dream." I hope, dear reader, you find yours.

Afterword

As the Assistant Director of the Jean Jennings Bartik Computing Museum and an editor on this autobiography, I hope you enjoyed reading about the life of Jean Jennings Bartik, which offers a rare, firsthand account of the people, places, and politics involved in the early, exciting days of computing, as much as I certainly did. I would like to thank Tim Bartik, Jean's son, and Bill Mauchly, John Mauchly's son, for reviewing and approving Jean's autobiography prior to publication. I also want to thank Mitzi Lutz, Dr. William E. Walden, and Dr. Michael Steiner for their time and effort on behalf of myself, Jean Jennings Bartik, and Dr. Jon T. Rickman. On a personal note, I want to thank Jean herself. I have no doubt that Jean is even now looking down from her heavenly *Camelot* with a broad smile, a glass of apricot brandy in hand, and Betty, John, and Kay by her side. Thank you for being an inspiration and yes, a "character." I will greatly miss you, Jean!

I had the distinct privilege of getting to know and work closely with Jean Jennings Bartik from 2002 to 2011. Jean's favorite motto was "luck beats brains"; however, while luck may have played a part in Jean's extraordinary story, her intelligence was unquestionable. The lady had brains and guts and a mouth that occasionally tumbled her into trouble. She also had heart! She was someone you would want to have at your side in a fight or when you're down and out. Jean knew the true meaning of friendship and what it took to stand strong and true in a world that was not always fair or kind.

Jean and Kay McNulty Mauchly Antonelli came to Northwest Missouri State University in 2002 to open the Jean Jennings Bartik Computing Museum. During an informal interview with me at that time, Kay and Jean addressed some of the controversies surrounding John Mauchly's work, including whether the BINAC, which is the first stored-program computer in terms of hardware, actually functioned or was as many have claimed a failure.

First I'd like to briefly examine Jean's assertion that John Mauchly, Pres Eckert, and the Moore School group came up with the idea for the stored-program computer and had already begun working on the design for the EDVAC independently of John von Neumann. The EDVAC was the successor to the ENIAC, which John von Neumann would later claim as his own work. According to both Kay and Jean, Mauchly and Eckert had written about automatic regulation or control of multiple calculations as early as December 1943 in a report about the ENIAC's progress, which Kay, as well as Jean, believed was an early statement referring to what we have come to know today as the stored-program computer. Additionally, Jean and Kay agreed that Presper Eckert clearly wrote about the concept for a stored-program computer in a January 1944 report on electronic calculations.[1] Jean uses these two examples in her autobiography as proof that John Mauchly and Pres Eckert were the originators of the stored-program computer concept, along with the fact that John von Neumann didn't come onto the scene until after Eckert and Mauchly were already working on the design for the EDVAC.

During my conversation with Kay and Jean, Kay specifically mentioned that her husband [John Mauchly] had written a letter, which was published in 1979 in *Datamation*, where he categorically stated that he and Eckert had worked out the stored-program architecture of EDVAC in 1944. The *Datamation* article supports Jean's version of events as laid out in her autobiography, and therefore, I would like to share several of its excerpts. In that article, John Mauchly stated,

> The EDVAC was the outcome of lengthy planning in which Eckert and I deliberately tried to overcome many problems of storage and control which were evident in the hasty "state-of-the-art" ENIAC System. Much of this planning took place in the early months of 1944, when most of the ENIAC design had been frozen.[2]

Mauchly went on to write that while they were building ENIAC, they were working on the design for the EDVAC:

> It was not until October 1944, that any Army Ordnance contract authorized work on EDVAC. We were still building ENIAC, and had to be sure that it was properly completed. That took over a year more. But all through 1944, and in 1945 as well, we were leading a "double-life."[3]

According to Mauchly, the first day that John von Neumann had security clearance to see the ENIAC and speak with them about the classified digital computer projects that they were working on was September 7, 1944.

> When von Neumann arrived, Eckert and I were asked to tell "Johnny" what our plans were, and we did. We started with our simple basic ideas: There would be only ONE storage device (with addressable locations) for the ENTIRE EDVAC, and this would hold both data and instructions.[4]

Once they realized that von Neumann saw the value in their design plans, Mauchly and Eckert went on to talk in detail about their ideas for EDVAC.

> Everyone could see how fascinated Johnny was with a subject which had somehow escaped his amazingly wide interests until [Herman] Goldstine told him of the Moore School Project. Like a child with a new toy, he could not put it aside. When his consulting duties required him to visit the Manhattan Project, he took off for New Mexico, but his mind was on our EDVAC architecture.[5]

Mauchly also says that von Neumann spent

> considerable time at Los Alamos writing up a report on our design for EDVAC. This MSS he sent to [Herman] Goldstine with a letter stating that he had done this as an accommodation for the Moore School group who had met with him. But Goldstine mimeographed it with a title page naming only one author—von Neumann. There was nothing to suggest that ANY of the major ideas had come from the Moore School Project![6]

Mauchly condemned Herman Goldstine for his unethical actions:

> Without our knowledge, Goldstine then distributed the "design for the EDVAC" outside the project and even to persons in other countries. Small wonder, then, that computer history gave von Neumann the credit.[7]

I found the *Datamation* letter very interesting and would encourage those interested in early computing to read the full article.

Dr. William E. Walden, who reviewed Jean's autobiography and who had been hired by Nick Metropolis on a Los Alamos project, confirms Jean and John Mauchly's version of events. According to Walden, John von Neumann had told Metropolis that he [von Neumann] had obtained the idea of the stored-program computer concept from a member of the ENIAC team.[8]

Following her work on the ENIAC, Jean was asked to join Mauchly and Eckert as a programmer when they formed their own computer company. Jean was a programmer for both the Binary Automatic Computer (BINAC) and the Universal Automatic Computer (UNIVAC). Jean asserted that the BINAC functioned well despite claims to the contrary. During our 2002 conversation, Jean stated,

The BINAC was demonstrated successfully to scores of people in Philadelphia and these demonstrations were reported in the October 1949 *Journal of the Franklin Institute*. The BINAC was also critically assessed by the Bureau of the Census (BOC) and the National Bureau of Standards (NBS). These two government agencies were invested in the BINAC's success because they were interested in purchasing the Eckert-Mauchly UNIVAC. If the BINAC worked, then they surmised that the UNIVAC would as well. Both [BOC and NBS] came away from the demonstrations highly satisfied with how the BINAC functioned.[9]

Jean's belief in the BINAC's success is one of several important themes in her autobiography and I am pleased to confirm that the statements she makes about the BINAC have been supported by a computer programmer from Northrop Aircraft. According to Roger Mills, who came to visit the Jean Jennings Bartik Computing Museum in 2008, Jean is absolutely right in her claim that the BINAC (which was comprised of two separate, identical machines, checking each other each clock cycle) was successful. Mills was hired as a computer programmer at Northrop Aircraft in January 1951 and his first job at Northrop Aircraft was the BINAC. In an email dated December 21, 2010, Mills, wrote,

My first program for the BINAC was "Nim." The BINAC versus a person with 64 squares and 64 items. The player going first could be selected by the person. The "classical" Nimm game is a game by two players. It consists of 16 matches in 4 rows. Two players alternately pick a certain number of matches and the one who takes the last match, loses.[10]

Mills went on to write that one successful engineering problem run on the BINAC was the

ray dome de-icing program. Northrop had two Friedan operators working 6 months on the steps to solve the function in order to check BINAC steps. The BINAC passed the operator steps in about 5 minutes and finished the program in 15 minutes.

According to John Mauchly's 1979 article in *Datamation*, Northrop took charge of the BINAC and the "various modules of the BINAC were roughly crated, shipped to California, and apparently ignored." Mills's December 12, 2010, email also confirmed Mauchly's statement: "the BINAC was set out in a parking lot under a tarp for 6 months before they started assembling it." Mills went on to add that after the BINAC was finally reassembled by the Northrop engineers, there were two major problems.

> The main set of vacuum tubes (radio tubes, I think they were 6L6s) had emission problems. One of the Northrop engineers designed and built an emission tester and 75% of the tubes directly from the factory were rejected. The other major problem was that to my knowledge, Northrop never was successful in running both computers to simultaneously check results along the high speed bus once it was moved from Philadelphia to California.[11]

Mills said, however, that the engineers were able to successfully work one of the two identical machines that comprised BINAC.

> All of our programs at Northrop were run on only one of the computers. I think the BINAC wasn't used as much as the other computing equipment due to the requirement for absolute octal programming and the program and data had to be in octal. However, the BINAC was still running and being used by Northrop when I left Northrop in April of 1953.[12]

Mills, like Jean, blames Northrop Aircraft for any problems with the BINAC, since Northrop never brought in any of the original BINAC engineers for help: "When I talked with Jean Bartik, she said that the BINAC probably would have been used more if Northop had let Eckert-Mauchly engineers come out to help install the BINAC."[13] Mills agreed with Jean's statement and was shocked that Northrop claimed the BINAC was classified as the reasoning for not bringing in the original engineers: "I was in the building that housed the BINAC, along with the CPC, and accounting machines, and I saw very little highly classified material, and there was none in the BINAC room. I have no idea why Northrop did that. It was dumb."[14]

As one of Jean's editors I will personally refrain from weighing in on the various debates surrounding the ENIAC, the EDVAC, and the BINAC. I wasn't there and could only make a secondhand argument at best. However, Jean was there and she makes a compelling case that Mauchly was maligned and credit was unfairly taken away from him and Presper Eckert. Most significantly, Jean's version of events surrounding the ENIAC, EDVAC, BINAC, and UNIVAC is supported by people who were there such as Joe Chapline, Betty Snyder Holberton, Kay Mauchly, John Mauchly, Presper Eckert, and Roger Mills just to name a few. So, as Jean was fond of saying—"Enough said."

>> Kim D. Todd, Assistant Director
>> Jean Jennings Bartik Computing Museum
>> Northwest Missouri State University
>> May 31, 2011

Notes

Preface

1. Herman H. Goldstine, *The Computer from Pascal to von Neumann* (Princeton, NJ: Princeton University Press, 1972), 229–30.

Chapter 1: The Originators, the Women, and the ENIAC

1. "Biggest, Fastest Calculator Built by ISC Physicist," Press Release, Ames, IA, April 7, 1942. The press release called the computing device a calculator rather than a computer. Copy in Penn Library/Exhibitions, "John W. Mauchly and the Development of the ENIAC Computer: The John Atanasoff Controversy" (http://www.library.upenn.edu/exhibits/rbm/mauchly/jwm7.html).

2. J. Presper Eckert, "Eulogy delivered by J. Presper Eckert in St. Anthony's Church, Ambler, Pennsylvania, at funder services on January 11, 1980," *Communications of the ACM* 23, no. 3 (March 1980): 145–46.

3. Brian Randell, "The Use of High Speed Vacuum Tube Devices for Calculating by John W. Mauchly, August 1942," in *Origins of Digital Computers: Selected Papers*, 355–58 (Berlin/Heidelberg: Springer-Verlag, 1982).

4. Jean Jennings Bartik, "My Conversations with Joe Chapline, 2003" (handwritten notes), Jean Jennings Bartik Papers, Jean Jennings Bartik Computing Museum, Northwest Missouri State University, Maryville, MO.

5. Presper Eckert and John Mauchly, "ENIAC Progress Report," Moore School of Engineering, University of Pennsylvania, December 31, 1943.

6. Herman Lukoff, "Disclosure of Magnetic Calculating Machine by J. Presper Eckert, January 29, 1944," in Lukoff, *From Dits to Bits: A Personal History of the Electronic Computer*, 207–9 (Portland, OR: Robotics Press, 1979).

7. Goldstine, *Computer from Pascal to von Neumann*.

8. Deposition of Jean J. Bartik, Box 12, and Deposition of Francis Elizabeth (Betty) Snyder Holberton, Box 14, ENIAC Patent Trial Collection, 1964–1973 [1938–1971 bulk], Record Group 8.10, University of Pennsylvania Archive; Barkley W. Fritz, "The Women of the ENIAC," *IEEE: Annals of the History of Computing* 18, no. 3 (1996): 13–28. See also Kathy Kleiman, *ENIAC Programmers Project* (http://eniacprogrammers.org).

9. IEEE Computer Society, "Richard F. Clippinger: 1996 Computer Pioneer Award" (http://www.computer.org/portal/web/awards/clippinger); John Giese, response to question of Jean Jennings

Bartik, in *Fifty Years of Army Computing: From ENIAC to MSRC: A Record of a Symposium and Celebration, November 13–14, 1996, Aberdeen Proving Ground*, edited by Thomas J. Bergin (ARL-SR-93), 70 (http://www.arl.army.mil/www/pages/shared/documents/50_years_of_army_computing.pdf); Deposition of Jean J. Bartik; Fritz, "Women of the ENIAC."

10. Presper Eckert and John Mauchly, "ENIAC Progress Report," December 31, 1943.

11. Lukoff, *From Dits to Bits*, 355–58.

12. Paul Halmos, "The Legend of John von Neumann," *American Mathematical Monthly* 80, no. 4 (April 1973): 382–94.

13. Ibid.

14. Kay McNulty Mauchly Antonelli Recollections, 2002, Jean Jennings Bartik Papers.

15. It was likely during this period that John von Neumann was exposed to large amounts of radiation, which probably caused his untimely death in 1957 at the age of fifty-three from bone or pancreatic cancer.

16. The ENIAC engineers used to laugh and say that Brainerd didn't even know how the ENIAC worked. He tried to manage without getting involved in any of the design problems.

17. John W. Mauchly (1907–80), transcript of interview by Henry Tropp, February 6, 1973, Computer Oral History Collection, 1967–1973, 1977, Box 13, Folder 14, Archives Center, National Museum of American History, Smithsonian Institution, Washington, D.C.

18. Signed and Notarized Statement by John von Neumann, May 8, 1947, #2011004, Jean Jennings Bartik Papers.

19. Ibid.

20. Because of Lovelace's skill as a mathematician and her physical beauty, Babbage called her "The Enchantress of Numbers." The U.S. Defense Department has a computer language called "Ada," named after her.

21. *General Report on Tunny with Emphasis on Statistical Methods* (aka *The Newmanry Report*) was prepared in 1945 and declassified in 2000. The report is available online at http://www.alanturing.net/turing_archive/archive/index/tunnyreportindex.html. A photo on page 332 of the report shows the women who ran the code-breaking programs at Bletchley Park; the photo was enhanced and reproduced in B. J. Copeland, *Colossus: The Secrets of Bletchley Park's Codebreaking Computers* (Oxford: Oxford University Press, 2010), photo #33. See also Computer History Museum, *Colossus: Breaking the Code*, video, 2011 (available online at http://www.computerhistory.org/revolution/birth-of-the-computer/4/82/2218) and the Bletchley Park website (www.bletchleypark.org.uk/). Prime Minister Churchill banned anyone involved with the Colossus project from talking about it for thirty-five years after the war. He was so concerned that the Soviet Union would obtain information about the group that he had all ten Colossus computers—and the buildings at Bletchley Park—destroyed after the war. The Colossus was rebuilt in 2007 and tested against a PC running the code-breaking software. The Colossus and the PC ran neck and neck.

22. IEEE Global History Network, "Milestones: Whirlwind Computer, 1944–1959," 2012 (www.ieeeghn.org/wiki/index.php/Milestones:Whirlwind_Computer).

Chapter 2: My Story

1. Six-foot-two and 200 pounds, Schottel made all-league in football in 1940 and 1941 and also earned letters in basketball and track. He entered the war and after it ended, played two years for

the Detroit Lions. He was used sparingly and scored only one touchdown in the NFL, but that came on a seventy-yard pass reception. He later coached the Northwest Missouri State Bearcats football team for eight seasons.

    2. WAVES, or Women Accepted for Volunteer Emergency Service, was a division of the U.S. Navy created during World War II to allow women to serve in stateside positions.

    3. Gail Collins, *America's Women: 400 Years of Dolls, Drudges, Helpmates and Heroines* (New York: HarperCollins, 2003), 371–96.

Chapter 3: Human "Computer" to ENIAC Programmer

    1. Ohm's Law is the basic relationship in electrical engineering. "E" is the voltage measured in volts. "I" is the current measured in amperes. "R" is the resistance measured in ohms. The equation means that the voltage drop across a resister is the current multiplied by the resistance.

    2. Kay McNulty Mauchly Antonelli Story, March 26, 2004, Jean Jennings Bartik Computer Museum.

    3. Ibid.

    4. The story about John Snyder and Robert Abrahams comes from an article by Jack Fried in the *Philadelphia Sunday Bulletin* of December 28, 1958.

    5. Goldstine, *Computer from Pascal to von Neumann* (229) wrote, "They [the ENIAC programmers] were trained largely by my wife, with some help from me." A total product of his fertile mind: Herman and Adele did no training of us whatsoever. Adele's manuals came out a year after we learned to program the ENIAC. Earlier, when I first came to Philadelphia, Adele had taught me some computing techniques for use with hand calculators, such as inverse interpolation, but in fact, I taught her to program the ENIAC. At no time did she teach any of the other programmers.

    6. Herman Goldstine claimed that he was in charge of all the arrangements for turning the ENIAC over to Aberdeen. If so, he did a horrible job of preparing for the "ENIAC girls'" arrival back from Aberdeen.

    7. Computers use various representations to store negative numbers. Nine's complement and ten's complement are two methods that were often used in decimal mechanical calculators, and in the ENIAC. Modern computers use the binary number system and represent negative numbers in two's complement. To subtract a number in a computer it is common to add the number in its complement representation.

A standard subtraction problem is

```
             259
Subtract     176
Equals      + 83
```

The same subtraction using complement arithmetic, where the tens complement of 176 is 824:

```
             259
Add          824
Equals      +083 (where the carry digit is truncated)
```

The sign of the numbers can also be represented by a 0 for positive and a 1 for negative. The final sign of the sum is determined by the binary sum of the individual sign digits plus the carryover digit. The binary sum of $1 + 0 = 1$ and $1 + 1 = 0$. For example:

	(1) 681 (tens complement for a negative 319)
Add	(0) <u>432</u>
Sum Equals	(1) 1113 = (0) 113 (binary sum of the carry digit and the sign digit)
Sign Equals	(1+1) 113 = (0) 113 (where the leading one thousands place is added to the sign digit)

8. Design and construction of the ENIAC were financed by the U.S. Army, Ordnance Corps, Research and Development Command, under a contract with University of Pennsylvania's Moore School of Engineering. The project, which developed from a proposal by John Mauchly and J. Presper Eckert, was code-named "Project PX" and was begun in June 1943.

9. Bob Jaffe, *Modern Marvels, The Creation of the Computer/Thinking Machine* (1995; New York: A & E Home Entertainment, 2005); Films for the Humanities and WGBH Television station, *The Machine That Changed the World* (Princeton, NJ: Films for the Humanities and Sciences, 1992).

10. In the computer science field, an argument is the input value, which is then evaluated by a function.

11. The memory bus trays and programming trays were eight feet long, one and a quarter inches thick, and nine inches deep. They could be extended in length by cabling two units together. The memory bus trays sat on top of the control switches for each unit (the accumulator or the multiplier divider/square rooter). The memory bus was connected to the unit with a cable consisting of eleven wires and a ground—one for each of the ten decade counters and one for the sign. Every unit that was connected to a particular memory bus needed the bus extended to reach the other units.

12. The program trays had eleven program lines that could be connected as input or output to start the operation or to signal that it was finished and go on to the next. They were plugged into a unit by a cable with a plug on each end. The program trays were stacked underneath the control switches on a unit.

13. Of the surrender on August 14, Kay writes that "Everyone was ecstatic. All of us had expected the war with Japan to continue for years, but the dropping of the atom bombs had changed all of that. I remember V-J Day, but it is all hazy because of the excitement. John Holberton took me to pick up my sister-in-law. Her husband and my brother, Pat, was in the South Pacific on Admiral Halsey's ship (the USS *Missouri*), and I knew she would be delighted. We went to downtown Philadelphia where there was wild cheering, singing, dancing, and laughing. Everyone was grabbing everyone else and kissing them. We were all so happy that the war was finally over. We were out of our minds with joy." Kay McNulty Mauchly Antonelli Story, March 26, 2004, Jean Jennings Bartik Computer Museum.

14. The *Wall Street Journal* interviewed me for a story on the ENIAC women on the fiftieth anniversary of the computer's creation. I told the reporter that it was a son of a bitch to program, and he of course latched onto that nugget and included it in his story. The *Journal*'s policy forbade the use of "son of a bitch" in print, but the reporter fought to keep the quote. An editorial meeting was hastily called, and the *Journal* reversed its policy for that instance, deciding that the expression really was the most appropriate way to convey the true difficulty of programming the ENIAC. To my knowledge, that is the single occasion when the *Wall Street Journal* has ever printed that phrase.

15. I would have two more perfect partners in my working life—Adele Goldstine and Arthur Gehring.

16. The function table was rather complex to program, and it took about five add times to get out a function. When we complained about this to Bob Shaw, he said—grinning mischievously—that he knew we would be happy to have some time to do other operations, so he had done it for us.

17. When I was asked by Hester to go out with them, I'd never seen John Sims before. He was a big man, not muscular, and rather ordinary looking. He and Pres had grown up together. Pres's wife, Hester, was pretty. Before that evening, I had only met her at the Moore School in the ladies room. When Hester gave birth to the couple's first son, John, Pres gave her a bright yellow Buick convertible, which Hester drove everywhere. It was quite spectacular. Following the birth of Pres and Hester's second son, Chris, Hester suffered from postpartum psychosis and was confined to the University of Pennsylvania's hospital thereafter. Hester came home for a visit one weekend and had hidden pills. She overdosed on the pills, lay down on the bed, and died.

John Eckert was quite brilliant. He fought in Vietnam and was wounded. He died in 2005. Chris grew up to be a bright, delightful man with a wonderful wife, Patti, and two sons, Cory and Ryan. All live happily in Atlanta, Georgia, where Chris works for a company that serves as the sales representative in the Southwest region of the United States for the chip manufacturer Advanced Micro Devices, or AMD. Chris credits his wife with making him "normal." I can still remember seeing Pres with his two beautiful little boys.

18. Dr. Hartree from England—the Cambridge professor who had built a differential analyzer model out of Meccano parts—loved the place. If we went there while he was in the United States, he always went with us and ate up a storm. England still had very heavy rationing from the war, especially meat, and he looked as though he were in heaven eating a perfect steak at Arthur's.

19. Fritz, "Women of the ENIAC," 1, 13, 27.

Chapter 4: Apricot Brandy and Nighttime Logic

1. The graph paper was about three feet square with one-inch squares traced in dark lines and, within them, quarter-inch squares defined by light blue lines. We wrote the program pulse as an alphanumeric combination using the letters A through Q and the numerals 1 through 11, and recorded it in a square below each unit that would be involved in the program sequence. If the unit was to receive a number, we would list the selector switch to be used (1 through 12), then show the settings of the operation switch (Alpha through Epsilon). If it was to send a number, we would list A for add, S for subtract, and AS for both add and subtract.

The ENIAC could send out the number and the nines complement at the same time on two different memory buses. Above and to the right of each operation, as marked on the graph paper, we placed a letter C if the accumulator was to clear before it received. Below the selector switch was another switch, with settings marked from 1 to 9, which selected the number of significant digits in the received number—that is, it determined where the number was rounded off. Below the selector switch was a repeater switch, which determined the number of times the unit was to perform the operation, ranging from one to nine. At the lower left, we listed the program input pulse. At the lower right, we listed the program output pulse (such as A-2).

Thus, one of the one-inch squares on our programming sheet might have looked like this:
[Alpha C]
[9]
[A-1 5 A-2]

What this shows is that the accumulator that is indicated at the top of the sheet is supposed to clear (C) before it receives five times on memory bus Alpha and to round off in the ninth digit position. The program pulse A-1 begins the operation and, when it is finished, the accumulator sends out program pulse A-2.

Along the left edge of the paper we would indicate the add time. Because the accumulator is to add five, it would end at add time 35 if it started at add time 30. Of course, the instructions written in the squares would vary for the different units.

2. Goldstine, *Computers from Pascal to von Neumann*, 230; and "Dinner and Ceremonies Dedicating the Electronic Numerical Integrator and Computer at the University of Pennsylvania, February 15, 1946," official program, on display at the Jean Jennings Bartik Computing Museum.

[Jean and Betty talked about their experiences preparing for the February 15 demonstration frequently over the years, including in interviews with the *Wall Street Journal*, the *New York Times*, the Institute of Electrical and Electronic Engineers, and Woman in Technology International; in oral histories for the Computer Oral History Collection at the Smithsonian Institute (Jean J. Bartik [1924–] and Frances E. [Betty] Snyder Holberton [1917–2001], transcript of interview by Henry Tropp, April 27, 1973, Computer Oral History Collection, 1967–1973, 1977, Box 3, Folder 6, Archives Center, National Museum of American History, Smithsonian Institution, Washington, D.C.), for the Computer History Museum (Oral History of Jean Bartik, Interviewed by Gardner Hendrie, July 1, 2008, Oaklyn, NJ, CHM #X4967.2009), and with Kathy Kleiman, who is preparing a documentary on the ENIAC women (eniacprogrammers.org); and in various documentaries (Bob Jaffe, *Modern Marvels, The Creation of the Computer/Thinking Machine* [1995; New York: A & E Home Entertainment, 2005]; Films for the Humanities [Firm] and WGBH [Television station: Boston, MA] *The Machine That Changed the World* [Princeton, NJ: Films for the Humanities and Sciences, 1992]). Both Bartik and Holberton also told of these experiences in their depositions for the ENIAC patent trial (Deposition of Jean J. Bartik, Box 12, and Deposition of Francis Elizabeth Snyder Holberton, Box 14, ENIAC Patent Trial Collection, 1964–73 [1938–1971 bulk], University of Pennsylvania Archive). In all of those years, nobody ever came forward to contradict their claim that they programmed the ENIAC or that they prepared the trajectory problem for the February 15 demonstration. —Ed.]

3. *Movietone News*, ENIAC newsreel footage with narration by Arthur Burks, The Moore School, 30 mins., The Computer History Museum (gift of Arthur Burks), Mountain View, CA.

4. The 1957 romantic comedy *Desk Set* (from the play by William Marchant) was loosely inspired by the romance between Kay and John Mauchly. Spencer Tracy played the inventor of the EMERAC and Katherine Hepburn played the head of the research department where "Emmy" was being installed. The machine's name, EMERAC, was an allusion to the ENIAC and the UNIVAC.

5. The details in this paragraph come from Betty's recollection, as told to Kathryn Kleiman.

6. Jack Davis, who was on the ENIAC team of design engineers, later told me that, after the banquet, he returned to the Moore School with Harvey Fletcher, a noted hearing specialist at Bell Laboratories, to go over the ENIAC with him some more, at Fletcher's request.

7. Lubkin was very bright but also quite arrogant, and was generally disliked. In fact, when Al Auerbach was at Underwood, he considered one of his major accomplishments to be the firing of Sam Lubkin.

8. Jean Jennings Bartik, "Notes on the Moore School Lectures, Summer 1946," #2011003, Bartik Papers.

9. Richard F. Clippinger, 1996 Computer Pioneer Award, IEEE Computer Society Awards (http://www.computer.org/portal/web/awards/clippinger).

10. Eckert and Mauchly, "ENIAC Progress Report," December 1943; and Lukoff, *From Dits to Bits*, 355–58.

11. Clippinger describes the project in Ballistics Research Laboratories Report No. 673, *A Logical Coding System Applied to the ENIAC*.

12. Nick Metropolis and Jack Worlton, in their paper titled "A Trilogy of Errors in the History of Computing," said that Adele tried to program the sixty-order code but couldn't until Nick in 1948 discovered that Aberdeen had a unit it had designed to translate many signals into one and translate the two digits from the function table into the program pulse to signal the execution of an instruction. Then he and Klare von Neumann, John's wife, did program it and ran his problem. That unit was no secret. I don't know what game the Goldstines were playing, but Adele worked alongside us and certainly had a copy of our programming, which had been done the previous year.

In any case, Goldstine in his book wrote that Adele and John von Neumann did the programming of the sixty-order code. He certainly knew that was false. My group was paid for delivering the sixty-order code, and we programmed Clippinger's problems using it. Later on, when external memory was added, the one-hundred-order code was discussed and the instruction set was expanded so that the two decimal digits read out from the function table could handle up to one hundred instructions.

Therefore, what Nick was talking about when he said that Adele tried and failed to program the sixty-order code is a complete mystery to me, unless he means that he and Klare von Neumann were involved in putting our sixty-order code on the ENIAC and setting up the function table switches to program the Monte Carlo problem. Herman Goldstine, Adele Goldstine, and John von Neumann certainly knew that my team originally and successfully programmed the sixty-order code instruction set.

13. This disconnection that the Moore School has with the ENIAC, and with the great advances made during that brief time at Penn, continues to this day. The school has just a few pieces of the ENIAC in a glass enclosure in a corner of the men's lounge. When I last saw the display, in 2002, there were no brochures telling about it, no labels or plaques to identify anything there in the room. There was a picture of the bigwigs on the wall, but, again, no identification of who they were. There was also a picture of some women going down a slide, but they weren't the ENIAC women. It's a sorry state of affairs, considering that my alma mater, Northwest Missouri State, has an entire museum devoted to technology.

Chapter 5: Surrounded by Brilliance

1. John Northrop, "Current Topics: BINAC Demonstrated, New Electronic Brain," *Journal of the Franklin Institute* 248, no. 4 (October 1949): 360–62.

2. Roger Mills, Northrop Aircraft, personal communications with Jean Jennings Bartik, Kim D. Todd, and Jon T. Rickman, 2009. Northrop Aircraft programmer Roger Mills talked to us about the BINAC when he visited the Jean Jennings Bartik Computing Museum on the campus of Northwest Missouri State University in Maryville in 2009, and donated several items to the museum that he used at Northrop Aircraft, including two BINAC manuals.

3. John Mauchly, "Letter to the Editor of *Datamation*: Stored Programs in the ENIAC, BINAC and EDVAC," 1979. Original typewritten document given to Jean Jennings Bartik by Kay McNulty Mauchly Antonelli from John Mauchly's personal papers, #2011005, Jean Jennings Bartik Papers.

4. When John Mauchly was hired in 1933, there were no physics majors at Ursinus and only three pre-med students needed a physics course. John spiced up his lectures to get noticed by students so they would want to take his courses. Did they ever! His lectures became the talk of the campus, and they were long remembered by his students there. In one of them, he fastened metal wheels from roller skates to the bottom of a board, set the board on a lab table, and stood on it to illustrate Newton's Laws of Motion. This was possibly the first skateboarding trick.

5. Bob went with my husband, Bill, and me to a Progressive Party rally at the Philadelphia Convention Center to see and hear Paul Robeson. Bill loved to sing songs made famous by Paul Robeson, such as "Go Down Moses" and (from the 1936 movie *Show Boat*) "Ol' Man River." Robeson supported Henry Wallace when he ran for president in 1948 on the Progressive Party ticket, and was even considered for the vice presidential spot on that ticket. Robeson was an ardent and outspoken supporter of Russian socialism because of the discrimination black people had suffered in the United States, and for that reason his recordings and films were withdrawn from circulation.

6. Michael Jay Friedman, "*See It Now*: Murrow vs McCarthy," from U.S. Department of State, *Edward R. Murrow: Journalism at Its Best*. America.gov Archive, June 1, 2008 (www.america.gov/st/democracyhrenglish/2008/June/20080601110244eaifas8.602542e-02.html).

7. Edward R. Murrow, *See It Now*, March 9, 1954, CBS News (http://www.cbsnews.com/video/watch/?id=1065699n).

8. Art's future wife, Kitty, told me that Art thought his salary was so high he would never make more than that, so he told her to plan to live on that amount. Kitty was adorable and she adored Art. She was gracious and charming and kept Art from being a workaholic.

9. Cathode-ray tube computer memory stored its data as dots on a TV-type screen, which had to be refreshed periodically to keep them intact. The mercury delay line stored data as streams of electrical pulses that were circulated as waveforms in a storage tank of mercury. The data circulated around and around, changing from pulses to waves to pulses and back to waves.

Micro-coding is a way to actually program the logical architecture of a computer. A storage device stored a long line of pulses, and each pulse triggered the execution of a logical operation, such as a read-out of a memory location or the storage of a number in a memory location. For each instruction, we had to define the logical operations that performed the execution of the instruction and then define what the micro-coded word looked like—i.e., what ones and zeros were in the word. We had to break up the total architecture into logical bits that could be combined to execute the computer's entire instruction set.

10. If a number carries over because it receives a carryover from the lower digit, that digit cannot produce a second carryover as a result of adding a carryover. Taking the worst case, let's suppose that 999 is added to 999. Without considering carryovers, the result is 888 with a carryover from the first, second, and third digits. Now send the carryover down the line, and the result is 1998. No digit position that had a carry can produce a delayed carry.

Now, let us suppose we have 909 added to 999. Without considering carryovers, the result is 898, with carries from the first and third digit positions. When we send the carryovers down the line, the result is 1808, with a delayed carryover from the second position. Then, sending the delayed carries down the line, we get 1898.

11. Both Pres and John were great teachers. I might ask for an explanation of something for a simple reason, but they would see its total implication and tell me all the ramifications of whatever I had asked about. They never questioned my reasons for asking. They liked questions, as questions helped them clarify their thinking. In fact, they encouraged questions. Plus, they were great listeners—they listened to every word. I think this is something people miss about geniuses: they learn so much because they are good listeners.

12. In 2001 the Philadelphia Orchestra moved to the Kimmel Center for the Performing Arts, but for many generations the Academy of Music was one of the greatest music halls in the world. Opened in 1857 and known as "the Grand Old Lady of Broad Street," it remains home to the Pennsylvania Ballet and the Opera Company of Philadelphia, making it the oldest functioning opera house in the United States.

13. Bernie Gordon went on to found Analogic, file more than two hundred patents, and develop most of the screening devices for airports. His original and high-tech work on combining digital and analog earned him the title "the father of analog-to-digital conversion."

14. See also Jean Bartik and Art Gehring, "Large versus Small Logic," from VIP Club, *Information Technology Pioneers*, 5.2 (http://vipclubmn.org/BlueBell.html#Bartik).

15. Welsh designed the tape loops in the UNISERVO—the primary I/O device on the UNIVAC—so it could keep up with the UNIVAC. In just the same way, Frazier kept up with Pres, as few around the place did. Frazier was about 5'8" tall and of medium build with brown hair. He was a bachelor and claimed that women were only after his money.

16. Lukoff, *From Dits to Bits*, 355–58.

17. In the 1920s, odds at racetracks were calculated by hand, which was slow and consequently inaccurate. On April 26, 1927, Harry Straus made a ten-dollar bet on a horse showing twelve to one odds at a racetrack in Havre de Grace. The horse won, and Straus went to the window expecting to collect about $120. However, the final odds—not announced until ten minutes after the race—were less than four to one, and Straus collected only $36. His disappointment spurred him to come up with an electromechanical system that would figure the odds of a horse paying off, display those odds on a large board, dispense tickets based on incoming bets, and show payouts. In just a few years' time, Straus's Totalisator—known colloquially as the "tote" board—was running pari-mutuel betting at nearly every racetrack in America, and it made Harry Straus a wealthy man. The Totalisator has itself now been replaced by computers that run specialized wagering software.

Chapter 6: Moving On, and the Glass Ceiling

1. For more on Northwest's Electronic Campus Program, see Jon Rickman and Dean L. Hubbard, *The Electronic Campus: A Case History of the First Comprehensive High-Access Academic Computing Network at a Public University* (Maryville, MO: Prescott Publishing, 1992); Hubbard and Rickman, *The Electronic Campus and Beyond* (Maryville, MO: Prescott Publishing, 2001); Hubbard and Rickman, "Northwest Missouri State University's Electronic Campus after Four Years," *The Journal: Technological Horizons in Education* 19, no. 3 (Oct. 1991): 91–92; and Jon Rickman, Kim Todd, Tabatha Verbick, and Merlin Miller, "The Evolution of the Electronic Campus: From a Communication System to an Educational Delivery System," in *Proceedings of the 31st Annual ACM SIGUCCS Fall Conference, San Antonio, TX, September 21–24, 2003* (New York: ACM, 2003), 65–69 (http://www.nwmissouri.edu/compserv/clientcomputing/AWARDS/pa26_Rickman.pdf).

2. In this latter capacity, Lou went to Japan to explore cooperation with the Japanese. That fell through because Japan insisted that any company located in Japan be Japanese-owned.

3. The 360 was the most important and successful computer IBM ever produced. Its major breakthrough was upward compatibility of mainframes, such as from the IBM 380/30 to the 360/40 to the 360/50. Also, it had a standard I/O interface so that all systems used the same one. Before this, each system had its own interface, so a lot of engineering time for a system was spent designing the I/O interfaces. This also meant other companies could design I/O devices for the 360, which gave rise to plug-compatible devices.

4. Ken Olsen had founded Digital Equipment in 1957 with Harlan Anderson and was president of the company. I attended all of the press conferences on computer products, so I heard him speak several times.

5. Eleanor and Bernedette worked for Auerbach Publishing's Mainframes service; Eleanor for the Data Handling service producing summaries of systems and devices. Bernedette later went to

work for Sperry UNIVAC. After I left, Auerbach brought her back to manage Auerbach Publications. Eleanor eventually became a freelance writer.

      6. Alison Oswald transcribed many of them (all of the women's); they are available at http://invention.smithsonian.org/resources/fa_comporalhist_index.aspx.

      7. In his 1968 *The Peter Principle*, Dr. Lawrence Peter describes how companies, when they want to get people out of the way, give them the "lateral arabesque" (named for a dance move)— they shuttle them to another position rather than firing them, which might cause problems.

Chapter 7: The Trial to Overturn the ENIAC Patent

      1. Alice Rowe Burks, *Who Invented the Computer? The Legal Battle That Changed Computing History* (Amherst, NY: Prometheus Books, 2003).

      2. Ibid., 86.

      3. Clark R. Mollenhoff, *Atanasoff: Forgotten Father of the Computer* (Ames: Iowa State University Press, 1988).

      4. Ibid., 81–86.

      5. Ibid., 62–66.

      6. According to USLegal.com "Prior art is a term used in patent law to broadly describe the entire body of knowledge from the beginning of time to the present. Prior art is everything publicly known before the invention, as shown in earlier patents and other published material. It is a barrier to obtaining a patent."

      7. Mollenhoff, *Atanasoff*, 81–86.

      8. Charles E. McTiernan, "Anecdotes: The ENIAC Patent," *IEEE Annals of the History of Computing* 20, no. 2 (1998): 54–58, 80.

      9. Findings of Fact, Conclusions of Law, and Order for Judgment, Judge Earl R. Larson, 1973 (Box 51, folders 2–4), Honeywell, Inc., *Honeywell v. Sperry Rand* Records (CBI 1), Charles Babbage Institute, University of Minnesota, Minneapolis.

      10. Alice R. Burks and Arthur W. Burks, *The First Electronic Computer: The Atanasoff Story* (Ann Arbor: University of Michigan Press, 1988), 181.

      11. Ibid., 201.

      12. John Mauchly, "Amending the ENIAC Story," *Datamation* 25, no. 11 (1979): 217–19 (reproduced on ENIAC/John Mauchly, at https://sites.google.com/a/opgate.com/eniac/Home/john-mauchly); An Interview with J. Presper Eckert, OH 13, by Nancy Stern, October 28, 1977, Sperry UNIVAC (Blue Bell, PA) (transcript online at http://conservancy.umn.edu/bitstream/107275/1/oh013jpe.pdf).

      13. Iowa State College, press release, "Biggest, Fastest Calculator Built by ISC Physicist," Ames, Iowa, April 7, 1942 (online at http://www.library.upenn.edu/exhibits/rbm/mauchly/jwm7.html).

      14. The ENIAC trial began on June 1, 1971, and ran until March 13, 1972.

      15. Jean Jennings Bartik, "John Mauchly, Arthur Burks and the Late Night Deal." Notes on conversations with Kay and John Mauchly, 1968–71, Jean Jennings Bartik Papers. Kay also recounted this incident in her March 26, 2004, autobiographical account, Kay McNulty Mauchly Antonelli Story, Jean Jennings Bartik Computer Museum.

      16. Dr. Jon T. Rickman, "The Late Night Deal," notes on conversation with Bill Mauchly,

2011, Jean Jennings Bartik Computer Museum.

    17. Burks and Burks, *First Electronic Computer*, 74, 377.

    18. J. Presper Eckert, "ENIAC: The Electronic Numerical Integrator and Computer," *The Computer History Museum Report* 16 (Summer 1986): 2–7.

    19. Alexander Randall V, "Q&A: A Lost Interview with ENIAC Co-inventor J. Presper Eckert," *ComputerWorld*, February 14, 2006 (http://www.computerworld.com/s/article/108568/Q_A_A_lost_interview_with_ENIAC_co_inventor_J._Presper_Eckert).

Chapter 8: The ENIAC Women in the Spotlight

    1. Presper J. Eckert, "List of ENIAC Firsts," speech given at the Eckert Research International Corporation in Japan, April 15, 1991, #2011007, Jean Jennings Bartik Papers.

    2. On November 13, 2009, the March of Dimes and Women in Technology presented the 2009 Heroines in Technology Lifetime Achievement Award to Kathryn "Kathy" Kleiman, the ENIAC Programmers Project founder. Since 1995, Kathy has spent years seeking recognition for the ENIAC women, as well as countless hours dedicated to documenting their story.

    3. Thomas Petzinger, "History of Software Begins with the Work of Some Brainy Women," The Front Lines, *Wall Street Journal*, November 15, 1996.

    4. Thomas Petzinger, "Female Pioneers Fostered Practicality," The Front Lines, *Wall Street Journal*, November 22, 1996.

    5. Jean Sammet was the primary developer of the FORMAC language at IBM, which eventually became FORTRAN. She also served as chair of the subcommittee that defined COBOL. Grace Hopper was on one of the committees under Jean that developed the COBOL program, which was based on the Flow-Matic compiler that Grace had developed at UNIVAC. For this reason, Jean called Grace the grandmother of COBOL. Betty Snyder Holbertson was assigned by her boss to be committee secretary so that she could monitor the committee's progress for Jean.

    Sammet wrote one of the classic books on programming, *Programming Language: History and Fundamentals* (Prentice Hall, 1969). Sammet was elected a Fellow of the ACM, served as president of that organization, and was also elected a Fellow of the Computer History Museum.

    6. This "hunk of wire" was actually a visual aid Grace used to explain the concept of nanoseconds because generals and admirals would often ask her why satellite communication took so long. She began handing out pieces of wire that were slightly shorter than a foot—the distance light travels in a nanosecond—and would then contrast these with a 1,000-foot-long roll of wire that represented a microsecond.

    7. Col. Paul Gillon had died on February 3, 1996, at the age of eighty-eight, nine months before the fiftieth anniversary celebration. Aberdeen brought his family there for the event, and his younger son, Brendan, a professor at McGill University in Montreal, attended in his place. Col. Gillon was Goldstine's ranking officer and assistant director of the Ballistic Research Laboratory, and was the one who came up with the name Electronic Numeric Integrator and Computer, or ENIAC for short.

    8. In fairness to both Goldstine and Brainerd, in the same lecture, Goldstine also conceded that "It should be said in connection with the above-mentioned grievances that Eckert and Mauchly felt with some justice that no one in the Moore School administration had any deep technical understanding of the ENIAC or EDVAC. There was truth in this. The way the dean organized things, Brainerd was so deeply immersed in all the administrative details of the research commitments of the Moore School that he did not have the time or strength to follow in detail the ENIAC or EDVAC projects."

9. Brooks, a software engineer and computer scientist, along with Gene Amdahl, managed the development of the IBM 360, and Brooks published *The Mythical Man-Month: Essays on Software Engineering* (Addison-Wesley, 1975) about the process.

10. The web address for the Jean Jennings Bartik Online Computing Museum is http://www.nwmissouri.edu/onlinemuseum/computing/index.htm.

11. Jean Jennings Bartik, "Eckert & Mauchly Corporation: The Technical Camelot," speech given at the 2006 dedication of the Eckert-Mauchly building as a historic site, #2011006, Jean Jennings Bartik Papers.

Afterword

1. Jean Jennings Bartik and Kay McNulty Mauchly Antonelli, interview by Kim D. Todd, April 2002, at the grand opening of the Jean Jennings Bartik Computing Museum; J. Presper Eckert, "Disclosure of Magnetic Calculating Machine," January 29, 1944.

2. John Mauchly, "Amending the ENIAC Story," *Datamation* 25, no. 11 (1979): 217–19 (https://sites.google.com/a/opgate.com/eniac/Home/john-mauchly).

3. Ibid.

4. Ibid.

5. Ibid.

6. Ibid.

7. Ibid.

8. Dr. William E. Walden, e-mail to Dr. Jon Rickman, August 4, 2011, Jon T. Rickman Papers.

9. Bartik and Antonelli, interview, April 2002.

10. Roger D. Mills, Northrop Aircraft programmer, e-mail to Kim D. Todd, December 21, 2010.

11. Ibid.

12. Ibid.

13. Ibid.

14. Ibid.

Index

A page number in **boldface** indicates an illustration on that page; an *n* following a page number indicates a note on that page; a *t* following a page number indicates a table on that page. All relationships within parenthesis relate to Betty Jean Jennings Bartik.

A

Aberdeen Proving Ground
    celebrates fifty years in computing, 184–87
    description of base, 66–67
    differential analyzer, 8–9, 23, 56
    recruiting of human computers, 8
    See also Bartik, Betty Jean Jennings, at Moore School and Aberdeen Proving Ground
Abrahams, Robert D., 74
accumulators
    BINAC, 125
    ENIAC, 22, 25, 75–76, 78–79, 80, 82, 84, 93–94, 96–97, 117
    round-off switch, 94
    two-accumulator test, 13–14, 177, 181, 185
Ada Lovelace Award, 20, 184
Advanced Research Projects Agency Network (ARPANET), 164
Aiken, Howard, 5, 98, 103
Alldredge, Forrest (brother-in-law), 29–30, 34, 38–39, 48, 58
Allen, Fran, 182, 183
Amad, Joseph, 49–52
Amdahl, Gene, 151, 189, 191, 219–20*n*9
American Federation of Information Processing Societies (AFIPS), 159
American Totalisator Company, 141, 142
analytical engine, 20, 201
Anderson, Harlan, 217*n*4
Antonelli, Severo, 177, 179
Association for Computing Machinery (ACM), 175, 183, 193, 219*n*5
Association for Women in Computing (AWC), 20, 184, 198
Atanasoff-Berry Computer (ABC), 168, 169, 171, 173–74
Atanasoff, John Vincent, 5, 76, 167, 168, 170, 171
atomic bomb, 14, 83, 84, 170
Auerbach, Al, 7, 86, 125, 128–29, **133**
Auerbach Corporation for Science and Technology, 155, 167
Auerbach, Isaac, 155, 158, 159–60
Auerbach Publishers
    gender discrimination at, 156–57, 160, 184
    reports, 156, 157, 158, 167
Automatic Sequence Controlled Calculator (ASCC), 98

B

Babbage, Charles, 19–20, 201
Ballistics Research Lab (Moore School), 20–21
Bartik, Alex (grandson), 196, 198
Bartik, Betty Jean Jennings, **1**, **3**, **63**, **78**, **81**
    and Bill Bartik
        children of, 151–52
        divorced from, 154–55
        marriage and honeymoon, **111**, 111–13, **112**
        meets and introduces to family, 104–5, 107
    childhood and education
        appendectomy, 33–34

Bartik, Betty Jean Jennings/ childhood and education, *cont'd*
    and athletics, 34–36, 50, **56**
    college years, 42–56
    desire to be alone when young, 31–32
    elementary education, 34
    family, 27–41, **32**
    high school, **38**, 38–40, 41–42
    and horse riding, 36–38
    learns to drive an automobile, 39
    religious background, 70
    summer jobs, 44–45, 53–54
    sweethearts of, 49–52
    and work habits, 200
  later years
    attends historic site celebration for EMCC, 191–92, **193**, **194**
    attends Moore School luncheon, 1986, 180–81
    attends 1985 reunion, 179–80, **180**
    honors, 189–93, **192**, 194, 195; honorary degree, 189–90; Hall of Fellows at Computer History Museum, 196; WITI Hall of Fame, **183**; homecoming grand marshall, 146–47
    resume, last official, 1996, 186
    speaking engagements, 188–89, **189**, 197, 198–99
    Wall Street Journal article on, 181–182
  at Moore School and Aberdeen Proving Ground
    appointment as "computer," 58, **59**
    interviews for job at, 65
    meets J. Mauchly, 75–76
    meets P. Eckert, 87–88
    in Philadelphia, 58–59, 61–62, 151
    programming trajectories, 21–22, 81, **81**, 84–85, 91–95
    and public demonstration of ENIAC, 23, 25–26, 97–99
    resigns from Moore School, 120
    selected as ENIAC programmer, 19, 20–21
    social life, 61–64, **63**, 69–70, 87–89, **89**
    as team leader for converting ENIAC to stored-program computer, 115–20
    training at Moore School, 60–61, 62, 67–69
    trains on ENIAC, 74–76
    trips with co-workers, 72–73
  political and volunteer work, 151
  professional life, after Moore School
    at Auerbach Publishers: as editor, 156, 157–158; and gender discrimination, 156–157, 158–159; resigns from, 159
    at Data Decisions, 164–65
    earns master's degree, 154
    at Electronic Control Company, 120
    at EMCC: asks for pay raise, 134; and BINAC, **123**, 127–128; interviews for job at, 120; partnership with A. Gehring, 136; and UNVIAC, 88, 122, **133**, 134, 135, 136–37, 138–39, 143
    at Honeywell, 162
    at Interdata, 160–62
    at Remington Rand: and gender discrimination, 144; gives UNIVAC presentation, 148, 150; interview by Goodman, 143; resigns from, 150; teaches Census Bureau programmers, 144, 145–46; work with to salesmen, 144–45
    at Systems Engineering Laboratories, 162
  videos about, 191
  working relationships
    with A. Goldstine, 17, 106
    with B. Snyder, 73–74, 84–84
    with H. Goldstine, 17, 21, 65, 106
    with J. von Neumann, 17
Bartik, Bill (husband)
  background of, 108
  divorce from Jean Bartik, 153–55
  employment, 137, 143, 150
  meets Betty Jean Jennings, 104–5
  meets family of Betty Jean Jennings, 107

and mercury delay line memory problem, 136–37
relationship with parents, 154
wedding and honeymoon of, **111**, 111–13, **112**
Bartik, Jane (daughter), 151, **152**, 189, 195
Bartik, Jonathan (grandson), 196, 198
Bartik, Mary (daughter), 151, **152**, 196–97
Bartik, Tim (son), 151, **152**, 182, 189, **192**, 196
Bartik, William, 108
Bartz, Carol, 182
Bell Laboratories, 5, 22, 67
Berry, Clifford, 5
Best, Neal, **32**
Bianco, Richard, **15**
Bilas, Fran, **81**, **89**
  attends 1985 reunion, 179–80, **180**
  background of, 79–80
  marriage to Homer Spence, 152
  professional life, 8, 19, 20–21, 79, 81
  social life, 88–89
BINAC (Binary Automatic Computer), 5
  computing power of, 125
  description of, **123**, 123–25, **124**, 128–29
  Eckert-Mauchly engineering team, **129**
  Short Code higher-level language for, 193–94
binary number system, 55, 102, 103, 122, 135, 211–12n7, 216n10
Bledsoe (Mr.), 150
Block, Ed, 157
Blumenthal, Ed, **133**
Bolar, Connie, 42, 46
Bonn, Ted, 104
Bradbury, Norris, 21
Brainerd, John Grist, 9, 14, 76, 87, 185–87
Brooks, Fred, 151, 191, 219–20n9
Brown, Jim, 157–58
Brown, Wister, 139–40
Bureau of the Census, 126, 143, 144, 206
Burks, Alice, 172
Burks, Arthur, **78**, 80
  background of, 86
  books, 172–73, 176
  on Eckert and Mauchly, 175, 176
  on Mauchly and Atanasoff, 172–73, 177–78

at Moore School, 7, 10, 84, 97–98, 103
Burr, Mary Ellen, 53–54
Bush, Vannevar, 8, 56
Byron (Lord), 19
byte, 189, 191

C

cards, 23, 25, 66, 67, 87, 94, 148, 150
carryover, 102, 135, 216n10
Chambers, Carl, 103
Chapline, Joe, 9, 109, 141, 191, 192–93
Chinitz, Paul, 148, 149, 191, 194
Chu, Jeffrey Chuan, 7, 10, 84, 85, 178
Churchill, Winston, 20, 210n21
Clapp, Judy, 198
Clippinger, Dick
  death of, 196
  personality of, 113–15, 119, 195–96
  receives Computer Pioneer award, 191
  security clearance denied, 131–32
  work on ENIAC, 11, 12, 113, 115, 116, 117
Clippinger, Dorothy, 114
coding, 134, 135, 216n9
Cohn, Roy, 130
Colbert, George, 55
CommunicationsWorld, 165
The Computer from Pascal to von Neumann (Goldstine), 11, 17, 95, 107, 187–88
computer languages, 182, 193–94, 219n5
computer museums, 189, 190, **190**, 191, 193, 194, 196
computers and calculators, early, 5, 13, 19, 20, 22, 60, 76, 98, 118, 126, 127, 128, 141, 168, 169, 171, 173–74, 210n21, 211–12n7, 212n8, 213–14n1
ComputerWorld, 164, 177
Cox, Joyce, 42, 51, 52
Cronkite, Walter, **145**
Crosby, Madeline, 62
Crosby, "Mama," 63–64
Crosby, Mary Jane, 63, 64
Cummings, Jim, **89**
Cunningham, Leland, 65
cybernetics, 97, 100

D

Data Communications magazine, 164
Data Decisions, 164
Datamation letter, 204–5
DataPro, 164
Davis, Jack, 10, 69, 121, 214n6
Davis, John, 84, 86
Dederick, Louis Serles, 79
Desk Set (film), 214n4
differential analyzers, 5, 8–9, 23, 56, 66, 67, 79, 192
Digital Equipment Corporation (DEC), 156, 217n4
Distributed Communication Architecture (DCA), 164
Distributed System Architecture (DSA), 164
Dow, Blanche, 43, 46, 146–47
    A World of Love (Harvey), 147
Dykes, Mattie, 44, 147

E

Eckert, Chris, 8, 191, 192, **194**
Eckert, Hester, 87
Eckert, John Presper (Pres), **6**
    book on, 172–73
    contracts with Northrop Aircraft to develop BINAC, **123**
    designs ENIAC, 10
    education of, 6–7
    and EDVAC, 10, 11, 14, 15, 16–17, 101, 172–73, 204–5
    first patent applied for, 7
    forms Electronic Control Company, 103
    meets Jean Jennings Bartik, 87–88
    patent case, 166–72, 176, 177
    personality of, 88, 137, 138
    and public demonstration of trajectory, 96, 98
    relationship with F. Welsh, 140
    relationship with J. Mauchly, 7–8, 86
    relationship with J. von Neumann, 14
    relationship with mother, 167
    and rotating drum idea, 140–41
    speeches by, 181
    and stored-program computer concept, 113
    teaches Moore School Lectures, 103
    and UNIVAC, **133**, 134–37, 138–40
    work on mercury delay line memory problem, 134–37
    writes proposal for computer, 9–10
    See also Eckert-Mauchly Computer Corporation (EMCC)
Eckert, Judith, 177
Eckert-Mauchly Computer Corporation (EMCC)
    declared historic site, 191–92, **193**
    financial and security problems, 130, 131–32, 141–42
    growth of, 134
    McCarthyism and, 130
    purchase by Remington Rand, 142
    See also BINAC (Binary Automatic Computer); UNIVAC (Universal Automatic Computer)
Eckert Research International Corporation (Japan), 181
EDSAC (Electronic Delay Storage Automatic Calculator), 104, 128
EDVAC (Electronic Discrete Variable Computer), **15**
    and J. Mauchly, 10, 11, 14, 15–17, 173, 204–5
    and J. von Neumann, 11–12, 14, 16, 17, 18, 172–73, 177
    mercury delay line memory for, 86–87
    patent rights, 15, 101–2, 177
    and P. Eckert, 10, 11, 14, 15, 16–17, 172–73, 204–5
    reports on, 14–17, 172–73, 177
Electrical Engineering for Defense Industries, 7
Electronic Campus program, 190
Electronic Control Company, 103. See also Eckert-Mauchly Computer Corporation (EMCC)
Electronic Delay Storage Automatic Calculator (EDSAC), 104, 128
Electronic Discrete Variable Computer. See EDVAC (Electronic Discrete Variable Computer)
ENIAC (Electronic Numerical Integrator and Computer), **100**
    in articles, books, and media, 17, 90, 95–96, 101, 129, 172–73, 176–77, 188, 191

computing power of, 22, 25, 125
debugging, 94–95
description of, 2, **3**, 22–23
designing and building of, 9–10
diagram of units of, **77**
divider/square rooter, 22, 76, 79, 82, 85, 86
errors, 102–3
logical block diagrams, 87, 138–39
memory bus, 82, 93
moved to Aberdeen Proving Ground, 108–9
multiplier, 22, 76, 78–79, 85
multiply test for stored-program, 118t
patent, 101, 166–72, 175
plugboard, 68
press demonstration of, 91, 99
programming, 82, 92–94, **93**, 116, 122, 212nn11–12, 213–14n1
public (scientific) demonstration of, 23, 25–26, 97–101
reports on, 14–16, 18, 141, 173
sixty-order code, 113
as stored-program computer, 11–12, 113, 115
trajectories, 3–4, 23–25, 76, 81, 84–85, 91–95
See also Eckert, John Presper (Pres); ENIAC patent; Mauchly, John William
Estrin, Thelma, 198
Ethernet, 164, 191
Everlof, Bernedette, 156–57, 160, 163–64, 217–18n5

F

farming, 29–30
Farnsworth, Philo, 7
FBI, 13–31, 125–26, 142
Federation on Computing in the United States (FOCUS), 159
Ficaro, Beatrice, 62, **63**, 112
firing tables. *See* trajectories
Fletcher, Harvey, 214n6
Fox, Eulaine, 55
Frankel, Mary, 21, 83
Frankel, Stan, 81, 83, 169–70

Franken, Margaret, 52
function tables, 22–23, 25, 76, 78, **81**, 94, 113, 116, 212n16

G

Galbraith, A. S., 117, 119
Gebremedan, Eleanor, 156–57, 160, 217–18n5
Gehring, Arthur, 120, **133**, 134
    and ENIAC stored-program, 116
    work on mercury delay line memory, 136–37
    work on UNIVAC, 134, 138–39, 143
Gehring, Kitty, 136
gender discrimination, 197, 198
    at Auerbach Publishers, 156–57, 160, 184
    and EEOC, 156–57, 158–59
    at IBM, 146
    at Remington Rand, 144
Giese, John, 117, 119
Gillon, Paul, 185, 219n7
Gingrich, George, **133**
Goldstine, Adele, 11, 12, 17, 65, 91–92
    at Moore School, 60–61, 105
    relationship with Jean Jennings, 106–7
    and stored-program computer concept, 116, 118
Goldstine, Herman
    on Brainerd, 185–86
    distributes "First Draft of a Report on the EDVAC," 14–15
    and ENIAC, 11, 12, 13, 21
    false claims by, 17, 95–96, 184–85, 197–98, 205
    idolization of von Neumann, 12, 18, 105–6
    inaccuracies in *The Computer from Pascal to von Neumann*, 187–88, 215n12
    as liaison between Aberdeen and Moore School, 8–10, 65, 87
    at Moore School, 60, 103
    offers trajectory computation job, 91–92
    personality of, 119
    at Princeton, 105–6
Goodman (Mr.), 143
Gordon, Bernie, **133**, 216–17n13
Gore, Al, 181
Gottlieb, Marvin, **133**

Grantham, Bobbie, **32**
Grantham, Glen, **32**
Gustafson, John, 173

H
Hake, Joseph, 44, 54, 56
Halmos, Paul, 12
Haney, John, 74
harmonic analyzer, 174
Harr, Luther, 148
Hartree, Douglas, 5, 56, 103, 104, 213*n*18
Harvey, David, 147
Helwig, Katherine, 53, 55
Herschel (cousin), 53
Hillegas, Jack, 155–56
Hofstadter, Douglas R.
Holberton, John, 76, 79, 152, 179, **180**
Hollar, John, **192**
Holt, Arlettie, 42–43, 51, 55
Honeywell, 162, 164
Honeywell v. Sperry Rand, 166–72
Hoover, J. Edgar, 142
Hopper, Grace, 20, 123, 126–27, 141, 148, 182, 192, 198, 219*nn*5–6
Horsfal, Frank, 43–44, 54
Hubbard, Dean, 190
human computers, 8, 19, 23–24, 25, 76, 81, 94
Husky, Harold, 10, 84, 87, 102, 103, 178, 184

I
IBM
    computer models, 151, 155, 189, 191, 198, 217*n*3
    gender discrimination, 146
    patent-sharing agreement with Sperry Rand, 171
    punch card installation, 67, 68
    Punched Card Computing Group (Los Alamos), 83–84
    System Service Girls, 56
    Systems Network Architecture of, 164
IEEE Computer Society, 90, 176, 191
Institute for Advanced Study (IAS; Princeton), 13, 117–18
instruction addresses, 116, 117
Interdata, 159, 160–62

Internal Revenue Service (IRS), 180–81

J
Jacobi, Kathe, 116
Jacobi, Marvin, 124, **133**
Jay, Betty, **133**
Jennings, Betty Jean. *See* Bartik, Betty Jean Jennings
Jennings, Bob (brother), 28–29, 37, 45, 47–48, **48**
Jennings, Egbert (uncle), 32, 38
Jennings, Eliza Jane Coffey (grandmother), 30, 32–33, 54
Jennings, Erma (sister), 28, 37, 38, 39, 47, 48, 58
Jennings, Fred (uncle), 30, 32, 36, 48
Jennings, Harold (brother-in-law and cousin), 44–45, **45**, 61, 73
Jennings, Kathleen (Kackie) (sister), 30–31, 37, 47, 48, 107–8
Jennings, Lula May (Lou) (sister), 29, 34, 35–36, 37, 44–45, **45**, 48, 61
Jennings, Lula Spainhower (mother), **27**, 28, 33–34, 38, 40–41, 43, 47
Jennings, Pat (uncle), 32
Jennings, Raymond (brother), 29–30, 37, 41, 47, 53
Jennings, Roy (uncle), 48, 54
Jennings, William (brother), 28, 47
Jennings, William Smith (father), 27–28, 32, 36–37, 38, 39, 47, 58
Johnson, Arthur J. (Johnny), 141
Johnson, Lyndon, 130
Johnsville Naval Air Station, 137
Jones, J. W., 54, 55, 146
Jones, Larry, **133**

K
Kalamazoo Area Math and Science Center (KAMSC), 198–99
Karr, Jeffer, 48
Kelly, John B., 71
Kelly, John B., Jr., 71
Kirby, Forrest (uncle), 40
Kirby, Gretchen Jennings (aunt), 39–41, **40**, 74
Kleiman, Kathryn, 181, 182, 191, **193**

Korzybski, Alfred, 43
Koss, Milly, 127, 191, 192, 198
Kozak, Al, **112**, 107

L
Lamkin, Uel, 48
Lane, Ruth, 56
Larson, Earl R., 166, 169, 170, 171, 174, 177
Levitt, Seymore, **133**
Lichterman, Ruth, **89**, **180**
    attends 1985 reunion, 179–80, **180**
    background of, 70
    death of, 180
    professional life, 19, 20–21, 66, 67–69, 80–81, 84, 85, 94
    marriage to Adolph Teitelbaum, 152
    religious background, 70
    social life, 69, 70
Lichterman, Simon, 70
Logical Block Diagrams, 87, 138–39
Lopker, Pamela Meyer, 182
Los Alamos Laboratory (New Mexico), 14, 21, 83–84
Lovelace, Ada, 19–20, 201
    Ada Lovelace Award, 20, 184
Lubkin, Sam, 101, 214*n*7
Lukoff, Herman, **133**

M
Mach, Ernst, 25, 90
Mach speed, 24, 25
Madeira, Amelia, 39, 41–42
marketing, 90
Marsden, Ethel, 198
Mars Rover, 183
Masoncup, Minerva, 68
Massachusetts Institute of Technology (MIT), 8, 20, 56, 97, 100, 167, 198
Mauchly, Bill, 191–92, **193**, **194**
Mauchly, John William, **6**, **89**, **110**
    and A. Burks, 175
    and BINAC, **123**, 193–94
    book on, 172
    Datamation letter, 204–205
    death of, 166
    education of, 6, 7
    and EDVAC, 10, 11, 14, 15–17, 101, 173, 204–5
    and ENIAC, 10, 96–97, 108–9
    family, 6, 109, 110
    forms Electronic Control Company, 103
    harmonic analyzer of, 174
    and J. Atanasoff, 173–76
    and Jean Jennings, **111**, 111–12, 120
    and J. von Neumann, 14, 16–17
    K. Mauchly on, 176
    marriage to Kay McNulty, **110**, 110–11, 152, **153**
    at Moore School, 10, 96–97, 108–9
    and P. Eckert, 7–8, 86
    and patent case, 166–72, 175–76
    personality of, 88, 95, 119
    security clearance and FBI report, 130–31
    and stored-program computer concept, 113
    teaching positions, 8, 103, 215*n*4
    and UNIVAC, **133**, 141
    writes proposal for computer, 9–10
    See also Eckert-Mauchly Computer Corporation (EMCC)
Mauchly, Mary, 109
Mauchly, Sebastian J., 6
Mauchly, Wendy, **193**
McCarthy, Joseph, 130, 132–33
McCarthyism, 130–34
McCartney, Scott, 129
McKeoun, Elizabeth, 164
McNamara, Robert, 31
McNulty, James, 71
McNulty, Kathleen "Kay," **75**, **89**, **110**
    addresses Moore School luncheon, 1986, 180
    attends 1985 reunion, 179–80, **180**
    background of, 71, 73
    death of, 194
    and ENIAC patent, 175, 176
    and Jean Jennings, 72, 110
    and J. von Neumann, 18
    marriage to John Mauchly, **110**, 110–11, 152, **153**
    marriage to Severo Antonelli, 179
    at opening of Jean Jennings Bartik Computing Museum, **190**
    professional life, 8, 13–14, 19, 20–21, 66, 67–69, 70, 75, 81, 84

religious background, 70, 73
McNulty, Kathleen "Kay," *cont'd*
    speaking engagements, 188–89, **189**
media
    ENIAC demonstration for, 91, 99, 100–101
    and public perception of ENIAC, 80, 101
Megamini processor, 159, 161
Meltzer, Phil, 109, 179
memory, 82, 93, 94, 141, **147**, 171, 212*n*11
    cathode-ray tube, 88, 134, 216*n*9
    mercury delay line, 86–87, 123, 125, 134–35, 136–37, 145
Menabrea, Luigi, 20
Metcalfe, Bob, 191, **192**
Metropolis, Nick, 21, 81, 83, 169–70
Michaels, Charlie, **133**
Milbanke, Anne Isabella, 19
Mills, Roger, 206, 207
Mitchell, Herb, 141
Mock, Bob, **133**
Mollenhoff, Clark R., 170
Molloy, John T., 161–62
Monroe, Pete, 69–70
Monte Carlo problem, 215*n*12
Moores, Calvin, 103
Moore School of Electrical Engineering, 1, **23**
    Ballistics Research Lab at, 20–21
    Lectures on Computer Design, 60–61, 62, 103
    luncheon for ENIAC's fortieth anniversary, 180–81
    See also Bartik, Betty Jean Jennings, at Moore School and Aberdeen Proving Ground
Morello, Fran, **133**
Morgenstern, Oskar, 12
Multinational Development of Women in Technology (MDWIT), 191
Mumma, Fred, 157
Murrow, Edward R., 133, 134

N

NASA, 137, 183
National Bureau of Standards (NBS), 206
National Cash Register Company, 142
National Semiconductor, 161

Naval Aviation Supply Office (ASO), 148
Naval Ordnance Laboratory, 170
Naval Ordnance Testing Station in Pasadena, 103
Neugebauer, Marcia, 182
Northrop Aircraft, 123–24, 125–26
Northrop, John K., 124
Northwest Missouri State Teachers College, 42–44, 46, 48–49
    electronic campus, 190

O

Office of Naval Research, 105
Office of Strategic Services (OSS), 104
Ohm's Law, 65, 211*n*1
Olsen, Ken, 217*n*4

P

Palmer, Catherine, 147
Passmore, Diane, 78
patents
    EDVAC, 15, 101–2, 177
    ENIAC, 101, 166–72, 175
    IBM-Sperry Rand patent-sharing agreement, 171
    and One-Year Rule (U.S. Patent Office), 168–69
PDP-9 (DEC), 156
Pender, Dean, 17
Pender, Harold, 8, 95, 185
Penny, Ruth, 62
Petzinger, Tom, 181–82
plugboards, 67, 68–69
Pratt & Whitney, 53–54
programming, 82, 92–93, **93**, 116, 212*nn*11–12, 213–14*n*1

R

Rademacher, Hans, 84, 102, 103
Randall (Dr.), 153
Randell, Brian, 10
RCA counter, 69
Reagan, Fonnie, 164
Rees, David, 103
Remington Rand
    lack of salesperson/customer training at,

147–48
  management at, 150–51
  purchases EMCC, 142
  See also Bartik, Betty Jean Jennings, at Remington Rand
Rickman, Jon T., 189, **190**, 191, **193**
Rullo, Tom, 158

S

Sammet, Jean, 182, 219*n*5
Schine, G. David, 130
Schlain, Ed, 116, 120
Schmitt, Bill, 191, 193
Schottel, Ivan, 42, 44
Scientific Advisory Committee, Ballistic Research Laboratory, **9**
Shafritz, Arnold, 155, 157, 167
Sharky, Pat, **189**
Sharpless, Thomas Kite, 10, 84, 85, 103, 178, 191
Shaw, Robert "Bob," 84, 86, 121
  at EMCC, 121
  and ENIAC, 84, 128, 212*n*16
  health problems of, 86, 128
  patent case and, 178
  personality of, 86, 127
  security clearance denied, 131
  and UNIVAC, **133**, 138
Sheppard, C. Bradford, 7, 86–87, 121, 127, **133**
Shirley, Donna, 182, 183
Shisler, Dorothy, 9, 185–87
Shriner, Ned, **133**
Sims, John, 87, 120, **133**, 213*n*17
Smolier, Jerry, **133**
Snark N-25 missile, 123, 127–28
Snyder, Betty, **1**, **3**, **75**
  attends 1985 reunion, 179–80, **180**
  awards, 20, 184, 191
  background of, 71, 73–74
  on B. Bartik, 104–5
  and COBOL, 182, 219*n*5
  at Electronic Control Company, 120
  at EMCC, 121, 141
  and ENIAC, 19, 20–22, 23, 25–26, 66, 67–69, 81, 84–85, 91–95, 97–99, 123
  gender discrimination and, 184
  and H. Goldstine, 17, 21

and J. Mauchly, 75–76
and Jean Jennings, 73–74, 84–84
marriage to John Holberton, 152
religious background, 70
suffers stroke, 183
and UNIVAC, 121, 122, **133**
Wall Street Journal article on, 181–82
Snyder, John, 73–74
Snyder, Monroe B., 71
Sowell, Shaunna, 182
Spears, Sally, 116
speed, Mach, 25
Spence, Homer, **89**, 152, **180**
Sperry Rand, 166–72
Sperry UNIVAC, 155, 160
Stad, Ben, **133**
Steeby, Dorothy, 42
Stibitz, George, 5, 67, 103
Stibitz machine, 22, 67
Stonesifer, Patty, 182–83
storage, magnetic tape, 121–22
"stored-program" computer, 10, 11, 113, 115
  hardware, 128
  origin of idea, controversy over, 11–12, 172
Straus, Harry, 141–42, 217*n*17
Strohbein, W. W., 107
Strowger, Almon, 141
Sweeney, Harold, 145
Sweet, Bill, 159, 160
Systems Engineering Laboratories (SEL), 162
System Service Girls (IBM), 56
Systems Network Architecture (SNA), 164

T

Tartaro, Bert, 155–56
Taub, Abraham, 11, 105
Taub shock wave program, 106
Teitelbaum, Adolph, 152, 179
Teller, Edward, 84
test program, 13–14, 21–26, 83, 85, 94, 95, 115, 128, 177, 181, 185
Todd, Kim D., 189, 190, 191
Todd, Lila, 62
Torvalds, Linus, 191, **192**
Totalisator (tote board), 217*n*17
trajectories, 8–9, 23–25, 60
Travis, Irven, 101, 102, 115, 116

Truex, Dorothy, 55
Truman, Harry S., 62, 63, 83
truncation errors, 84, 102–3
Turing, Alan, 5, 117–18
    A. M. Turing Award, 183, 188

U

UNIVAC (Universal Automatic Computer), 5, 86, 88, 90
    backup for, 88, 134, 135, 139, 143
    Census Bureau purchase of, 144
    cycling unit, 167–68
    description of, 121–23
    Eckert-Mauchly crew, **133**
    Logical Block Diagrams for, 138–39
    predicts 1952 presidential race, 134
    printer for, 139–40
    UNIVAC I, **147**, 149
University of Pennsylvania, 7, 56
Ursinus College, 6, 7, 8, 109, 130, 215n4
Usandivaras, Americas, 52–53
U.S. Census Bureau. *See* Bureau of the Census
U.S. Patent Office, 168, 169, 170

V

vacuum tubes, 7, 123
Veblen, Oswald, 10
von Neumann, John
    and atomic bomb, 84
    background of, 12–13
    books, 12
    and EDVAC, 11–12, 18, 173, 177
    and "First Draft EDVAC Report," 14, 16–17, 172–73, 177
    and Moore School Lectures, 103
    publications, 13
    and stored-program computer concept, 113, 116, 118–19
    and U.S. Navy computer project, 170
    von Neumann architecture, 16
von Neumann, Klare, 215n12

W

Walden, William E., 205
Wallace, Bettie Claire, 50, 55
Wallace, Peter, 157, 158
Wallington, Patricia, 183
Wall Street Journal, articles, 181–82, 188, 212n14
Wang, 164
Warren, Reed, 14, 186
Weiner, Jim, 97, 100, **133**
Welch, Joseph, 132–33
Welsh, Frank, **133**
Welsh, Frazier, 138–39, 140
Wendell, Doug, **133**
Wescoff, Marlyn, **89**
    attends 1985 reunion, 179–80, **180**
    background of, 70–71
    and ENIAC, 19, 20–21, 94, 66, 67–69, 80–81, 85
    and Jean Jennings, 72–73
    marriage to Phil Meltzer, 109, 152
    religious background, 70
Wickman, Debra (daughter-in-law), 196
Wilkes, Maurice, 103, 104
Williams, Christopher (grandson), 197
Williams, Christopher (son-in-law), 196–97
Williams, Jacob (great-grandson), 197
Williams, Jamie (grandson), 197
Williams, Jesse (grandson), 197
Wilson, Lou, 7, 86, **133**, 155, 157, 217n2
Winsor, Paul, **133**, 155, 157, 167–68
women in the military, 46
Women in Technology International (WITI) Hall of Fame award, 182–83, **183**
World War II, 13, 44–47, 61, 62, 83, 212n13
Wright-Patterson Air Force Base, 56

X

Xerox, 164

Y

Yalow, Rosalyn, 183

Z

Zeliff (Mr.), 41
Ziff-Davis Publishing, 164, 165
Zuse, Conrad, 5